UNDERSTANDING YOUTH CRIME

Understanding Youth Crime

An Australian Study

Edited by

JOHN S. WESTERN
University of Queensland, Australia

MARK LYNCH
Crime and Misconduct Commission, Queensland, Australia

EMMA OGILVIE
Department of Premier and Cabinet (QLD), Australia

Routledge
Taylor & Francis Group

LONDON AND NEW YORK

First published 2003 by Ashgate Publishing

Reissued 2018 by Routledge
2 Park Square, Milton Park, Abingdon, Oxon OX14 4RN
711 Third Avenue, New York, NY 10017, USA

Routledge is an imprint of the Taylor & Francis Group, an informa business

Publisher's Note
The publisher has gone to great lengths to ensure the quality of this reprint but points out that some imperfections in the original copies may be apparent.

Disclaimer
The publisher has made every effort to trace copyright holders and welcomes correspondence from those they have been unable to contact.

A Library of Congress record exists under LC control number: 2003057861

ISBN 13: 978-1-138-70909-6 (hbk)
ISBN 13: 978-1-138-70907-2 (pbk)
ISBN 13: 978-1-315-19838-5 (ebk)

Contents

List of Figures and Tables

List of Contributors

David Chant

Dr David Chant completed his Ph.D. in mathematical statistics at the Research School of Social Sciences, Australian National University. He has held various statistical appointments at the ANU and The University of Queensland, and the chair of social statistics at the University of Essex, UK. He is presently pursuing his research interests in the applications of statistical techniques across the spectrum of psychiatric research as a Principal Research Fellow in the Department of Psychiatry at The University of Queensland.

Wing Hong Chui

Dr Wing Hong Chui graduated from Cambridge University with a Ph.D. in Criminology. He has been a Lecturer in the Department of Social Work and Probation Studies at the University of Exeter and in the School of Social Work and Social Policy at The University of Queensland. He has recently been appointed as an Assistant Professor in the School of Law at the City University of Hong Kong. His areas of interest include social work with young people and offenders, and criminology and criminal justice.

Denise A. Durrington

Denise A. Durrington is a doctoral student in the School of Social Science at The University of Queensland. She obtained a BSc (Hons) in the area of Psychology at the same university in 1996. She has worked as a researcher on the Sibling Study and is presently a researcher on a program focussing on injury in young adults for Injury Prevention and Control Australia.

Abigail A. Fagan

Dr Abigail A. Fagan received her Ph.D. in Sociology from the University of Colorado at Boulder. She is currently employed on a Post-Doctoral Fellowship at The University of Queensland, where she is involved in two longitudinal research projects investigating adolescent involvement in crime. Her areas of interest within criminology include crime prevention, gender and crime, and female offending.

Ross Homel

Professor Ross Homel is Foundation Professor of Criminology and Criminal Justice at Griffith University, and is also Deputy Director of the Australian Key Centre for Ethics, Law, Justice and Governance. He was from February 1994 to

April 1999 a part-time Commissioner of the Queensland Criminal Justice Commission. He has a particular interest in the prevention of crime, substance abuse and injuries, and has designed, implemented and evaluated several large community-based crime prevention programs.

Lisa Kennedy

Lisa Kennedy is currently a doctoral candidate in the School of Social Science at The University of Queensland. She has held positions in the public service and at The University of Queensland where she has been responsible for various crime research projects and program evaluation. She completed her Bachelor of Social Work (Hons) at the University of South Australia and her Masters in Social Welfare Administration and Planning at The University of Queensland.

Robyn Lincoln

Robyn Lincoln is an Assistant Professor in Criminology at Bond University on the Gold Coast, Australia where she has taught since 1994. She has previously worked at Queensland University of Technology as a lecturer, at The University of Queensland as a tutor and researcher, and at the Australian Institute of Aboriginal and Torres Strait Islander Studies in Canberra as Senior Editor with Aboriginal Studies Press. She was previously Managing Editor of the Journal of Sociology and Editor of the Australian Journal of Social Issues.

Mark Lynch

Dr Mark Lynch is Deputy Director of the Research and Prevention Division, Crime and Misconduct Commission. He has previously been employed as Executive Manager of the Juvenile Justice Branch, Department of Justice and as a Research Fellow at The University of Queensland. He received his Ph.D. on reconceptualising youth 'at risk' of criminality in 2002.

Stephanie McGrane

Stephanie McGrane received her Bachelor of Social Work from The University of Queensland. She has previously been employed as a Research Assistant on the Sibling Study. She is currently involved in youth justice conferencing within the Youth Justice Program, Department of Families, Queensland Government.

Ian O'Connor

Professor Ian O'Connor is Deputy Vice-Chancellor (Teaching and Learning) at Griffith University, Queensland. He has published extensively in the area of juvenile justice and juvenile crime, paying particular attention to the range of family and social factors associated with adolescent criminality. He is the author of Social Work and Welfare Practice (1998), Juvenile Crime, Justice and Corrections

(1997) and Contemporary Perspectives on Social Work and Human Services (1999).

Emma Ogilvie

Dr Emma Ogilvie is currently Principal Research Officer in Criminal Justice Research, Department of the Premier and Cabinet in the Queensland Government. At the time of writing she was a Sibling Study Research Fellow in the School of Social Science at The University of Queensland, and was previously a Criminology Research Council Postdoctoral Fellow at the Australian Institute of Criminology.

Rosie Teague

Rosie Teague is currently a doctoral candidate in the School of Criminology and Criminal Justice, Griffith University. She received her BSc (Hons) from the University of Birmingham in 1995. Her research and professional areas of interest include violence and crime prevention, community intervention programs and family violence.

John S. Western

Professor John Western has researched and published extensively in the areas of social inequality, class, ethnicity and social problems. He has been a Principal Investigator on a variety of large-scale research projects including the Professions Study and the Class and Stratification Project. He currently holds an Emeritus Professor position in the School of Social Science at The University of Queensland.

Acknowledgements

The authors of the chapters in this volume wish to record their thanks to a number of individuals without whose assistance this study would not have been possible. Firstly, we would like to acknowledge the assistance of Paul Wilson, a leading Australian criminologist, who in the early stages of the Sibling Study project helped shape its direction and then more recently provided valuable advice on how it should proceed. Our industry partners, the (then) Queensland Criminal Justice Commission, the State Government Department of Justice and Attorney General, and the (then) Corrective Services Commission in the persons of David Brereton, Ken Levy and Trevor Carlyon, matched in 'cash and kind' the funds provided by the Australian Research Council and ensured that the project had the resources to enable it to be undertaken. The Queensland Government Department of Families also played a crucial role in the project by facilitating our contact with young people on Supervised Orders and assisting the research conducted in the juvenile detention centers. Queensland Education was also helpful in arranging our access to sixteen government schools in the South East Queensland area. In the final stages of the preparation of this book additional funds were made available by Injury Prevention and Control (Australia) Ltd. (IPCA). These funds assisted us in bringing the phase of the project reported here to a successful conclusion.

Our respondents from 16 government schools, state schools in the Australian system, from the court system and juvenile detention centres, and from the streets of Brisbane, taught us a lot. At times they were somewhat bemused by our naivety, but they co-operated with us in good spirit and were pleased to provide an account of 'their side' of the story.

The manuscript would not have reached its final form without the expertise of Irene Saunderson and Jill Pappos, and we are of course delighted that Ashgate share with us a belief in the importance of this study and have provided this opportunity for our manuscript to see the light of day.

Finally, the authors of the chapters in this book, which includes the three editors, are equally culpable for the final product, which does not necessarily reflect the views of the agencies identified above, nor those of the organizations by which we are gainfully employed.

Chapter 1

The Sibling Study: Theory, Research and Guiding Principles

Mark Lynch, Stephanie McGrane, Emma Ogilvie and John S. Western

Introduction

At the heart of sociology is the Hobbesian question of why it is that people conform to normative structures. In a very real sense, the writings of the 'founding fathers' of sociology, Marx, Weber and Durkheim, constitute a seminal body of work aimed at revealing the hitherto hidden reasons for the conformity of people to the dominant values and ideas of the day. As a field of sociology, criminology shares this interest in the basis of conformity; however, what marks out criminology as a discipline in its own right is its focus upon why it is that (some) people do not conform and instead embrace criminality in a (perhaps) explicit rejection of the norms and values of the day.

Any examination of the factors associated with criminality and conformity is vastly more complicated than a simple listing of the characteristics of 'baddies' and 'goodies'. Risk factors consistently associated with criminality, such as poverty, family abuse and inadequate social support mechanisms, are not the exclusive prerogative of offenders. Similarly, protective factors such as socio-economic advantage and high levels of family support are not the exclusive preserve of non-offenders. As sociologists and criminologists, we are surprisingly ill-equipped to explain why it is that some adolescents from backgrounds characterized by neglect and marginalization do not engage in criminal behaviours while others from very advantaged backgrounds, with high levels of access to educational and cultural capital, do. Finally, but most importantly, we are especially poorly equipped to explain how it is that adolescents who do engage in crime may nonetheless simultaneously adhere to many of the norms and values of their non-offending counterparts. Our difficulty in explaining this contradiction points very directly to our inability to satisfactorily theorize both the nature of, and relations between, conformity and criminality.

To date, the major criminological explanations of conformity and criminality have developed on the basis of very different conceptions of the nature of human beings and human social relations. However, despite their differences, these divergent schools of thought are alike in the way in which, until quite recently, they tended to focus upon particular aspects of either conformity or criminality.

For example, control theory, the school of thought most explicitly dependent upon the concept of conformity, uses the concept to both signal and highlight law-abiding behaviours. To over generalize, for control theorists, deviance is taken for granted and it is conformity that must be explained. Somewhat similarly, developmental approaches draw upon the notion of conformity to investigate 'protective' factors, which may shield youth from dangerous and risk-taking behaviours, some of which are criminal. In contrast, classic strain theory begins with the premise that virtually all individuals accept the dominant cultural values, but that some may adopt illegitimate means to attain the goals enshrined in these values. For strain theorists, it is conformity that is taken for granted and deviance that must be explained. This focus is not dissimilar to the orientation central to the differential association theory pioneered by Sutherland. Differential association theorists emphasize the importance of significant others in the lives of adolescents, in that criminal behaviours are acquired when the values and judgments characterizing one's immediate social milieu run counter to the values of the larger society.

Notwithstanding their differences, each of these approaches yields important insights into how and why it is that the social order is characterized by certain enduring features. While most people conform most of the time, many people nevertheless engage in criminality at certain times and in certain circumstances. In seeking to disentangle the factors underpinning both conformity and criminality, criminology addresses the fundamental issues defining the social sciences. Criminology may have begun as a relatively junior player in the sociological arena, but with each advance in our understanding of conformity and criminality, it stakes a larger claim upon the broader terrain of the social sciences.

With these issues in mind, the objective of this introductory chapter is threefold. Firstly, to provide a brief overview of the key ways to date in which criminologists have sought to reconcile the tensions between conformity and criminality. Secondly, to describe in broad terms the research design of the Sibling Study project, and, thirdly, to outline how we see the Sibling Study research as making a substantive contribution to the current debates concerning law-breaking and law-abiding behaviours. In order to address these (related) objectives, it is useful to begin by very briefly considering the four theoretical orientations that have most decisively shaped the development of criminology as a discipline in its own right.

Social Control

Those who see the world from a social control perspective take as their starting point the view that humankind is essentially hedonistic, aggressive and manipulative, necessitating well-developed psycho-social barriers in order for individuals to adhere to the social order. Developing from the work of Travis Hirschi (1969), this approach seeks to explain the deviant and/or criminal by problematizing conformity. It asks the question: why is it that people conform? The social bond between individuals and society is central to the theory and consists of four major elements: attachment to significant others, commitment to social conformity, involvement in conventional activities, and belief in the moral validity of existing social norms. Delinquent and criminal behaviours are said to result from a fracturing or weakening of these bonds.

Gottfredson and Hirschi have further developed this perspective, claiming that criminality can be understood as a subset of behaviours in which individuals prioritize immediate pleasure over long-term consequences. The crucial factor underpinning this preference is 'self-control', or the 'tendency to avoid acts whose long-term costs exceed their momentary advantages' (Gottfredson and Hirschi, 1990:3). This is not to say that low self-control *causes* criminality, but, rather, that individuals with low self-control are the most likely to take advantage of opportunities for criminality and/or reckless acts in general.

There is considerable empirical support for this position, and, as a result, it has markedly influenced criminological research over the past three decades. Indeed, a survey identified more than seventy publications using the concept of control (Kempf, 1993). Hirschi's approach has been used to explain the gendering of crime (Hagan, Gillis and Simpson 1985, Zager 1994), school experiences and delinquency (Empey and Lubeck 1971, Kruttschnitt *et al* 1986, Cernkovich and Giordano 1992, Zingraff *et al* 1994) and perhaps most extensively, the impact of family on delinquency.

The interest in the influence of family-related factors upon delinquency has typically involved a concern with both family structure (including 'broken' homes) and the nature of intra-familial relationships. Two major findings from studies examining these issues have been, firstly, that adolescent offenders are disproportionately likely to come from single parent families (Rosen and Neilson, 1978; Haskell and Yablonsky 1982), and, secondly, that an inverse relationship exists between attachment to parents and delinquency, regardless of social class or ethnicity (Hirschi 1969, Hindelang 1973, Gibbs, Giever and Martin 1998). Of these two factors, parental attachment has consistently proved to be the stronger predictor of adolescent offending.[1]

Despite the apparent strength of these findings, recent longitudinal research suggests that social control variables actually have a rather weak effect on adolescent offending (see Kempf 1993, Greenburg 1999, Thornberry 1987 1994, Agnew 1985 1991a). However, it may be that future longitudinal studies should more closely examine the impact of social bonds among pre-adolescents (Agnew 1991a). The argument here being that family and school factors have a significant impact on the formation of delinquent predispositions during pre-adolescence, but that their importance declines during adolescence, when the peer group becomes more influential.

---

1 Moreover, recent studies have concluded that the overall relationship between broken homes and delinquency is not as strong as was first thought (Free 1991, Wells and Rankin 1991, Kennedy 1999).

Developmental Perspectives

A related approach focuses on the 'pathways' of adolescent trajectories (Cairns and Cairns 1994, Farrington 2002, Robins and Rutter 1990),[2] in which it is recognized that there are multiple pathways to conformity and criminality and that different individuals may choose alternative routes to these outcomes. A considerable body of research is currently aimed at identifying possible developmental pathways that lead to crime and substance abuse, with considerable attention being paid to risk and protective factors that may influence individuals during critical transition points in their lives (National Crime Prevention 1999, see also Bor, Najman, O'Callaghan, Williams and Anstey 2001, Greenwood, Model, Rydell and Chiesa 1996, Keating and Hertzman 1999, Loeber and Farrington 1994). The social context is a crucial element identified in this approach, particularly the level of support available to those choosing different paths (Homel, Lincoln and Herd 1999). Developmental theorists can thus be seen to be working to identify those pathways that are injurious to adolescents and the broader community, and those pathways that are beneficial.

Developmental approaches have been criticized, however, particularly with respect to their conceptualization of 'risk'. It has been argued that programs based upon 'at risk' transition points serve to define youth as 'the problem' (Lubeck and Garrett 1990), in that 'young people who do not conform to the standards of the mainstream are identified as 'at risk', requiring specific attention to bring them into line with the mainstream' (Wyn and White 1997:52). This scepticism regarding the explanatory power of developmental and social control approaches invites attention to other ways of understanding the conditions for criminality and conformity. It is to these perspectives that we now turn.

Strain Theory

Classical strain theory argues that while most people adhere to the dominant values of society and so share the desire for material success, status and prosperity, many lack the legitimate means to fulfil these desires. Problems arise not because people have rejected societal goals, but because, in order to realize these goals, they have had to resort to illegitimate means such as theft or property crime. For early strain theorists, such as Robert Merton (1938), the primary motivating factor for criminal behaviour was the desire for monetary success. Merton (1938) argued that deviance arose from the fact that America's socio-cultural system encouraged a perception at odds with reality, that upward social mobility was universally possible. Having accepted the dominant cultural markers of success, if people

---

2   It should be noted that these approaches are being compared due to their common interest in 'protective' factors. Nonetheless there are important differences, with control theory being more focused upon integration into society, and developmental approaches being more interested in the complex interactions between biology, family, peers and culture which serve to protect people from criminal trajectories.

could not achieve wealth via legitimate means, they would then turn to crime in order to satisfy the socially constructed desires they experienced. Subsequent developments in strain theory have both challenged and broadened Merton's perspective so as to include other pressures that may encourage nonconforming conduct in some people in some circumstances.

Beginning with a commitment to Merton's original formulation, Cohen (1955) sought to take into account the importance of social class. Arguing that delinquency was significantly class-based, Cohen maintained that the delinquent subculture arose out of a need by working class youths to 'get even' with an unfair society: 'The delinquent subculture takes its norms from the larger culture but turns them upside down. The delinquent's conduct is right, by the standards of his subculture, precisely because it is wrong by the norms of the larger culture' (Cohen 1955:28). Importantly, this is one of the first attempts to position delinquency as an exercise of conformity to a subcultural set of standards and values, rather than as non-conforming behaviour with respect to wider norms.

Cloward and Ohlin (1960) also argued that young people were forced into deviancy because they could not achieve the universal goals of status and wealth. The specific nature of this delinquency, however, is dependent upon the particular neighbourhood in which the delinquent adolescent lives. Accordingly, in neighbourhoods where there was an established adult criminal subculture, young thieves and robbers could be recruited into the larger subculture (thereby maintaining the criminal subculture). Rather than view conformity and deviancy as an enduring aspect of social systems with essentially fixed characteristics, Cloward and Ohlin describe an altogether more fluid and evolutionary process.

Since the late 1960s, the relevance of strain theory to sociological/criminological studies on juvenile crime has increasingly been questioned. It has been widely claimed that the approach is unsupported by the empirical evidence (Hirschi 1969, Box 1971, Kornhauser 1978); that it is both class- and gender-biased (Hirschi 1969, Gottfredson and Hirschi 1990); and that it is actually a special type of control theory Burton and Cullen 1992, Cullen 1984, Hirschi 1969). Yet, as Passas and Agnew (1997) argue in defense of the theory, there are an increasing number of criminologists who are re-examining the empirical evidence, conducting more sophisticated tests, and, as a result, refining and extending the theory.

In particular, Agnew and White's General Strain Theory (GST) (Agnew and White 1992), a broader reformulation of the original approach has fostered renewed interest in the strain perspective. GST recognizes that there may be a variety of sources of strain, including the failure to achieve positively valued goals, the removal of positively valued stimuli, and the presentation or threat of negative stimuli (Agnew and White 1992). It is the focus given to negative life events and their relationship to delinquency that distinguishes GST from other classical delinquency theories, such as control and differential association, which tend instead to concentrate on positive relationships (or lack thereof) (Hoffman and Su 1997:47).

In the first explicit empirical analysis using GST, Agnew and White (1992) demonstrated that a composite measure of strain, based on negative life events and negative relationships with others, was as good a predictor of delinquency and adolescent drug use as a composite scale comprising social control and social learning variables. In a similar study, Paternoster and Mazerolle (1994) confirmed the finding that several dimensions of general strain were positively related to involvement in a wide range of delinquent acts. Further, this analysis suggested that strain had the indirect effect of 'weakening the inhibitions of the social bond and increasing one's involvement with delinquent peers' (1994:235).

Other research reports that the relationship between stressful life events and delinquency and drug use is similar for male and female adolescents (Hoffman and Su 1997; Grossman *et al* 1992). These latter findings tend to contradict the theoretical analysis of gender and crime provided by Broidy and Agnew (1997), who concluded that while both males and females experienced anger in response to strain, the 'anger of females [was] more likely to be accompanied by depression, guilt, anxiety, and related states' (1997:287). It was assumed that these accompanying states would reduce the likelihood of aggressive criminal behaviour and increase the likelihood of self-destructive and escapist actions. Broidy and Agnew (1997) argue that the failure of the empirical studies to find sex differences is due to the fact that only certain types of strain were examined, the negative emotion measures used were limited or absent, and, finally, only minor forms of aggression or crime were considered.

Differential Association

While social control theory argues for the importance of strong social bonds for the maintenance of social conformity, and strain theory asserts the importance of 'means/ends' relationships, differential association highlights the significance of social learning. At the heart of Sutherland's (1947) approach is the concept of cultural diversity and the fact that there are many forms of consensus in society. Rather than there being a single (or dominant) conventional set of norms, Sutherland suggests that there is a wide range of subcultures with very different norms. Some emphasize violation of the law and others emphasize conformity to it. Delinquency is an expression of conformity to (subcultural) norms that run counter to the values of the wider society. The emphasis here is on learning to conform to the expectations of *significant others* within one's own cultural milieu. In this sense, differential association theory differs markedly from control theory, in its suggestion that delinquent impulses are learned (and contingent) rather than universal.

A substantial body of empirical studies has provided general support for the differential association thesis. Research into the dynamics of peer relationships has consistently found that involvement with delinquent peers is a powerful predictor of engaging in delinquent or criminal behaviour (Thompson *et al* 1984, Johnson *et al* 1987, Matseuda 1988, Agnew 1991b, Empey and Stafford 1991, Warr 1993, Mears *et al* 1998). Three relatively recent studies (Agnew 1991b, Warr 1993, Mears *et al* 1998) that utilized data from the National Youth Survey (NYS), a longitudinal, national survey of 1,725 adolescents, all supported the influence of peer associations on delinquency. In examining peer attachment factors, Agnew (1991b) found that a high level of interaction with peers who engage in serious delinquency, as opposed to low or moderate levels, significantly contributed to involvement in serious delinquent acts.

In the second analysis, Warr (1993) examined the usefulness of differential association theory in interpreting the age-crime relationship among young people. Although conceding that friendships, including those with delinquent peers, tended to last beyond adolescence (i.e. the 'sticky friend' phenomenon), Warr (1993:25) contended that, like the age distribution of crime itself, 'the role of peers is transitory, rising and falling quickly during a relatively brief period of life'. The relevance of peers in the lives of young persons was found to be strongest during the middle to late teen years, but declined thereafter.[3]

In the third analysis, Mears *et al* (1998) investigated gender differences in delinquency to determine whether females were differentially affected by exposure to delinquent peers. Their analysis provided support for the notion that males were substantially more likely than females to have delinquent friends and were 'more strongly affected by delinquent peers than females' (Mears *et al* 1998:263). The authors also observe that the moral judgment of females was able to sufficiently reduce and even eliminate the impact of delinquent peers. Finally, they conceded that the study did not support the idea that attitude transference among adolescents was the sole or primary mechanism for the transmission of delinquency.

If differential association theory has a fundamental shortcoming, it is the difficulty entailed in using it as a general framework for conceptualizing delinquency. Increasingly, ideas drawn from differential association theory are being integrated with important elements of other theoretical approaches in broader attempts to offer a more complete explanation of delinquency (see Matsueda 1988, Reinarman and Fagan 1988). For example, the results of two studies that investigated the role of peers (Johnson *et al* 1987) and the attachment to parents (Dembo *et al* 1986) in the aetiology of adolescent drug use both suggested some interactive effects between differential association and social control theory.

Review

Given these different theoretical perspectives and their varying levels of empirical support, what conclusions might we draw about adolescent criminality? Clearly, no single approach to explaining crime is entirely satisfactory. The lines between the approaches are increasingly blurring, as social scientists attempt to compensate for the weaknesses of some approaches by 'grafting' on stronger aspects of other approaches.

---

3   This finding would seem to contradict the idea that delinquent behaviour declines with age and, as Warr acknowledged, further scrutiny is needed to adequately interpret the implications of this phenomenon.

The more rigorous our empirical demands of particular theories, the more counterproductive overly partisan approaches appear. The social sciences are not like some of the natural sciences, where if one approach is proved, other approaches are necessarily disproved. In other words, an increased quantum of empirical support for differential association (for example) does not somehow mean that control theory (for example) is weakened by an equivalent amount. The 'trick' therefore is not so much the identification of a 'one size fits all' theory, but, rather, the identification of the many different contexts and turning points in the pathways to crime and conformity, and the recognition that different theories are all relevant (to a greater or lesser extent at different points in time) in explaining these processes. Theoretical perspectives, such as strain, control, differential association and learning theory, all have something important to reveal about the complex process whereby experiencing the social world transforms children into adults. Central to this transformative process characterizing the adolescent years is a grappling with social forces encouraging conformity on the one hand and criminality on the other.

What this all points to is the problematic nature of the very concepts of criminality and conformity. It is all too easy to position these concepts as markers for attitudes and behaviours that are the polar opposite of one another. But, does anyone really believe we can so neatly dichotomise matters? If an individual fails to conform to the prevailing norms and values of their society because their expression of conformity to those values is atypical or deviant, are they necessarily criminal? Similarly, if an individual seemingly does conform to the norms and values of the day, but this adherence is based upon problematic understandings of those values, are they actually conformist? Who is the conformist and who is the criminal: the 14 year old girl who steals in order to pay her mother's drug debts, or the 16 year old boy who informs on a co-offender in order to hasten release from prison through a demonstration of rehabilitation? It is precisely these sorts of questions that arise when we consider the implications of the different theoretical perspectives touched upon thus far. Answering questions of this sort, however, requires comprehensive data drawn from very diverse adolescent groups/subcultures. It is precisely this breadth of data that are available in the Sibling Study research project described in this book. The Sibling Study project provides a means of empirically addressing the conformity/criminality question from a wide variety of theoretical perspectives.

The central focus of the Sibling Study research program is the identification of those factors that contribute to adolescent engagement in illegal behaviours, and those that inhibit such engagement. With this focus in mind, the study has been framed since its inception by a concern to take account of the major schools of thought within contemporary criminology. The result of this commitment has been a coordinated research program equipped to simultaneously examine the impact of a broad range of potential causal factors on young people's involvement in the criminal justice system.

Study Design

The Sibling Study research design was developed in order to permit a detailed comparison of the trajectories of serious offenders and non-offenders. These comparisons were to be based upon data from a 65-page self-report questionnaire containing in excess of 200 questions. This questionnaire was developed with the explicit intention of empirically operationalizing the major theoretical perspectives outlined earlier and exploring the range of potential influences on crime including demographic characteristics, as well as structural, neighbourhood, family, and individual factors that we have already described. A number of established scales were used, including the Attitudes to Self and Others Scale (Feeney and Noller 1996, Feeney, Noller and Hanrahan 1994), the Delinquent Disposition Scale (Paternoster and Mazerolle 1994), the Parental Bonding Instrument (Parker, Tupling and Brown 1979), the Attitude to Authority Scale (Rigby and Schofield 1985), the Australian Self-Report Delinquency Scale (Mak 1993) and the Low Self-Control Scale (Grasmick, Tittle, Bursik and Arneklev 1993).

In addition, a number of questions were developed that were considered to be of specific relevance to Australian young people. For example, questions were included concerning sexual orientation and activity (of those 13 years and older), body image, cultural 'tastes', access to public amenities, ethical decision-making and perceptions of their environment. Qualitative data to elicit further details regarding the nature of young people's trajectories through adolescence were also collected.

Three key features distinguish the Sibling Study research design. Firstly, the design is quasi-experimental, incorporating four discrete cohorts. Secondly, wherever possible the sample draws upon mixed-sex sibling pairs aged between 12 and 18 years and not separated in age by more than three years. Thirdly, the study is planned as longitudinal. Respondents were first interviewed in 1995, followed by a second wave of interviews in 1998/99, and it is anticipated that a third wave of interviews will be conducted around 2003/2004.

The use of mixed-sex sibling pairs was perhaps the most innovative feature of the research design. This strategy was adopted in order to exploit the well-established finding with respect to juvenile criminality that males typically offend at around five times the rate of females (Chesney-Lind 1997, Ogilvie, Lynch and Bell 2000, Triplett and Myers 1995). With this finding in mind, the notion guiding the initial project development was that the identification of those aspects of socialization closely associated with the gendering of young people was simultaneously also likely to identify the factors associated with the sex effects so consistently observed in studies of adolescent offending. By using mixed-sex sibling pairs, there was obviously also some degree of control being exercised over the potentially confounding effects of background or home environment.

The quasi-experimental research design was utilized in order to acquire respondent groups of particular relevance to the research goals. In order to maximize the dependent variable, offending young people, and minimize the standard error associated with multivariate analyses of the determinants of juvenile criminality, adolescents officially identified as criminal offenders were over-sampled. For the same reason, young people deemed to be 'at risk' or 'vulnerable' (as they are arguably better described) were also over-sampled. In order to compare the criminal activities of these youth with adolescents likely to have lower rates of crime, a third group was obtained, which included young people drawn from a range of South East Queensland high schools. Finally, a small cohort of Indigenous young people from urban areas was also included in the study.

The longitudinal aspect of the design was also an important defining feature. In particular, the ability to re-interview respondents over time permits a rare opportunity to examine trajectories from late childhood to early adulthood.

A number of assumptions were implicit in the design strategy. Firstly, it was assumed that criminality was a socially learned behaviour, rather than a 'hard-wired' biological imperative. Moreover, it was assumed that adolescence represented a particularly important period of learning masculinity and femininity (i.e. gender roles and behaviours). It was further assumed that the process of illuminating the social bases of *learned gender* would by corollary reveal key aspects of whatever it is that propels some young people (disproportionately male) into criminal trajectories.

Covariance Structures Within the Sibling Study Data

While the unique aspects of the Sibling Study research design provide for an unusually broad range of inquiry, they also introduce covariance structures regarding the inter-sibling correlations that need to be considered. The presence of very marked sibling correlations could undermine the extent to which findings from the data analysis might be generalized to the larger population of young people in Australia. However, to the extent that sibling correlations are present in the data, they are (perhaps surprisingly) modest. Exploratory analyses were undertaken to examine whether there was a relationship between older and younger siblings and self-reported offending. Total scores were calculated from 32 items on the Australian Self-Report Delinquency Scale (Mak 1993). There was no significant relationship in siblings' self-reported offending for either the School cohort ($r=0.05$, $p<0.40$) or the Offender cohort ($r=-0.08$, $p<0.65$). However, there was a significant association in self-reported offending among siblings from the Vulnerable group ($r=0.43$, $p<0.05$). Nonetheless, the Vulnerable cohort is the smallest of the three primary cohorts and only 32 per cent of the cohort had a sibling that also participated in the study. This rate is obviously low compared to the School cohort, in which 83 per cent was part of a sibling pair. Given these data, it was deemed unnecessary in the essentially exploratory analyses included in this book to control for sibling effects. The issue is examined in more detail in Chapter 9 (see summary below) and will be further explored in future analyses based on the longitudinal data.

Sibling Study Sample

Table 1.1 presents information regarding the four cohorts of the Sibling Study. As shown, these vary in size, with the largest group drawn from South East Queensland schools ($n= 678$), followed by the Offender cohort ($n=225$), the Vulnerable cohort ($n=160$), and the urban Indigenous cohort ($n=62$). It is also important to note that the number of mixed-sex sibling pairs also varies across the four groups. While almost 83 per cent of the School cohort is made up of sibling pairs, both the Vulnerable and Offender groups have slightly more than 30 per cent sibling pair components, while there are no sibling pairs in the urban Indigenous cohort.

Table 1.1   The Sibling Study cohorts

Cohort	n	Percentage of Total Sample	Paired Siblings (% of Sample)	
School	678	60.27	562	(82.9)
Vulnerable	160	14.22	52	(32.5)
Offender	225	20.00	68	(30.2)
Indigenous	62	5.51	–	
Total	1125	100.00	682	(60.6)

It is important to note that, in the analyses reported in the majority of the following chapters, the Indigenous cohort is not included due to its small sample size, but Indigenous young people are the subject of Chapter 9. The methods used to select the other three cohorts varied and are described in detail below. The qualitative component of the study is also described.

The School Cohort

In early 1994, the Director-General of the Queensland Department of Education was approached in order to seek departmental support for administration of the Sibling Study questionnaire to high school students aged between 12 and 18 years old (inclusive). Approval for the project was obtained and the Director-General forwarded letters in support of the research to the principals of 23 Brisbane high schools. The Department of Education nominated these 23 schools as constituting a reasonably even 'spread' of schools in terms of a departmental measure, the Index of Relative Disadvantage[4] determined largely by the socio-demographic characteristics of the families from which the students in each school came.

As a result of the Director-General's letter, as well as subsequent discussions with the Sibling Study Consortium, 16 high schools agreed to participate in the research. Despite a small over-representation of least disadvantaged schools, the

---

4   This measure is no longer used by the Queensland Department of Education.

final (School) sample frame and distribution of respondents contained a good distribution of schools in terms of the Index of Relative Disadvantage. In fact, the Queensland Department of Education advised the Consortium that they considered the final sample a close approximation to the population distribution of both Queensland schools and students/respondents. With this mind, it is not unreasonable to treat the School cohort as broadly representative of the population of young people aged between 12 and 18 years in Queensland in the mid-1990s.

The Vulnerable Cohort

In the initial thinking about the study, the specification of 'Vulnerable' was only loosely defined. This group was always envisaged as incorporating young people who were demonstrably at risk of coming into formal contact with the juvenile criminal justice system, in terms of some clearly defined criteria. However, the problematic nature of the concept of 'at-risk' designation (see, for example, Bessant 2001, Hil 2000) made it difficult to determine appropriate criteria on which to select respondents for this cohort. Advice was sought from the (then) Department of Family Services and Aboriginal and Torres Strait Islander Affairs who had responsibility for the management of *Care and Protection Orders* for young people as to what criteria might most sensibly be employed. On the basis of the advice obtained, 'at-risk' was operationalized as adolescents who were chronically marginalized/disadvantaged. This definition meant a sub-sample of young people known to a range of government and non-government social support services (for precisely these reasons) who could be invited to participate in the research project. In addition, a limited number of respondents were obtained directly from the 'street' as well as via word-of-mouth from other respondents. The 'street' respondents were obtained exclusively from one inner city location acknowledged by the police, support agencies and the respondents themselves as being a 'hang' for the target group. The word-of-mouth (i.e. 'snowball') contacts were almost exclusively obtained as a consequence of respondents contacted through support agencies persuading friends in the same position as themselves to participate.

Slightly less than half this cohort (*n*=71) was obtained through the access provided by various support agencies; a further 44 respondents came from the 'street' interviews and 45 from word-of-mouth snowballing. The proportion of this cohort comprising sibling pairs was 32 per cent. In general, the Vulnerable cohort contains a small percentage of sibling pairs, but this is not surprising given the characteristics of this group (i.e. chronically marginalized and disadvantaged youth).

A sense of the Vulnerable respondents can perhaps be gained by noting the following example. A support agency had agreed to permit Sibling Study researchers to talk to their clients about the research and arrange the participation of those young people willing to take part in the project. A Sibling Study researcher arrived at the agency at 7:30am on what was officially recorded as the coldest day of 1995. Two very lightly clad young people (a male/female couple) were found attempting to sleep on the open verandah of the agency premises. Not only was it exceptionally cold and exposed on the verandah, but also at 5:00am the automatic garden sprinklers had turned on and immediately drenched the young couple. The couple was friendly and unassuming, but was primarily concerned with seeking warmth, coffee and cigarettes until later in the day when they were confident they could obtain a meal and a bed from the Salvation Army.

This couple was typical of many of the young people being assisted by the different support agencies. Unemployment, (poly)substance abuse, high mobility, 'criminal' peer networks, a history of traumatic life-events, limited education and a relaxed attitude towards criminality all contribute to the basis upon which this group are deemed to be 'at risk' or *vulnerable* to suffering the impact of marginalization which may lead to offending or self-harmful behaviours. It should also be noted that these social support agencies also represented a 'first stop' for many young people after being discharged from a youth detention centre.

The Offender Cohort

The Offender cohort was derived from three sources within the juvenile criminal justice system. Roughly equal numbers of respondents were drawn from youth detention centres ($n = 72$), 'appearances' at the Children's Court ($n = 77$) and young people on 'supervised orders' ($n = 76$). Although each of these three categories contains respondents readily identifiable as 'offenders', there are nevertheless some differences between these groups that need to be acknowledged.

The Detention Centre Respondents

The Detention Centre respondents included all incarcerated females and slightly more than half of all incarcerated males in detention centres in South East Queensland at the time of the interviews. Respondents were interviewed over a three-month period in early 1995. As revealed in qualitative interviews (described in more detail later in this chapter), at least half of the 72 respondents clearly fall at the more serious end of the offending spectrum. Although property crimes were the most common, this group also included respondents detained for murder, attempted murder, (child) rape, armed robbery and aggravated assault.

Not surprisingly, there are relatively few sibling pairs within this cohort. The inability to access siblings largely derived from a lack of knowledge by some respondents as to the location of siblings, as well as a desire by some respondents to protect siblings from the perceived invasive nature of the questionnaire.

The Children's Court Respondents

The 77 respondents interviewed at the Children's Court were obtained by approaching young people appearing in court (particularly for sentencing) and seeking their agreement to be interviewed. This procedure was approved by the responsible department, the (then) Department of Family Services and Torres Strait Islander Affairs. In addition to adolescents who were convicted and/or sentenced, this group comprises a number of respondents who had earlier been convicted of an offence and who were in court to support a friend appearing in relation to some offence. Interestingly, these individuals also included a number who were members of one of the few genuine youth 'gangs' in Brisbane (as opposed to the looser networks that are better described as 'crews'), the 'Toombul Boys' (widely recognized for taking pride in their reputation for being 'staunch' and a preparedness to engage in criminality for both fun and profit).

Although this sub-category includes more sibling pairs than does the incarcerated group, the final number of paired siblings was only 14. This low yield derives from most respondents believing they had more immediately pressing concerns than 'helping out Uni wankers'.

The Supervised Orders Respondents

With the assistance of the (then) Department of Family Services and Torres Strait Islander Affairs, young people aged between 12 and 18 years who were 'on file' as having been or currently on a supervised order, were contacted by mail by Sibling Study researchers. Young people on *Care and Protection Orders* or on an order for a *Status Offence* (running away from home, for example) were excluded from consideration. Although a total of 76 respondents was obtained over a seven-month period through the use of this procedure, given that more than 1000 letters inviting participation were sent out, this initiative was without doubt the least successful research strategy employed.

Perhaps because these young people were in the community rather than detention and had their cases resolved rather than in process, a much larger number of paired siblings was obtained with respect to this sub-sample than obtained in court or detention. Of the 76 respondents in this group, 52 were members of a sibling pair. One consequence of this strategy is the potential for 'diluting' the sample through the inclusion of non-offending siblings within this group. Whilst a degree of dilution is undoubtedly the case, this is not as great a concern as might be expected. Fully 100 per cent of this group (including siblings) reported having 'done something against the law,' although this does of course include some relatively minor transgressions. However, the fact that those who *had* come into formal contact with the criminal justice system had received supervised orders rather than non-supervised orders or detention, also points to the medium-level nature of their offences. This sub-category should thus be viewed as disproportionately comprising lower- to medium-level offenders who had been apprehended and (some) offending siblings who had not been apprehended.

The Qualitative Sample

As noted, qualitative interviews were conducted with 30 serious offenders (15 female and 15 male) incarcerated in two Queensland detention centres. Interviews were voluntary and semi-structured, following the general topics covered in the questionnaire, but also allowing respondents to direct the topics covered in the interviews if they preferred. With respect to obtaining contextual information, the respondents were treated 'as a witness who can report on the events being studied' (Wright and Bennett 1990:142). Interviews were conducted over a period of three months, taking approximately two and a half hours at a time, with most respondents interviewed between two and 15 times over the three-month period. The male sample is comprised of four boys aged 15 years, eight aged 16 years, two aged 17 years and one aged 14 years. In comparison, the female sample comprised seven girls aged 16 years, five aged 15 years, two aged 17 years and one aged 14 years. There were seven non-Indigenous girls and eight non-Indigenous boys, six Aboriginal and/or Torres Strait Islander girls and four Aboriginal and/or Torres Strait Islander boys, two Maori boys, one Tongan girl and one Tongan boy, and one girl who refused to identify herself as either Indigenous or non-Indigenous. (For a more detailed overview of the qualitative methodology see Ogilvie 1999.) In order to protect the anonymity of respondents, pseudonyms are utilized throughout the chapters in which qualitative data are used.

Now that the guiding principles, research instrument, design and sample selection of the Study have been discussed, we turn briefly to a consideration of some demographic characteristics of the young people comprising the sample.

Characteristics of the Sample

Sex

As can be seen in Table 1.2, the Sibling Study sample comprises a predictable variation in the sex distribution across the cohorts. Although the School and Vulnerable cohorts contain relatively equal numbers of females and males, the Offender cohort comprises 71 per cent male and 29 per cent female respondents.

Table 1.2 The Sibling Study cohorts by sex

Sex of Respondent	Cohort					
	School		Vulnerable		Offender	
	n	%	*n*	%	*n*	%
Female	348	51	82	51	65	29
Male	330	49	78	49	160	71

The disproportionate level of males derives from the much smaller number of females sentenced to detention for serious offending (see Alder and Hunter 1999, Carrington 1993, Ogilvie 1996, Ogilvie and Lynch 2001). The slight discrepancies with respect to the School and Vulnerable cohorts are the result of a policy decision made during the interviewing phase of the research. Same-sex siblings who sought to participate were accepted as respondents; likewise, respondents were not excluded if their opposite-sex sibling ultimately decided not to participate in the research.

Age

Table 1.3 outlines the age distribution of the three cohorts. As can be seen, respondents vary in age from 12 to 19 years. The Vulnerable and Offender groups are closely matched in age, with mean ages of 15.5 and 15.6 years, respectively, while respondents in the School cohort are somewhat younger, having a mean age of 14.4 years.

Table 1.3   Mean ages of the Sibling Study cohorts

Cohort	*n*	Mean Age (Years)	Minimum Age	Maximum Age
School	671	14.4	12	18
Vulnerable	141	15.5	12	19
Offender	221	15.6	12	19

Note: Excludes 11 year old respondents (*n*= 6), respondents older than 19 (*n*=16) and respondents for whom no age was recorded (*n*=8).

Socio-Economic Disadvantage

Based on their home address, Sibling Study respondents were given a score on the measure of socio-economic disadvantage developed by the (then) Queensland Government Statistician's Office, the Index of Relative Disadvantage. The distribution of these scores collapsed over a five-point scale for the total sample is shown in the first column of Table 1.4.

As can be seen, the group is evenly distributed across this measure. The 17 per cent of respondents from suburbs deemed to be most disadvantaged are neatly matched by the 18 per cent of respondents from suburbs deemed to be least disadvantaged. The single largest category of respondents (21 per cent) is from suburbs midway between these two extremes.

A more focused appreciation of this measure can be gained by considering it with respect to the three cohorts of interest. The relevant data are provided in the second, third and fourth columns of Table 1.4. As we might expect, 24 per cent of the School cohort fall into the least disadvantaged category, followed by 15 per cent of the Vulnerable group and 11 per cent of the Offenders. However, when we turn to the most disadvantaged category we find both the School and Offender cohorts at 18 per cent, whilst fully 29 per cent of the Vulnerable cohort live in areas classified in this way.

Table 1.4   Collapsed Index of Relative Disadvantage for the total sample and each cohort (column percentages)

Level of Disadvantage	Total Sample	School	Cohort Vulnerable	Offender
1 – Most Disadvantaged	17	18	29	18
2 –	13	10	30	23
3 –	21	24	13	33
4 –	19	24	14	15
5 – Least Disadvantaged	18	24	15	11
n	991	676	125	190

Note: Missing values=72, *n*=991.

The Sample by Parental Presence in the Household

As shown in the first column of Table 1.5, 58 per cent of respondents recorded their household as including both their mother and father. A further 16 per cent listed a mother but no father, while six per cent of the young people reported having no parents in their home. Once again, a better appreciation of these data can be obtained by examining the distribution with respect to the three samples of interest. The data are provided in columns two to four of Table 1.5.

Very marked differences between the three samples in terms of family structure can be observed. The high level of dual (mother/father) carer families shown in the first column of the table appears to be very much a function of the characteristics and size of the School cohort. When the data are examined more closely, 77 per cent of the School respondents report both a mother and father in their household, but only 43 per cent of the Vulnerable cohort and 29 per cent of the Offender cohort do so. Similarly, 12 per cent of the School respondents report having a mother only in their household, compared to six per cent of the Vulnerable cohort but 27 per cent of the Offender cohort. Likewise, whilst only two per cent of the School respondents report a father-only family structure, this was reported by six per cent of respondents in both the Vulnerable and Offender samples.

Perhaps the most telling data relate to households in which neither a mother nor a father is present. Whilst less than one per cent of the School cohort report living in such a household, 23 per cent of the Vulnerable cohort and 17 per cent of the Offenders report this family structure. And finally, while only one per cent of the School group report living with relatives, six per cent of the Vulnerable group and 13 per cent of the Offender cohort report doing so.

Table 1.5   Parental presence in the household for the total sample and each cohort (column percentages)

Parental Presence	Total Sample	School	Cohort Vulnerable	Offender
Mother and Father	58	77	43	29
Mother and Step-Father	6	6	7	8
Father and Step-Mother	1	1	1	1
Mother Only	16	12	6	27
Father Only	3	2	6	6
No Parents	6	0	23	17
Relatives (no parents)	5	1	6	13
n	1033	670	149	214

Note: Missing values=40, *n*=1033.

These last two tables in particular highlight graphic differences in the relative social advantage of the three cohorts. How this translates into differences in experiences with the juvenile justice system will be one of our major concerns in the chapters that follow.

The Nature of These Chapters

Each of the chapters that follow has been developed to examine a range of attributes thought to be associated with criminality and conformity. As a result, they explore key background factors of class, gender, and age, as well as the mediating factors of family dynamics, peer relationships, social networks, and individual characteristics, as they impact upon self-reported offending, involvement with the juvenile justice system, and victimization. The chapters are as follows:

Chapter 2: Offending Behaviours: Situated Choices and Consequences
John S. Western, Mark Lynch, Emma Ogilvie and Abigail A. Fagan

In this chapter, the authors provide an initial examination of the data from the Study, with the primary purpose of examining whether the immediate pathways to criminality are different across the cohorts and for females and males. The chapter begins by focusing on the types of crimes young people from different social groups commit and the motivations they report as underpinning their offending Whether the cohorts have different opportunities for access to criminality, whether they place different values on the censure of social groups, how they perceive the likelihood of being caught or punished and, overall, what effect this has on their decisions about criminality and conformity are all considered.

Chapter 3: Age and Offending: Characteristics and Criminological Factors
Mark Lynch, Emma Ogilvie and Wing Hong Chui

Age makes a difference to offending, and in this chapter the authors trace the changing meaning of offending that is associated with movement away from childhood and towards adulthood.

Chapter 4: Gender and Offending Behaviours: Opportunity, Motivations and Manifestations
Emma Ogilvie and John S. Western

There are marked gender differences in terms of opportunity, motivation, engagement and the 'experience' of criminality. Ogilvie and Western highlight some of these while drawing on both quantitative and qualitative data from the Sibling Study. At the same time, they suggest some possible alternatives to commonly accepted explanations of gender differences.

Chapter 5: Gender and Offending Attitudes: Criminality, Compliance and Complexity
Emma Ogilvie

In this chapter, Ogilvie raises further questions about current explanations of gender and offending, and suggests alternative strategies for understanding femininity, masculinity and criminality. In particular, she argues that for young females at least, 'gender specific' explanations are more useful in explaining non-criminal conformist behaviours, than they are in explaining criminal behaviours.

Chapter 6: Social Inequality, Alienation and Socio-Economic Position
John S. Western

Western argues in this chapter that social class differences lead to social inequality, and that increasing social polarization contributes to the development of anomic structures. Both social inequality and the low self-esteem that flows from anomic structures may impact on criminality. Data from the Sibling Study are drawn upon in considering these issues.

Chapter 7: Family Influences and Delinquency
Lisa Kennedy, Ian O'Connor and John S. Western

The ways in which parenting practices including parental support and supervision influence reported delinquent behaviour among the cohorts are considered by the authors of this chapter. They report that maternal care seems more important than paternal care in providing an environment for conformity. Age, gender and family structure also appear to impact on the effects of parenting practices.

Chapter 8: The Influence of Siblings on Delinquency
Denise A. Durrington, Abigail A. Fagan and David Chant

Sibling similarities in delinquent behaviours provide important insight into the causative factors for delinquency. Durrington, Fagan and Chant begin an analysis into this complex relationship and point the way for further research, suggesting that other characteristics of the family may also be important in understanding the relationships uncovered.

Chapter 9: Urban Indigenous Young People: Criminality, Accommodation or Resistance
Mark Lynch, Abigail A. Fagan, Emma Ogilvie and Robyn Lincoln

This chapter focuses on urban Indigenous youth and self-reported criminality. The authors draw attention to the ways in which criminality appears to represent an act of 'resistance' for some Indigenous young people and discusses the ways in which this resistance is accommodated within Indigenous cultural values. The chapter explores aspects of family, neighbourhood, education, and peer-networks, as risk/protective factors.

Chapter 10: Adolescent Victimization and Involvement in Crime
Abigail A. Fagan, Ross Homel, Ian O'Connor and Rosie Teague

Victims and perpetrators of crime are often one and the same. The authors review previous research and examine the relationship between victimization and later offending as revealed by data from the Sibling Study. The reciprocal nature of the relationship is commented upon, and the need for longitudinal data to sort out the causal pathways is discussed.

Chapter 11: Criminality and Conformity: Implications for the Future
Mark Lynch, Emma Ogilvie and John S. Western

This chapter draws together the findings from the preceding chapters in terms of their collective policy implications. Low self esteem, unstable families, a lack of maternal care, and for some youths, a lack of parental supervision, are found to increase the likelihood of criminality over conformity. As well, age, gender and cohort membership all impact on the conformity/criminality divide. Because of the complexity of the causal pathways into criminality, the authors conclude that no single intervention strategy is likely to reduce adolescent offending across the board. Researchers and policy makers need to work collaboratively to identify the range of interventions likely to prove fruitful.

Conclusion

This first chapter has drawn attention to the centrality of the issues of conformity and non-conformity to the social sciences generally and criminology specifically. The major theoretical perspectives with respect to conformity and non-conformity have been briefly described and the ability of the Sibling Study research project to address divergent orientations has been highlighted.

In addition, in this chapter we have tried to convey a sense of both the complexity and the comprehensiveness of the Sibling Study data. As demonstrated, the study's underlying philosophy, as well as the research design, has ultimately resulted in a sample which can reasonably be expected to yield detailed understandings of the factors underpinning both offending and desistence from offending. In particular, the quasi-experimental research design allows tightly focused comparisons of offending of three very different populations of youth, those from the School, Vulnerable and Offender cohorts. In addition, the unusually high proportion of females, as well as the selection of mixed-sex sibling pairs, provides a rare opportunity for a close examination of gender-associated pathways to crime.

Chapter 2

Offending Behaviours: Situated Choices and Consequences

John S. Western, Mark Lynch, Emma Ogilvie and Abigail A. Fagan[1]

Introduction

This chapter begins our exploration of adolescents' involvement in crime. It starts by focusing upon the opportunities that adolescents see as available to them to offend, and the choices they make as to whether or not to do so. It is at this point that we introduce the main measure of self-reported offending, the Australian Self-Report Delinquency Scale (ASRDS) (Mak 1993), which we will return to on a number of occasions throughout this book. A variety of offending behaviours are included in this measure, and the analyses detail the number of young people reporting involvement in crime in general, as well as in particular types of offences. Exploring offending in more detail, the chapter next describes factors associated with adolescents' most recent offences, such as whether the act was planned or spontaneous or committed alone or with friends. Adolescents' attitudes towards the law are then considered, including their perceptions of whether or not they will be caught while offending, as well as their knowledge of laws and punishment. The chapter ends by examining whether or not respondents plan to commit additional crimes in the future.

Unlike subsequent chapters, this overview is primarily descriptive in nature and is not intended to test specific theories of offending. However, some perspectives, particularly deterrence, shaming, and rational choice theories, and their relationships to the findings, are briefly discussed. In addition, the ways in which offending behaviours and motivations for crime are affected by gender and cohort membership are examined throughout the chapter. Thus, the analyses focus on the extent to which cohort membership and gender influence young peoples' perceptions of opportunities for criminality, their actual involvement in crime, their belief that they will be caught or punished for such transgressions, and their decisions to offend or conform in the future.

---

1 The authors gratefully acknowledge the generous assistance provided by Denise A. Durrington with the statistical analyses reported in this chapter.

The focus of the chapter, then, is not so much upon general structural factors associated with crime, but rather on the ways in which adolescents understand criminality and conformity at a more personal level.

Opportunities to Offend

Before we consider the illegal acts young people report committing, we must consider whether they perceive opportunities to offend. Obviously, not all individuals will have equal opportunities to break the law. For example, many who commit white-collar crimes will be employed in high-level, management positions. Similarly, some criminologists assert that boys have more opportunities to commit crime, perhaps because they are less supervised by their parents and more likely to 'hang out' with friends or spend time in public spaces (Felson and Clark 1998, Jensen and Brownfield 1986). Conversely, it is argued that girls have fewer chances to break the law, as they typically spend more time at home, under more careful supervision. Nonetheless, females may have greater opportunities to commit certain types of crime, particularly those consistent with their gender role, such as shoplifting (Steffensmeier 1993). In addition, some feminists assert that girls' and women's opportunities for crime are constrained by the gendered contexts in which they live and work, so that females enact crime in different ways than men (Maher 1997, Miller 1998).

Opportunities for crime were assessed in the Sibling Study by asking: 'Have you ever had a chance to do something you knew was against the law or thought was probably against the law?'. Overall, 62 per cent of the respondents report that they had such an opportunity. Consistent with the literature, differences in opportunities are found by sex and cohort. Not unexpectedly, males report more opportunity to engage in criminal activities than do females, with 68 per cent of the boys, compared to 58 per cent of the girls, reporting opportunities. While this sex difference is statistically significant, it is not large. However, greater differences can be seen between the three cohorts. Specifically, the Offenders are most likely to report the opportunity to commit a crime (86 per cent), followed by the Vulnerable (68 per cent) and School (53 per cent) cohorts.

There are gender differences between the cohorts as well. In the Offender and Vulnerable cohorts, boys are markedly more likely than girls to report the opportunity to do something against the law (see Table 2.1). However, these differences are not apparent in the School cohort. Instead, equal numbers of boys and girls report opportunities for crime.

Table 2.1   Cohort and sex differences in the percentage of respondents who had the chance to do something against the law

	School	Cohort Vulnerable	Offender
Female	54	60	70
n	(333)	(81)	(61)
Male	52	76	92
n	(314)	(76)	(154)

Note: Numbers in brackets are the totals on which the percentages were calculated.

Respondents were also asked to describe the specific crimes they had the opportunity to commit, including one or more of the following offences: bag snatching, shoplifting, graffiti/tagging, burglary, stealing, vandalism, and using drugs or alcohol. As shown in Table 2.2, respondents' opportunities for offending again varied by sex and cohort, with girls generally, and those in the School cohort, reporting fewer opportunities to commit specific types of offences.

Boys in all three cohorts report greater opportunities for bag snatching, graffiti, burglary, car theft and vandalism, while girls report greater opportunities for shoplifting and using alcohol. Gender differences are almost non-existent with respect to drug use. The relative prevalence of drug and alcohol use among the sample is perhaps a reflection of their cultural prominence, which in this society results in heightened opportunities for young people to illegally access such substances.

Expected differences by cohort are also found, with respondents in the School cohort reporting fewer opportunities for offending than those in the Vulnerable cohort, who report fewer opportunities than those in the Offender cohort. Differences between the three groups are also smallest for the most commonly reported offences of shoplifting, alcohol use, and drug use, suggesting, again, that all young people have much the same opportunity to engage in these types of offences. These sex and cohort differences are further explored in Chapter 4.

Involvement in Crime

Having the opportunity to commit a crime is, of course, quite different from taking advantage of the opportunity. So, in this section, we identify the number of respondents who report engaging in offending behaviours.

To determine their level of offending, respondents were first asked whether or not they had 'actually done something you knew was against the law or thought was probably against the law'. Although a very high proportion of young people reported having had the opportunity to offend (62 per cent), a smaller number reported actual involvement in crime, with 43 per cent of all respondents indicating that they had broken the law. Not surprisingly, offending varies by sex, with more males reporting breaking the law. Slightly more than half the females (52 per cent), but only one-third (38 per cent) of the males reported *never* having committed a crime, and only one-fifth of the females (19 per cent), but just under one-third of the males (31 per cent), reported having committed six or more offences.

Table 2.2   Cohort and sex differences in the percentage of respondents who had the chance to commit offences

	School		Cohort Vulnerable		Offender	
	Female	Male	Female	Male	Female	Male
Bag Snatch	2	9	22	31	23	45
Shoplift	59	45	80	69	80	80
Graffiti	19	30	51	54	43	54
Burglary	3	9	29	46	39	65
Steal a Car	2	6	29	44	43	58
Vandalism	13	30	41	49	36	52
Use Drugs	50	51	84	76	73	75
Use Alcohol	74	62	90	69	82	75
n	183	168	49	59	44	146

Cohort differences are also apparent and are even more striking than sex differences. Of the School cohort, 58 per cent had never done anything illegal, and only ten per cent had done something illegal six or more times. In comparison, only 15 per cent of the Offender cohort reported having never done something illegal, but 59 per cent reporting having committed an illegal act six or more times. Once again, the Vulnerable cohort falls in between these two extremes, with over one-third (38 per cent) stating that they had never done anything illegal while 41 per cent admitted to committing illegal acts on six or more occasions.

Gender differences are not consistent across the cohorts. In fact, they are virtually non-existent within the School sample, where 58 per cent of the girls and 57 per cent of the boys report no illegal acts, while 11 per cent and nine per cent of the same groups report six or more offences. In contrast, gender differences are marked in the other two groups, with boys committing more offences. Among the Offenders, 30 per cent of the girls but only nine per cent of the boys report no illegal acts. For the Vulnerable group, 47 per cent of the girls, compared to 29 per cent of the boys, report committing no illegal acts. Boys in each of the two cohorts are more likely than girls to report six or more acts, with 67 and 39 per cent, respectively among the Offenders, and 45 per cent, compared to 37 per cent, of the Vulnerable group doing so.

Age of Onset

Respondents were also asked to report the age at which they 'first did something you knew was against the law or thought was probably against the law'. While longitudinal investigations of crime vary in their estimates of the average age of onset for offending, it is generally accepted that most offenders begin their criminal careers during adolescence, and very few begin after age 18. However, the specific age at which offending begins may vary according to characteristics of the offender. For example, there is much evidence that individuals who have longer and more serious criminal careers also begin offending at earlier ages, compared to other offenders (Blumstein, Cohen, Roth and Visher 1986, LeBlanc and Loeber 1998). It is less clear, however, whether female and male offenders have similar ages of onset, as this issue has been largely overlooked (Piquero and Chung 2001).

In the Sibling Study, the results indicate that many young people commit their first illegal act at a very early age. Of those who reported ever committing a crime, the average age of onset was 11.7 years, and 13 years was the age at first offence most commonly cited by respondents. In addition, 31 per cent report committing their first crime when they were younger than 11 years old, 40 per cent when aged 11–13, 25 per cent when aged 14–15, and only five per cent when aged 16 or older.

This pattern of early offending is similar for females and males, although males are somewhat more likely to begin their offending at earlier ages. Before the age of 11, 24 per cent of girls and 35 per cent of boys report having committed an act they believed to be against the law. Equal numbers of girls and boys (approximately 40 per cent) report their age of onset as between 11 and 13 years of age, while 32 per cent of girls and 19 per cent of boys report an age of onset between age 14 and 15. Only five per cent of both females and males delayed offending until they were 16 years old. The School group, perhaps not unexpectedly, begins offending somewhat later than the Vulnerable and Offender cohorts, but all three groups are likely to have committed their first offence before age 16.

The sex differences in age of onset are not the same across all cohorts, however. Table 2.3 indicates that while boys are earlier starters in both the School and Offender cohorts, there are virtually no differences in the Vulnerable group: over half of both the boys and girls had done something against the law before they were 11 years of age.

Table 2.3   Cohort and sex differences in the age of onset
(column percentages)

Age	School		Vulnerable		Offender	
	Female	Male	Female	Male	Female	Male
Under 11	22	40	53	51	27	47
11–13	37	34	20	29	31	30
14–15	36	21	23	15	35	18
16 and over	5	3	4	5	7	5
n	138	150	49	66	52	145

Overall, the findings regarding the age of onset confirm prior research that adolescents often begin their offending at a very early age. Likewise, they provide additional evidence that more frequent offenders (i.e. boys and those in the Vulnerable and Offender cohorts) have earlier ages of onset. While these findings present rather basic illustrations of the relationship between age and offending, this area will be further explored in Chapter 3.

The Nature of Delinquency

As noted in the beginning of this chapter, our examination of offending behaviour was based upon the 37-item Australian Self-Report Delinquency Scale (ASRDS) (Mak 1993). At this point, we need to consider the ASRDS measure in more detail. Each item in the scale describes a discrete act, and respondents are asked to report whether or not they had committed each act during the previous 12 months. Four of the 37 acts are so-called 'lie' items, used to determine response habituation and social desirability. The other items all describe offending behaviours that range in seriousness, including playing tricks on the telephone, property crimes such as break and enter, personal violence such as fighting and other illegal acts, such as using drugs and alcohol.

The Sibling Study researchers made several changes to the original ASRDS scale. The original wording of several items was modified to simplify the language, and an item on cheating on games machines was omitted, as it was seen to duplicate the 'cheated or stolen from dispenser machines' item. Two other items originally asked respondents whether they had used LSD or abused barbiturates. Ecstasy and speed use were added to the LSD item, and the barbiturates item was modified into a question that specified using pills, puffers or medicine for fun when the respondent was not sick.

Table 2.4 includes the complete list of items contained in the (modified) ASRDS, as well as the percentages of respondents reporting each offence, by cohort and sex. Importantly, habituation and social desirability do not appear to be major factors in the pattern of responses, given the high endorsement of the four 'lie' items (marked with asterisks in the table).

Table 2.4   Self-reported delinquency, by cohort and sex (percentages reporting involvement)

ASRDS Item	School (*n*=548)	Vulnerable (*n*=141)	Offender (*n*=196)	Female (*n*=418)	Male (*n*=467)	Total (*n*=885)
1. Driven unregistered car	5	20	34	6	21	14
2. Driven without licence	19	29	61	16	42	30
3. Driven after drinking	4	21	27	4	18	2
4. Raced with other cars	6	17	32	5	21	14
5. Joy riding in stolen car	3	20	38	7	20	13
6. Stolen parts from a car	4	23	30	5	20	13
7. Stolen a bicycle or parts	4	18	28	5	18	11

ASRDS Item

Participation Rate

	School (n=548)	Vulnerable (n=141)	Offender (n=196)	Female (n=418)	Male (n=467)	Total (n=885)
8. Seen an R-rated film	18	29	43	19	31	25
9. Not kept a promise*	57	55	57	60	55	57
10. Bought alcohol	23	53	67	33	42	38
11. Drinking in a public place	14	50	59	25	34	30
12. Not paid an entrance fee	17	32	47	17	34	26
13. Skipped class/school	22	45	58	30	37	34
14. Run away from home	8	31	38	14	22	18
15. Shoplifted	16	48	55	21	37	30
16. Stolen money of <$10	20	38	31	22	28	25
17. Stolen money of >$10	7	42	53	12	33	23
18. Been late*	77	79	75	79	75	77
19. Break and enter	3	28	51	7	27	18
20. Stolen from a dispenser	9	28	29	8	24	17
21. Damaged private property	11	36	40	10	32	21
22. Started a fire	4	17	15	4	12	8
23. Damaged public property	5	29	32	8	21	15
24. Damaged school property	12	37	34	15	26	21
25. Graffiti on public places	14	38	40	21	26	24
26. Gone against parents*	64	73	80	69	69	69
27. Group fight	20	37	58	22	40	31
28. Beaten someone up	14	36	53	14	37	26
29. Used weapon in a fight	5	20	37	5	24	15
30. Used force to get things	8	29	36	12	23	18
31. Used marijuana/hash	18	60	65	29	41	36
32. Used ecstasy/acid/speed	2	36	37	11	19	15
33. Used medicines for fun	6	29	28	12	17	15
34. Forced sex	2	4	4	2	4	3
35. Telephone tricks	35	45	43	35	42	38
36. Nasty phone calls	12	26	26	13	21	18
37. Told lie*	76	74	82	77	77	77

* Denotes a lie item.

As would be expected, the survey responses reveal that criminal involvement varies by sex and cohort. Females consistently report lower levels of offending behaviour, although the male-to-female ratio varies depending on the crime committed, ranging from about 1.3 for graffiti to around 5.5 for ever used a weapon in a fight. In addition, sex differences are lowest for some of the most commonly reported offences, such as vandalism and drug and alcohol use.

Cohort effects are also found, and, as with sex differences, these effects vary depending on the offence reported. Overall, offending is least likely to occur in the

School cohort, followed by the Vulnerable and Offender cohorts. However, members of *all* cohorts report committing vandalism and drug/alcohol use at reasonably high levels. In fact, nearly 20 per cent of the School cohort reported cannabis use in the preceding 12 months, while 60 per cent of both the Vulnerable and Offender cohorts also reported using cannabis. It is also important to note the relatively high rates of involvement in violent crimes. While it may not be surprising that more than 50 per cent of the Offender cohort reported having beaten somebody up, it is remarkable that more than a third of the Vulnerable cohort also report this offence, as do 14 per cent of the School cohort.

While these percentages are very informative, it is also useful to reduce the data into a more manageable and readily interpretable form. In fact, the self-reported items have been subject to several data reduction procedures, which have resulted in several sub-scales of reported offending. First, the items, excluding the four 'lie' questions, were subjected to a principal components analysis, followed by an oblimin rotation. The principal components analysis revealed that the first component had an eigen value of 11.9, and accounted for 38.4 per cent of total variance, while the next five components accounted for a further 20.7 per cent of variance. All items, with the exceptions of items 34 and 35 from Table 2.4, had factor loadings greater than 0.4 on the first factor. As a result, a 31-item general delinquency measure was constructed (i.e. excluding the four 'lie' items and items 34 and 35). Scale scores were based on the number of reported offences and, as a consequence, ranged from 0 to 31.

The oblimin rotation of the first six factors produced the solution shown in Table 2.5. Included are items defining the factors. All items with factor loadings above 0.30 are listed, together with measures of scale reliability, Cronbach's alpha, derived from the inter-correlations of the items comprising each factor. The analysis was based on 628 'primary' siblings: one sibling randomly selected from each pair in the School cohort and the sibling with whom first contact was made in the other two cohorts. A further analysis including the 'secondary' siblings produced a very similar solution. Scale scores were calculated in the same manner as was used for the generalized measure, with scores ranging from 0–4 for assault and public disorder, 0–5 for drug and alcohol use and vandalism, and 0–6 for theft and burglary. Overall, the analyses demonstrate that there are good grounds for using these factors to examine rates of self-reported delinquency. In particular, scale reliability as measured by Cronbach's alpha is high. Moreover, face validity is high, as each factor is defined by a set of items which identify related offending behaviours, including assault, illegal vehicle use, public disorder, drug and alcohol use, theft and burglary and vandalism, and together, these six sub-scales provide a comprehensive coverage of total criminal involvement.

Table 2.5   Items, factor loadings and Cronbach's alphas for the Australian Self-Report Delinquency Scale (*n*=722)

Item	Factor Loading
Factor 1: Assault (alpha = 0.76)	
27 Taken part in group fight	0.633
28 Beaten someone up	0.790
29 Used a weapon in fight	0.556
30 Used force to get something	0.404
Factor 2: Illegal vehicle use (alpha = 0.85)	
1 Driven an unregistered car	−0.731
2 Driven without a licence	−0.635
3 Driven when drunk	−0.584
4 Raced with other vehicles	−0.718
5 Driven a vehicle without permission	−0.583
6 Stolen things or parts from vehicle	−0.536
Factor 3: Public disorder (alpha = 0.67)	
8 Seen an R-rated film	0.392
12 Not paid an entrance fee	0.402
13 Skipped class/school	0.501
14 Run away from home	0.301
Factor 4: Drug and alcohol use (alpha = 0.83)	
10 Bought alcohol	−0.760
11 Drinking in a public place	−0.744
31 Used marijuana/hash	−0.676
32 Used ecstasy/acid/speed	−0.393
33 Used medicine for fun	−0.311
Factor 5: Theft and burglary (alpha = 0.84)	
7 Stolen a bicycle or parts	0.434
15 Shoplifted	0.586
16 Stolen money of <$10	0.676
17 Stolen money of >$10	0.561
19 Break and enter	0.402
20 Stolen from a dispenser	0.427
Factor 6: Vandalism (alpha = 0.79)	
21 Damaged private property	0.362
22 Damaged property by starting a fire	0.747
23 Damaged public property	0.486
24 Damaged school property	0.661
25 Graffiti on public places	0.408
36 Made nasty phone calls	0.554

Note: The Cronbach's alphas are based on final compositions of the sub-scales, with item 36 dropped from Factor 6 (vandalism) because of its incompatibility with the manifest content of the factor.

Table 2.6 presents information regarding offending for the overall measure of delinquency, as well as each of the sub-scales, for females and males. Not surprisingly, the results demonstrate significant gender differences in offending, with boys committing more offences than girls overall, and for particular types of crime. In fact, boys' mean scores of offending for each category of crime are higher than are girls', and larger percentages of girls report no participation in overall crime or particular types of offences. The extent of sex differences depends on the criminal act, with more for public disorder crimes and drug and alcohol use, compared to more serious types of offences. As shown in Table 2.6, approximately three-fourths of girls (79 per cent) report committing no illegal vehicle use, assault, theft, or vandalism offences, compared to approximately half of the boys, while just over half of the girls report never committing public disorder or drug and alcohol offences, compared to 47 and 37 percent of the boys.

Table 2.6   Self-reported offending for generalized delinquency and the six ASRDS sub-scales, by sex (column percentages)

	Female	Male
Generalized Delinquency		
No Offence	28.0	17.0
1 Offence	15.0	12.0
2–3 Offences	19.0	11.0
4–5 Offences	14.0	12.0
6–12 Offences	15.0	19.0
More Than 12 Offences	9.0	29.0
n	440.0	490.0
Mean	6.1	8.1
SD	7.2	8.0
Illegal Vehicle Use		
No Offence	79.0	52.0
1 Offence	12.0	15.0
2–3 Offences	7.0	17.0
4 or More Offences	3.0	16.0
n	440.0	490.0
Mean	0.4	1.4
SD	1.0	1.8
Assault		
No Offence	70.0	47.0
1 Offence	18.0	19.0
2–3 Offences	11.0	26.0
4 or More Offences	2.0	8.0
n	440.0	490.0
Mean	0.5	1.2
SD	0.9	1.4

	Female	Male
Theft		
No Offence	66.0	47.0
1 Offence	18.0	15.0
2–3 Offences	10.0	20.0
4 or More Offences	7.0	19.0
n	440.0	490.0
Mean	1.2	1.6
SD	1.7	1.9
Public Disorder		
No Offence	54.0	37.0
1 Offence	22.0	25.0
2–3 Offences	19.0	27.0
4 or More Offences	5.0	11.0
n	440.0	490.0
Mean	1.2	1.4
SD	1.4	1.4
Drug and Alcohol Use		
No Offence	57.0	47.0
1 Offence	14.0	12.0
2–3 Offences	19.0	26.0
4 or More Offences	10.0	15.0
n	440.0	490.0
Mean	1.2	1.5
SD	1.6	1.7
Vandalism		
No Offence	70.0	54.0
1 Offence	17.0	16.0
2–3 Offences	8.0	20.0
4 or More Offences	5.0	10.0
n	440.0	490.0
Mean	0.6	1.1
SD	1.1	1.5

Table 2.7 details respondents' involvement in each type of offence by cohort. The familiar pattern of marked cohort differences in offending can be observed. The means for the School cohort are considerably lower than the other cohorts', for each type of crime, and a significant number (31 per cent) had not participated in any of the acts in the generalized measure of delinquency. In addition, the majority (60 to 77 per cent) of young people in the School cohort had not committed any of the acts contained in the any of the six sub-scales (see Table 2.7). In contrast, only two per cent of the Offender sample reported *never* committing any of the acts in the past 12 months, and approximately three-quarters had engaged in at least one act in each of the sub-scales of offending behaviour. Offenders were most likely to report using drugs and alcohol (over 80 per cent reported one or more offences),

but least likely to report vandalism (35 per cent reported no acts of vandalism). The Vulnerable cohort was more similar to the Offender cohort than the School cohort, with only 14 per cent reporting not having engaged in any of the offending behaviours and over half reporting one or more offences in each of the sub-scales (with the exception of illegal vehicle use).

Table 2.7   Self-reported offending for generalized delinquency and the six ASRDS sub-scales, by cohort (column percentages)

		Cohort	
	School	Vulnerable	Offender
Generalized Delinquency			
No Offence	31.0	14.0	2.0
1 Offence	18.0	8.0	4.0
2–3 Offences	19.0	9.0	8.0
4–5 Offences	14.0	10.0	11.0
6–12 Offences	13.0	23.0	25.0
More Than 12 Offences	6.0	36.0	51.0
n	599.0	145.0	199.0
Mean	3.1	9.7	12.8
SD	4.2	8.4	8.0
Illegal Vehicle Use			
No Offence	77.0	57.0	32.0
1 Offence	14.0	10.0	14.0
2–3 Offences	7.0	18.0	23.0
4 or More Offences	3.0	15.0	31.0
n	638.0	154.0	210.0
Mean	0.4	1.3	2.3
SD	0.9	1.8	2.1
Assault			
No Offence	70.0	47.0	24.0
1 Offence	17.0	18.0	21.0
2–3 Offences	11.0	27.0	38.0
4 or More Offences	1.0	8.0	17.0
n	642.0	156.0	216.0
Mean	0.5	1.2	1.9
SD	0.9	1.4	1.4
Theft			
No Offence	68.0	40.0	29.0
1 Offence	19.0	13.0	10.0
2–3 Offences	11.0	19.0	27.0
4 or More Offences	3.0	29.0	35.0
n	618.0	151.0	210.0
Mean	0.6	2.0	2.5
SD	1.1	2.1	2.1

	School	Cohort Vulnerable	Offender
Public Disorder			
No Offence	61.0	38.0	23.0
1 Offence	23.0	18.0	19.0
2–3 Offences	15.0	39.0	43.0
4 or More Offences	2.0	5.0	15.0
n	637.0	152.0	208.0
Mean	0.6	1.3	1.9
SD	1.0	1.3	1.4
Drug and Alcohol Use			
No Offence	67.0	29.0	18.0
1 Offence	15.0	11.0	9.0
2–3 Offences	17.0	27.0	42.0
4 or More Offences	1.0	33.0	32.0
n	631.0	154.0	213.0
Mean	0.6	2.3	2.7
SD	1.1	1.9	1.7
Vandalism			
No Offence	74.0	40.0	35.0
1 Offence	14.0	20.0	21.0
2–3 Offences	10.0	22.0	28.0
4 or More Offences	2.0	19.0	16.0
n	642.0	154.0	214.0
Mean	0.5	1.6	1.6
SD	0.9	1.7	1.6

Before considering circumstances associated with respondents' most recent offences, it is perhaps useful to briefly reflect on the major themes that have emerged in the data presented so far. Although the majority of our sample has never knowingly done anything against the law, more than half have had the opportunity to do so, and the data demonstrate that girls and those in the School cohort are least likely to perceive opportunities for offending. In addition, a substantial proportion of those with the opportunity to break the law report having committed a crime, with offences ranging from less serious acts to more violent crimes. Not surprisingly, girls and those in the School cohort report fewer offences than boys and those in the Vulnerable and Offender cohorts. Finally, the majority of young people committed their first criminal act at a very young age (before age 12), with boys and those in the Vulnerable and Offender cohorts beginning even earlier than girls and respondents in the School cohort.

The Most Recent Criminal Act

In order to learn more about the nature of and circumstances surrounding respondents' criminal activities, young people were asked to describe in detail the most recent offence they had committed. Specifically, they were asked whether or not the act had been planned more than a day in advance, if it was committed alone or with friends, and how much they talked with their friends about the crime after it was committed.

In response to the first issue, only 25 per cent of offenders reported that their offence was planned more than a day ahead of time, indicating that offending in this study is largely spontaneous. No sex differences are found, as 25 per cent of both girls and boys reported planning their offence in advance. The extent of planning did vary somewhat by cohort, with Offenders less likely to plan their offences than the School and Vulnerable cohorts. Nonetheless, members of all three cohorts tended to enact their offences without extensively thinking about them more than a day in advance.

These results run counter to the predictions of rational choice theory, which posits that crime occurs *after* offenders make rational decisions about the potential rewards of crime outweighing the risks of apprehension and/or the costs of being sentenced by the courts (Clarke and Cornish 1985). Rather than viewing crime as a spontaneous event, rational choice theorists believe that 'offending is purposive behaviour, designed to benefit the offender in some way. Offenders have goals when they commit crimes, even if those goals are short-sighted and take into account only a few of the benefits and risks at a time' (Felson and Clarke 1998:7). Thus, it is assumed that at least some planning will occur before criminal action takes place. However, this process did not occur for most respondents in the Sibling Study.

Respondents were also asked to report whether or not they committed their last offence alone or with others, as there is a substantial body of evidence that crime is more a social event than a solitary effort, and that a large proportion of offences occur in the company of others (Reiss and Farrington 1991). The Sibling Study data confirm this finding, in that only one-quarter (26 per cent) of those who reported breaking the law indicated that they acted alone. Boys are more likely than girls to report being on their own during the commission of a crime, with 32 per cent of boys and 15 per cent of girls stating that they acted alone. For girls, crime is much more a group activity, with nearly two-thirds (60 per cent) reporting that their most recent criminal act involved two or more friends, compared to less than half (41 per cent) of the boys.

Cohort differences are not great, with all groups more likely to have been in the company of one or more friends than acting alone. However, the Vulnerable group are marginally more likely to have committed their last offence alone (31 per cent), compared to the other two groups (School cohort 23 per cent, Offender cohort 27 per cent), while those in the School cohort are somewhat more likely to be with a group of friends when offending.

Crime as a social, rather than an individual, activity is most strongly apparent among the girls in the School cohort, with two-thirds having committed their most recent offence in the company of two or more friends, compared with slightly more than half (55 per cent) of the girls in the other two cohorts. There are virtually no cohort differences for the boys, with around 40 per cent of each group accompanied by two or more friends on their most recent escapade.

Overall then, these findings reinforce the view that crime tends to occur in groups, particularly for the girls and members of the School cohort in this study. In addition, the results support the importance of peer alliances in leading to involvement in crime. Given the fact that crime is social rather than individual for most offenders, it is somewhat surprising that the great majority of these young people, across both sexes and cohorts (82 per cent), spent only a little time discussing their crimes with their friends.

Getting Caught

For those who break the law, getting caught is akin to an occupational hazard. And presumably, those who make a habit of offending are more likely to be caught. In the Sibling Study, the School cohort does not break the law very often, the Vulnerable group does so more frequently, and the Offenders, particularly the boys, make a regular habit of it.

When those who had broken the law were asked whether or not they had ever been caught, boys were more likely than girls to answer in the affirmative. More specifically, 68 per cent of boys, compared to 49 per cent of girls, report having been caught offending, and those in the Offender cohort are more likely to reporting having been caught (87 per cent), compared to members of the Vulnerable (64 per cent) and School cohorts (39 per cent).

Gender differences are maintained within the cohorts, with girls in all three groups less likely to have been caught. Offender boys are the least likely to escape the law, as only eight per cent report never having been caught. The girls are a little more successful, however, with 25 per cent having never been caught. Among the Vulnerable group, 25 per cent of the boys, but nearly half of the girls, have never been caught. Similarly, in the School cohort, nearly half the boys (42 per cent), but two-thirds of the girls (64 per cent), have escaped capture.

Arguably, our sampling strategy is at work here, and it is not surprising that those in the Offender cohort have the greatest likelihood of begin caught. The gender differences are not as straightforward. While boys in each cohort may be more likely to get caught because they commit more offences, it is possible that girls may be experiencing some bias by the criminal justice system. For example, the 'chivalry' hypothesis predicts that girls will be less likely to be arrested or processed through the criminal justice system, based on their status as female and the notion that they must be shielded from such experiences. Thus, it is possible that even when girls commit similar number of offences as boys, they will be less likely to be caught or punished by police.

Exploring escaping capture in a little more detail, the data reveal that the majority of girls (66 per cent) had been caught one or two times, in comparison to 48 per cent of the boys. However, a reasonable proportion of both the girls and the boys (19 per cent and 25 per cent, respectively) had been caught six or more times.

Expected cohort differences are also seen. Within the School cohort, the vast majority of those caught had only been caught once or twice (79 per cent), with only nine per cent having been caught six or more times. This is in stark contrast to the Offender cohort, in which 40 per cent had been caught once or twice and 34 per cent had been caught six or more times. Once again, the Vulnerable cohort falls between these groups.

As these results demonstrate, the frequency of offending (not surprisingly) does impact on the number of times respondents report being caught. Among the Offender and Vulnerable cohorts, where offending is noticeably more a way of life, breaking the law six or more times increases the likelihood of being caught quite substantially, and, interestingly, gender differences are not great. More specifically, of the Offenders who have broken the law six or more times, 68 per cent of the boys and 67 per cent of the girls have been caught on at least three occasions. Similarly, among the Vulnerable group who have broken the law six or more times, 56 per cent of boys and 63 per cent of girls have been apprehended at least three times. In contrast, those reporting between three and five offences are much more likely to escape the wrath of the law. These results are somewhat less supportive of the chivalry hypothesis posited earlier, indicating that differential processing by the criminal justice system may not occur for girls and boys who commit large numbers of offences.

Motivations for Conformity and Crime: The Relevance of Shaming, Deterrence and Rational Choice Theories

The next section examines possible motivations for offenders' criminality and conformity. Several criminological theories provide some insight into these motivations, including 'shaming', deterrence, and rational choice. Although differing in their specific tenets and recommendations for criminal justice policies, all three theories hypothesize that offenders who are concerned about being caught will be less likely to offend. Braithwaite (1989) and Grasmick and Bursik (1990) are probably the best known advocates of 'shaming' (although see also Cochran, Chamlin, Wood and Sellers 1999), with the former particularly known for his elaboration of the role of shame in restorative justice processes (see Strang and Braithwaite 2001). In a rather similar vein, Grasmick and Bursik (1990) suggest that 'significant others' and 'conscience' both function as agents of social control, to deter criminal behaviour in a less formal and more diffuse fashion than the bureaucratized operations of the criminal justice system. In contrast, deterrence and rational choice theorists advocate more formal sanctions to dissuade offenders from pursuing crime. Specifically, deterrence theorists advocate that crime will be reduced if harsh sanctions are imposed on offenders. Thus, if offenders are aware of these punishments and believe they will occur, they will be less likely to enact criminal behaviours. As previously discussed, rational choice theory posits a similar process, in that offenders carefully weigh the costs of offending (including the potential for being caught and punished) against the benefits they will gain from the act. All three perspectives assume, then, if the cost is great enough, criminality becomes an unappealing lifestyle choice.

We consider the relevance of these ideas by examining the extent to which young people worry about being caught for offending, believe they will be caught, and are familiar with possible punishments for offending. First, respondents were asked whether or not they would worry if caught by the police. In fact, the majority (74 per cent) reported that they would worry a lot. There is a significant gender difference, however, in the likelihood of being worried about being caught by the police. Although a majority of both females and males would worry a lot, the girls are much more likely to worry than the boys: 87 per cent report worrying a lot compared with 70 per cent. There are cohort differences as well, with members of the School cohort much more likely to report worrying a lot (88 per cent), compared to the Offender and Vulnerable cohorts (at 60 per cent in both cases).

As shown in Table 2.8, gender differences in the extent of worrying are maintained within the cohorts, although at different levels. For example, virtually all the girls in the School cohort reported that they would worry a lot if caught by the police, but a smaller, though substantial, proportion of boys would also do so. These proportions are smaller in the Vulnerable and Offender cohorts, but the gender differences nonetheless remain.

Table 2.8   Cohort and sex differences in the percentage of respondents who would worry a lot if caught by the police

		Cohort	
	School	Vulnerable	Offender
Female	94	71	74
	(*n* = 333)	(*n* = 79)	(*n* = 57)
Male	82	48	55
	(*n* = 314)	(*n* = 73)	(*n* = 150)

These results suggest some support for shaming and deterrence theories, in that it is likely that those who worry more about being caught (i.e. girls and those in the School cohort) will refrain from offending. To explore this possibility in more detail, we examined the ways in which levels of concern at being caught vary with the frequency of offending. Table 2.9 includes only those who would worry a lot about being caught by the police, by cohort and sex. The results confirm that those who commit fewer delinquent acts are more apt to worry about getting caught by the police. Thus, girls and those in the School cohort who commit fewer offences are more likely to worry about getting caught, relative to boys and those in the Vulnerable and Offender cohorts. Although these results present further support for shaming and deterrence theories, the relationship between offending and worrying may be more complex than this. For example, it is also possible that increased involvement in crime may serve to 'inoculate' young people against worrying about being caught, so that, as the number of offences increases, worry about getting caught decreases. However, further analysis using longitudinal data is needed to explore this temporal sequence in more detail.

Table 2.9   Cohort and sex differences in the frequency of illegal acts and worrying a lot about being caught by police (percentage who would worry a lot)

| | | Number of Times Carried Out an Illegal Act | | | | |
		Never	1–2 times	3–5 times	6 or more times	*n*
School	Female	95	93	97	86	182
	Male	89	81	86	72	159
Vulnerable	Female	83	86	83	52	38
	Male	75	67	36	41	58
Offender	Female	–	81	100	64	41
	Male	–	72	61	51	140

Similar results are found when examining young people's worries about being caught by parents, although adolescents are somewhat (though not greatly) less concerned at being caught by their parents than by the police, with 60 per cent of all respondents reporting that they would worry a lot about getting caught by their parents (compared to the 74 per cent who would worry about getting caught by the police). In terms of gender differences, it is not surprising that girls are more worried (74 per cent worry a lot) than boys (54 per cent worry a lot).

Members of the School cohort are far more likely to be worried about being caught by their parents than those in the other two cohorts. Virtually all (98 per cent) adolescents in the School cohort would worry a lot or worry a little if they thought they were going to be caught by their parents, while around a quarter (22 per cent) of the Offender and Vulnerable groups wouldn't worry at all. Once again, gender differences also appear within cohorts, with girls in each group clearly worrying more than boys. More specifically, 80 per cent of the School girls would worry a lot if caught by parents, compared to 66 per cent of boys, but, interestingly, the remainder of both groups would worry a little. In the other two cohorts, sizeable numbers of girls and boys would not worry at all, but girls are still more disposed to worry. Thus, parental norms appear stronger in the School cohort, and impinge more markedly on girls than boys.

Consistent with the deterrence and shaming theories, when we examine the relationship between frequency of offending and worry about getting caught by parents, we find that those who worry a lot are less likely to commit offences. Conversely, the data also suggest that, as young people commit greater numbers of illegal acts, they will be less likely to worry about being caught by their parents.

There are clearly different levels of concern about getting caught, which seem to be related to levels of participation in criminal behaviour. With increasing participation, concern about getting caught drops off. But what about the chances of getting caught?

Focusing on the last time they did something against the law, we asked respondents: 'How much chance did you think there was of getting caught the last time you did something against the law?'. Somewhat surprisingly, perhaps, the majority of young people (76 per cent) felt there was little to no chance they would be caught breaking the law, and only six per cent said they were certain they would get caught, while the remainder said that there was a pretty good chance of getting caught or they were almost certain they would be. Interestingly, there were virtually no gender differences in responses.

The cohorts differed slightly. Between two-thirds and three-quarters of the Vulnerable and Offender cohorts were fairly optimistic about their chances of escape. These results provide some support for rational choice theory, in that the more likely young people are to believe that the benefits of crime outweigh the costs (i.e. getting caught), the more likely it is that they will break the law. However, the situation appears more complex for the School cohort. This group is even more optimistic than the other young people about escaping the law, as 84 per cent stated that there was no chance or not much chance of their getting caught. It is somewhat difficult to interpret these findings. It may be that these adolescents, who have less of a 'career' in crime behind them, may be suffering from false confidence. Alternatively, they may have gauged their visibility to the police extremely well.

While all groups were reasonably optimistic about escaping the law, the Vulnerable cohort and Offenders were perhaps a little more cautious, not least because of their greater involvement in illegal activities. In the unlikely event of being apprehended, then, were they aware of the punishment that might befall them? It appears that the majority were aware. More than two-thirds (68 per cent) of respondents who reported committing an offence reported knowing the punishment for breaking the law. Again, gender differences are not apparent. More significant differences were found between the cohorts, as only 59 per cent of the School cohort reported that they were aware of the punishment if caught by police, compared to over three-quarters of the other two cohorts. Nonetheless, the majority of respondents from all groups claimed that they knew the punishment for breaking the law.

The correspondence of views between girls and boys in the three cohorts regarding knowledge of punishment is quite remarkable. In the School cohort, the same proportion of boys and girls (59 per cent) believed they knew the punishment they would receive if caught. In the Vulnerable cohort, the percentage is somewhat higher, but still similar for girls and boys (78 and 75 per cent, respectively). There are comparable figures for the Offenders (72 per cent of girls believed they knew the punishment, compared to 80 per cent of boys).

Overall, these results provide little support for deterrence theory, as those who commit more offences (i.e. those in the Vulnerable and Offender cohorts) are even more likely to know the punishment for doing so, they are not deterred by knowledge of criminal sanctions.

Future Plans for Crime

Finally, young people were asked to report whether or not they would commit their most recent crime(s) again. Overall, the respondents were mixed in their answers to this question, with approximately one-third believing they would never commit the crime again, one-third stating that they might, and the remaining one-third indicating that they would commit the act in the future. Responses do not vary by sex although some differences are reported by cohort. Somewhat surprisingly, members of the Offender group are most likely to never 'do this thing again', while the Vulnerable cohort is most likely to affirm that they would offend again. The School cohort comes between these extremes and is the most ambivalent of the three, with nearly equal proportions in the categories of 'never', 'maybe' and 'yes'. When interpreting these results, we should not forget, of course, that the Offender cohort is made up of young people appearing in court, on supervised orders, or in detention centers, whereas the Vulnerable cohort respondents are relatively 'free', albeit marginalized.

Girls and boys within the cohorts adopt similar positions. Thus, both female and male Offenders are most likely to say they would not offend again, both sexes in the Vulnerable cohort are most likely to say they will offend, and girls and boys in the School cohort are equally undecided as to whether they will or will not commit the same crime in the future.

Conclusion

A substantial body of data has been presented in this chapter, aimed at providing an overview of some key aspects of adolescent offending. The discussion has provided some broad brush stokes of the types of offending young people from the Sibling Study engage in, and importantly, the contexts in which they find themselves 'being' criminal. This has included a variety of commonly examined areas, such as opportunities available to commit crime, specific crimes chosen, and age of onset for offending, as well as less extensively examined areas, such as respondents' perceptions of their chances of getting caught or awareness of probable punishments if caught offending.

To summarize the findings, we see that girls and those in the School cohort are less likely to perceive opportunities for offending, compared to boys and those in the Offender and Vulnerable cohorts. Similarly, when we look at those who actually take advantage of the opportunities to offend, the boys and those in the Vulnerable and Offender cohorts are more likely to seize the day. Moreover, these groups tend to commit more serious and violent acts, while differences in offending are less noticeable for more common and minor acts, such as shoplifting, vandalism, and drug and alcohol use. Finally, while most young people commit their first illegal act at a relatively early age, usually before the age of 13 years, boys are somewhat more likely than girls to be early starters.

Regarding the specific offences committed, the findings reported in this chapter reinforce prior research that most criminal acts are social, rather than individual. The results also reveal that, somewhat contrary to rational choice theory, these acts also tend to be spontaneous, with offenders failing to plan their offences ahead of time. With regard to worry about being caught, it is interesting to note that most young people, even those in the Offender cohort, would worry a lot if caught by their parents or the police. And, not surprisingly, those who report the highest level of worry (i.e. girls and those in the School cohort) commit the fewest numbers of crimes, providing some support for deterrence and shaming theories. However, these results may also be interpreted as suggesting that the more often young people commit crime, the less likely they are to worry about getting caught. It would seem that, as for so many endeavors, increasing experience of offending reduces any attendant anxieties.

As this example illustrates, many of the findings presented in this chapter provide mixed support for shaming, deterrence, and rational choice theories espoused by many criminologists. In fact, the results can be seen to either confirm or disconfirm these perspectives, depending on how one chooses to interpret the data. Thus, while it is possible to be persuaded that traditional explanations can satisfactorily explain adolescent offending, one might also take the view that these findings suggest a series of equally important pointers of altogether different types of explanations regarding adolescent offending. That is, these data may be indicators of quite different social processes from those typically drawn upon in 'classical' explanations of why some young people engage in crime.

The challenge, then, is how best to develop theories of adolescent behaviour which 'cope' equally well with data that are consistent, and data that are at odds, with traditional or mainstream approaches to adolescent offending. Such an endeavor is not the objective of this particular chapter, however. Instead, the more modest aim has been to lay out in fairly general terms the dimensions of adolescent offending behaviours. Thus, we leave it to the authors of subsequent chapters to examine this data in more detail, to reach a better understanding of the ways in which criminological theory can be utilized to explain adolescent crime and conformity.

Chapter 3

Age and Offending: Characteristics and Criminological Factors

Mark Lynch, Emma Ogilvie and Wing Hong Chui

Introduction

The aim of this chapter is to examine the relationship between age and offending by focusing on the kinds of criminal behaviour reported by the Sibling Study respondents at different stages in adolescence. Age is often advanced as a crucial determinant of young people's behaviour and involvement in crime. Emler and Reicher argue that 'the age distribution is the single most conspicuous feature of recorded criminal offences' (1995:73). The nature of this age distribution has led some researchers to argue that youth is the most 'criminogenic'[1] age (Shoemaker 1996, Farrington 1997, Mukherjee 1997, Muncie 1999, Jenson, Potter and Howard 2001).

One plausible explanation for adolescence possibly being an especially criminogenic stage of life is that adolescence is the transition from childhood to adulthood and as such is widely accepted as a period of some 'storm and stress' (see Bessant, Sercombe and Watts 1998, Coleman and Hendry 1999). During adolescence, most young people are engaged in a process of 'carving out' for themselves a degree of material and emotional independence. For some, this process may be marked by the pursuit of illegitimate excitement and the thrill of rebellion. In Australia at least, it is not uncommon for young people to be involved at some point in relatively minor criminality or anti-social behaviour such as underage drinking, graffiti, shoplifting and fighting—though they may not necessarily be either caught or prosecuted (see Rutter, Giller and Hagell 1998).

An alternative, but equally plausible explanation for apparently high levels of offending among young people, is that their 'visibility' in public spaces leads to heightened levels of 'stops and searches' by police (Finnane 1994, White 1994). Support for this phenomenon is also found outside Australia—notably in Britain (Flood-Page, Campbell, Harrington and Miller 2000). As Wundersitz notes 'it could be argued that a high proportion of juveniles are apprehended for break/enter

---

1   Such studies indicate that adolescence is a life-stage when young people begin to commit crimes and which is often associated with petty offences such as shoplifting and gang fights.

offences, not because they are more likely than adults to commit such crimes, but because their immaturity and inexperience make them easier for police to catch' (1996:130).

Whatever the actual reality of the situation, age/crime relationships are more complicated than a simple combination of a stressful stage of life coupled with heightened visibility. The very concepts of youth and crime are problematic and contested (see Farrington 1986, Warr 1993). What exactly is the age range we should classify as youth? How should we define criminality? There are no universally accepted answers to these questions. More critically, there are no valid or reliable statistics as to the true extent and nature of youth crime, irrespective of how these terms are defined. As Muncie notes, 'what is known about young offending is a social construction—a product of particular social reactions and policing practices which become embedded as fact, not only in official statistics, but also in popular and political discourses' (1999:45). Officially recorded offences (i.e. that recorded on the administrative data bases of police and courts) will always represent the tip of an iceberg whose actual size is unknown. In addition, age may be differentially associated with different types of criminal acts, and issues of gender may further complicate this effect. As Ogilvie (1996) and Ogilvie, Lynch and Bell (2000) argue, the relationship between adolescent crime and gender is more complicated than simply 'boys do more' (see also Carrington, 1993 and Chapter 5 in this book).

In order to obtain a 'fix' upon the nature of adolescent crime, three issues are typically addressed. First, what is the age of onset of offending? Second, what is the peak age for offending? And third, what types of offences do young people commit? In considering these three issues, it is important to recognize that quite different sources of data are frequently employed to identify age of onset and the peak offending age. Age of onset is most often determined on the basis of self-report data, while the peak age of offending is most often determined on the basis of administrative data obtained from police and courts (with type of offending drawing upon both sources).

One consequence of the different data sources that have been drawn upon to explore the association between age and offending is a degree of inconsistency in the picture that emerges from the available data. It is reasonably clear, however, that regarding the age of onset, 'early starters' are likely to offend more and more likely to persist in offending than are 'late starters' (Graham and Bowling 1995, Moffitt 1993, Piquero and Chung 2001). For example, on the basis of police arrest data, Piquero and Chung (2001) demonstrate that early onset offending (i.e. before age 14) correlates positively with serious offending by age 18 and predicts the seriousness of offending even when controlling for other factors. However, the authors find that the multivariate relationship is significant for males, but not females (Piquero and Chung 2001).

In terms of the peak age of offending, Wolfgang, Figlio and Sellin (1972) report that the peak arrest age amongst a male cohort born in 1945 was 16 years. Similarly, Farrington (1995) reports the peak age in terms of the prevalence and frequency of offending is around 17 years of age (again, for males only). Somewhat counter to this data, Graham and Bowling (1995) report a peak age for offending of 21 years for males and (very interestingly) 16 years for females. Whilst these differences in observed peak ages may derive from the different data sources being used, we should also be mindful of the point made by Rutter, Giller and Hagell who assert that officially recorded data regarding the peak age of offending:

> ...like all other features of the crime statistics, will to some extent reflect changes in criminal justice policy and practice, such as changes in recording practices and 'informal' actions with apprehended offenders (Farrington and Burrows, 1993). It is crucial to keep a close eye on these changes in the peak age, as they may reveal critical influences on criminal behaviour, and to untangle the relative contributions of broader social changes and those within criminal justice policy (1998:77).

It is also important not to lose sight of the fact that peak age of offending varies with respect to different types of offences. For example, Greenwood, Petersilia and Zimring (1980) report that the peak arrest age is lowest for vandalism and highest for homicide, and Graham and Bowling (1995) report a peak age for 'expressive' property offences[2] of 14, compared with 16 for violent behaviour, 17 for serious offences, and 20 for drug and acquisitive property offences, for males. The peak ages for females are 15 for property, expressive, and serious offences; 16 for violent offences; and 17 for drug offences (Graham and Bowling, 1995).

These issues of onset and peak age of offending are important and need more systematic attention than has perhaps been the case to date. It is not the aim of this chapter, however, to discuss these issues in detail or attempt some sort of resolution (or reconciliation) of the different pictures derived from diverse data sources. Instead, the aim is to use the Sibling Study data in order to focus more directly on a third issue: the social characteristics of different age groups and the sorts of offences associated with them.

The strategy employed is to divide the Sibling Study data into three age-defined sub-samples, corresponding to early, middle and late adolescence, to explore developmental changes as adolescents move through their teenage years.[3] Following this division, the chapter examines the ways in which these three age groups engage in criminality. This is followed by consideration of a small group of variables that may go some way towards explaining age-defined differences in reported offending.

---

2   'Expressive' property offences normally include vandalism and arson.
3   The term 'late' is used here for convenience. Some that might argue that the period of late adolescence is actually 'later' than the age group being discussed here. This is a plausible argument, however it might equally plausibly be suggested that the first few years beyond 18 are better described as 'early adulthood'.

Age Distribution in the Sibling Study

Dividing the sample into three age groups corresponding to early, middle and late adolescence, we find that 25 per cent of the total sample falls into the youngest group of 11 to 13 year olds, 41 per cent fall into the middle category of 14 and 15 year olds, and the remaining 34 per cent comprise the oldest group of 16 to 19 year olds.

In terms of the gender differences of the three age groups, as can be seen in Table 3.1, there is a reasonable enough balance of female and male respondents in each age group. Females are however somewhat over-represented in the younger group (27 per cent compared with 23 per cent) and conversely under-represented in the older group (29 per cent compared with 39 per cent). This skewing of the data (females towards the younger group and males towards the older group) will need to be kept in mind when interpreting sex and age effects in later sections of the chapter.

Table 3.1   Age differences of females and males (row percentages)

Sex	11–13 Years	14–15 Years	16–19 Years	n
Female	27	44	29	487
Male	23	38	39	550

At first sight, the use of three age-defined sub-samples may appear problematic given the fact that the Sibling Study data also comprises three discrete cohorts (i.e. the School, Vulnerable, and Offender cohorts). And indeed, as can be seen in Table 3.2, the ages of each of the three cohorts are substantially different. The School cohort is markedly younger than the Vulnerable cohort, and even younger compared to the Offender cohort. Whereas 32 per cent of the School cohort fall into the youngest group and 23 per cent are in the oldest group, for the Offender cohort, only 10 per cent are within the youngest group and fully 59 per cent are within the oldest group. The Vulnerable group falls in between, with 18 per cent in the youngest group and 46 per cent within the oldest group.

The substantially larger size of the School cohort, compared to the Vulnerable and Offender cohorts, also results in significant differences when we turn to row percentages. Of the 11–13 year old group, a very substantial 81 per cent is from the School cohort and 72 per cent of the 14–15 year old group is from this cohort. In contrast, only 44 per cent of the oldest group is from the School cohort, even though this cohort is larger than the other two combined.

That the Vulnerable respondents are generally older than the School cohort, and the Offender respondents are older than the Vulnerable cohort is not surprising. The Offender cohort is by definition a cohort of respondents whose offending has been so persistent and/or serious that they have come into formal contact with the juvenile criminal justice system. In particular, a substantial proportion of the Offender cohort was drawn into the Sibling Study because they were incarcerated in a juvenile detention centre. Progression to this point, both in terms of undertaking the offending and being subject to a formal response by the state, takes time.

Table 3.2   Ages of the three cohorts (row and column percentages)

Age Group		School	Vulnerable	Offender
11–13 years (*n* = 261)	Row	81	10	9
	Column	32	18	10
14–15 years (*n* = 422)	Row	72	12	16
	Column	45	36	31
16–19 years (*n* = 354)	Row	44	19	37
	Column	23	46	59

Age and Crime

This section begins by examining the offending behaviour of all three age groups. The reasoning here being that if there are no observable differences between the three age-defined sub-samples in terms of factors such as levels of offending and 'criminal' self-identity, then there is very little to be gained by examining developmental changes arising from age differences in adolescent criminality.

The first variable of interest is the ASRD scale. Using the 31 ASRD items, we can create a simple summative measure of self-reported offending simply by tallying the number of offences reported. If we then calculate the mean score on the ASRD offending scale, we observe the expected differences across the three age-defined groups. As shown in Table 3.3, there is a clear and unambiguous increase in the magnitude of the mean scores as we move from the younger to older age groups. For the 11–13 year old group, the mean level of offending is 3.6 self-reported offences in the past 12 months. This compares with a mean of 6.1 offences for the 14–15 year old group, and a mean of 9.4 for the 16–19 year old group.

Table 3.3   Mean scores on the ASRDS by respondents differing in age

Age Group	Mean Score on the ASRDS
11–13 years (*n* = 222)	3.6
14–15 years (*n* = 363)	6.1
16–19 years (*n* = 319)	9.4

The differences observed across this variable provides us with persuasive indicators that developmental changes in offending are indeed being captured by the quantitative data, and, therefore, more detailed examination of the effects of (and relationships between) a wider range of factors/variables is warranted.

'Unpacking' the ASRD Measure of Offending

At this point we need to recognise that the construction of the ASRD measure of offending may be clouding important differences in the offending patterns of adolescents as they move through their teenage years. Less serious offences are essentially carrying the same weight as very serious offences. To take things to the absurd for the sake of clarification—if 100 per cent of the offending of the 11–13 year old respondents was minor in nature, 50 per cent of the offending of the middle group was minor, and 50 per cent was major; and 100 per cent of the offending of the oldest group was major in nature—we would never recognise these differences by comparing scales scores. In order to determine whether there are substantive differences in the types of offending engaged in by the various age groups, as well as determining the extent to which there are changes in the amounts of offending, we need to 'unpack' the offence types as measured by the ASRD scale. To do so, we use the six sub-scales of offending described in Chapter 2, which include vehicle-related, theft, public disorder, assault, drug and alcohol, and vandalism offences.

The procedure followed at this point is to score as '1' the reporting by respondents of engagement in any of the activities defined by the grouped ASRD items (i.e. reporting any one of the activities results in a score of '1', as does reporting all of the activities in the sub-scale). Respondents who do not report engaging in any of the grouped items are scored '0'.

Table 3.4 presents the involvement by respondents in each of the six offence types. As can be seen, there is a consistent pattern, in that younger respondents tend to report fewer crimes, for each offence type. In some instances, the differences between the groups are substantial. For example, while 19 per cent of the 11–13 year old group report at least one drug or alcohol offence, 72 per cent of the 16–19 year old group does so. Similarly, whilst only 16 per cent of the 11–13 year old group report vehicle related offences, 56 per cent of the 16–19 year old group report this category of offence. Even with respect to public disorder offences, which we might have expected to be particularly reported by the youngest group (as it includes offences such as going to R-rated films, running away from home, and not paying entrance fees), we find 24 per cent of the 11–13 year old group reporting engaging in this category of offending, compared with 34 per cent of the 14–15 year old group, and 52 per cent of the 16–19 year old group.

**Table 3.4 Age differences in types of offences
(row percentages and mean scores)**

Age Group		Theft	Public Disorder	Assault	Drugs and Alcohol	Vandalism	Vehicle-Related	*n*
11–13 yrs	%	30	24	29	19	23	16	261
	Mean	0.75	0.39	0.61	0.36	0.51	0.28	
14–15 yrs	%	41	34	42	40	39	27	422
	Mean	1.19	0.60	0.84	1.02	0.90	0.61	
16–19 yrs	%	49	52	50	72	45	56	354
	Mean	1.84	0.92	1.19	2.23	1.08	1.36	

Note 1: Row percentages sum to greater than 100 because respondents report more than one offence type.
Note 2: The mean scores are calculated on the basis of summed responses to the items in each offence category (not reported = 0, reported = 1). The minimum possible score for each category is 0, and the maximum score is 5 for vehicle-related offences, 7 for theft, 3 for public disorder, and 5 for drugs and alcohol, vandalism and assault, corresponding to the number of items in each sub-scale.

The method used to calculate these percentages may, however, introduce a new artefact that makes it inappropriate to draw inferences about the frequency of offending. That is, because reporting engagement in any of the items within an offence category results in a score of '1,' as does reporting engaging in all of the items, the possibility exists that the percentage data are misleading. If, for example, it was the case that all the respondents in the youngest group reported engaging in only one of the theft category items, whereas all the respondents in the oldest group reported engaging in all seven theft items, the two groups would nevertheless have the same final score or reported percentage. Thus, this measure cannot accurately estimate the frequency of offending.

With this possibility in mind, the mean scores obtained by summing the item scores in each offence category are also included in Table 3.4. These mean values confirm the appropriateness of making inferences about frequency on the basis of the percentages by demonstrating that in every case there is a clear increase in frequency of offending associated with increases in age. For example, the mean score on the five-item drugs/alcohol measure is 0.36 for the 11–13 year old group, compared with 1.02 for the 14–15 year old group, and 2.23 for the 16–19 year old group. Similarly, the mean score on the five-item vehicle-related measure is 0.28 for the 11–13 year old group compared with 0.61 for the 14–15 year old group and 1.36 for the 16–19 year old group.

Exploring the data further, Table 3.5 reports the levels of engagement in each category of offending as a proportion of the total offending of each age group. For example, '5' in the second row and column of the table indicates that five per cent of all offending by the 11–13 year old group is for vehicle-related offences. As can be seen, when the data are reconfigured in this way, a slightly different picture emerges.

Table 3.5   Age differences in types of offences as a proportion of total offending (row percentages)

Age Group	Theft	Public Disorder	Assault	Drugs and Alcohol	Vandalism	Vehicle-Related	*n*
11–13 yrs	55	18	16	3	3	5	147
14–15 yrs	57	14	15	5	5	3	317
16–19 yrs	57	18	8	12	3	2	310

With two or three exceptions, Table 3.5 reveals a surprising degree of stability in the categories of offences committed by each age group. There is little to suggest in these data that the nature of the actual offences committed by adolescents' changes in any very marked way as they get older. Instead, it appears that the changes that do occur are largely frequency-related.

For example, 55 per cent of the offending of the youngest group falls within the theft category. This compares with 57 per cent for both the older groups. Similarly, 18 per cent of the offending of the youngest group falls within the public disorder category. This compares with 14 per cent for the middle group and 18 per cent for the oldest group. There are exceptions to this pattern of relative stability across age groups, however. In the case of the drugs and alcohol category, whilst only three per cent of the offending of the youngest group falls within this category, 12 per cent of the offending of the oldest group does so. In a surprising reversal of expected results, we also find that 16 per cent of the offending of the youngest group falls within the assault category, compared with eight per cent of the offending of the oldest group. This same downward trend is observed with respect to the vehicle-related category, with five per cent of the offending of the youngest group concerned with motor vehicles, but only two per cent of the offending of the oldest group.

The data in Tables 3.4 and 3.5 suggest that, exceptions to the general pattern notwithstanding, for offending adolescents, the movement through the teenage years is associated with an increase in the preparedness to commit particular types of crimes, rather than any particularly marked increase or decrease in the range of crimes the individual is prepared to commit. This interpretation is based upon the argument that this is the most immediately obvious inference that can been drawn from data that show a high degree of stability in terms of the proportional representation of the different offence categories across the three age groups, coupled with a consistent increase with age in the frequency of offending across all offence categories.

Further evidence in support of this interpretation comes from considering just one example of a particular category of offending. While Table 3.5 shows an admittedly proportional narrowing of engagement in assault offences (from 16 per cent for the youngest group to eight per cent for the oldest group), if we examine each age group's actual levels of engagement in each of the assault offences, we see a reasonably clear increase in offending with age. Table 3.6 shows, for example, that while only 18 per cent of the youngest group had deliberately hurt or beat someone up in the preceding 12 months, 33 per cent of the oldest group reported having done so. Similarly, while only 11 per cent of the youngest group had used a weapon in a fight, 22 per cent of the oldest group reported having done so.

Table 3.6   Age differences in five assault offences (percentage reporting each offence)

Assault Items	11–13 yrs	14–15 yrs	16–19 yrs
Taken part in a fight between two or more groups	24 (62)	31 (131)	39 (141)
Deliberately hurt or beat somebody up	18 (45)	26 (110)	33 (129)
Used anything as a weapon in a fight	11 (27)	9 (39)	22 (80)
Forced someone to give you things	9 (24)	16 (68)	24 (89)
Forced someone to do sexual things when they didn't want to	2 (5)	4 (15)	3 (10)

Note: Bracketed numbers are totals on which percentages are based.

It would thus seem from these data that with increasing age there comes an increasing involvement in a range of offences. The decline in proportional involvement in particular offence types with age is just a reflection of the fact that the absolute increase in particular offence categories with age is greater in some instances than others, with a consequent impact on the proportionality of offences. Importantly, the 'unpacking' of the offence types making up the composite ASRD Scale measure also indicates that the data derived from analyses using the total scale measure do not differ substantially from analyses of the disaggregated items. This means we can reasonably safely adopt the simpler and more straightforward strategy of using the complete ASRD measure as a dependent variable in subsequent analyses when explaining age effects in a multivariate context.

Criminological Factors

We now briefly describe several variables that bear upon factors/concepts that we believe to be implicated in the relationship between age and crime, including neighbourhood context, family context, and victimization status.[4] These variables will then be included in multivariate analyses further explaining the age/crime nexus.

Neighbourhood Context

In considering the issue of neighbourhood context, there are both objective and subjective measures we can take into account. In an objective sense, we can obviously draw upon the Index of Relative Disadvantage that was discussed initially in Chapter 1. For the purposes of this chapter, we will be using the collapsed Index of Relative Disadvantage, which includes the five categories ranging from most disadvantaged ('1') to least disadvantaged ('5'). It is interesting to note here that 16–19 year old group appears as the most disadvantaged compared with 11–13 year old group, which is more likely to be least disadvantaged (Table 3.7).

Table 3.7   Age differences in the Index of Relative Disadvantage (row percentages)

Age Group	(1)	(2)	(3)	(4)	(5)	*n*
11–13 yrs	16	12	22	25	25	257
14–15 yrs	16	15	26	21	21	408
16–19 yrs	25	17	25	18	16	312

(1) = Most Disadvantaged → (5) = Least Disadvantaged.

In terms of more subjective dimensions of neighbourhood context, we can draw upon two questions that explicitly address how respondents feel about their neighbourhood:

- are the people in the area where you usually live friendly?
- would you like to move to a different area to live if you could?

---

4 It needs to be noted that these three variables are not being positioned as the only variables of importance. Arguably, factors such as education, sense of self and peer relations (among others) could also have been included in the analyses. Unfortunately, given the limited space available, it was decided to simply focus on three key variables that could provide indicators of developmental change across adolescence.

All respondents overwhelmingly reported that the people in their neighbourhoods were either very or fairly friendly. Among the youngest group, 90 per cent felt this way compared with 86 per cent of the 14 to 15 year old group and 83 per cent of the oldest group.

In contrast, however, there is a statistically significant age effect with respect to the desire to move from the neighbourhood. As reported in Table 3.8, the respondents from the oldest group are much more likely than those from the two younger groups to indicate a desire to move (35 per cent compared to 19 per cent for both of the younger groups).

Table 3.8   Age differences in the level of desire to move from neighbourhood (row percentages)

Age Group	I'd like to move	I'd rather stay	I'm not sure	*n*
11–13 yrs	19	59	22	251
14–15 yrs	19	57	24	413
16–19 yrs	35	41	24	344

Family Context (Family Structure and Quality of Parenting)

As with the neighbourhood variables, family context can be assessed using both objective and subjective measures, which include family structure and quality of parenting in this case. The family structure variable used here is a simple measure indicating whether there was no parent/adult carer, a single parent or two parents in the respondent's household. As can be seen in Table 3.9, there is an obvious and unsurprising age effect. The younger the respondents, the less likely they are to be living in a household in which there is no parent present (from three per cent in the youngest group to seven per cent for the middle group and 20 per cent for the oldest group). Likewise, the older the respondent, the less likely they are to be living in a two-parent household (81 per cent are living with both parents in the youngest group, 75 per cent for the middle group and 57 per cent for the oldest group). We have already seen (Table 3.2) that the cohorts differ in age, with the School-based sample the youngest and the Offender cohort the oldest, so the above relationships may have as much to do with cohort as age. We will explore these relationships further shortly.

Table 3.9   Age differences in family structure (row percentages)

Age Group	No Parent in Household	One Parent in Household	Two Parents in Household	*n*
11–13 yrs	3	16	81	256
14–15 yrs	7	18	75	412
16–19 yrs	20	23	57	344

The number of parents in a household does not of course necessarily tell us very much about the quality of parenting within the household. Children may grow up in a two-parent household and yet experience very little love and affection from either parent. Conversely, children may grow up in a single-parent household and yet experience very high levels of affection from two parents (albeit that one parent is non-residential). The Sibling Study questionnaire includes a series of questions[5] about the levels of emotional support experienced from each parent during childhood (see also Chapter 7).

On the basis of these questions, parental support was classified into three categories: 'high parental support from two parents', 'high parental support from one parent' and 'no high levels of parental support'. Because age and cohort are related, we need to examine the cohorts separately to fully understand the significance of age for level of parental support. The relevant data are shown in Table 3.10.

As can be seen, the same pattern exists in each cohort: high parental support from both parents is most likely among the youngest group. High support is reported by 77 per cent of 11–13 year old group in the School cohort, 74 per cent in the Vulnerable cohort, and 47 per cent of those in the Offender cohort. Overall, however, high parental support from both parents is most likely in the School cohort, even among the oldest age group, with over half reporting high levels of support from both parents. High support from both parents is least likely in the Offender cohort, reported by less than half of the youngest group and one-third or less of the other two groups. In the Vulnerable cohort, a sizeable number of the youngest group (74 per cent) report high support from both parents, but less than half of the other groups do so. Clearly, the data lends support to the proposition that lack of parental support in childhood can be a precursor of offending in adolescence.

---

5   Questions are taken from the care scale of the Parental Bonding Instrument (Parker, Tupling and Brown 1979 (see Chapter 7 for more details).

Table 3.10 Age differences in parental support in the three cohorts (row percentages)

Age Categories By Cohort	No High Levels of Parental Support	High Parental Support from One Parent	High Parental Support from Two Parents	*n*
School Cohort				
11–13 yrs	5	18	77	190
14–15 yrs	10	19	71	268
16–19 yrs	13	24	63	148
Vulnerable Cohort				
11–13 yrs	22	4	74	23
14–15 yrs	23	34	43	44
16–19 yrs	41	20	39	59
Offender Cohort				
11–13 yrs	21	32	47	19
14–15 yrs	30	37	33	51
16–19 yrs	34	36	30	106

Adolescent Victimization

In Chapter 10, the issue of victimization and its relationship to self-reported offending is considered in some detail. At this point, we will look briefly at victimization and how the likelihood of its occurrence is affected by age.

The Sibling Study questionnaire includes questions regarding whether or not respondents have been the victim of a crime and whether or not 'bad things' have ever happened to respondents. By drawing upon responses to these two questions, it becomes possible to construct a measure of the proportion of respondents who report being a victim of serious, unfortunate events. When answering these questions, some respondents listed problems routinely faced by most people in adolescence, such as problems with boyfriends/girlfriends; however, responses of this type have not been included in the constructed variable. In total, a surprisingly high 24 per cent of the sample report being the victim of traumatic events and/or criminal offences (the latter comprising roughly two-thirds of all reported experiences).[6]

---

6 Experiences of trauma include: racial harassment; sexual harassment; death of a family member or significant other; suicide attempt by significant other; separated from parents; fostered/adopted out; health problems; family alcohol use; family member arrested; and being bullied. Types of criminal victimization include: sexual assault; sexual abuse; physical assault; attempted murder; attempted sexual assault; attempted physical assault; maltreatment; robbery; stalking; police harassment; abduction/attempted abduction; threatened with violence; theft; break and enter; and car theft/vandalism. See Chapter 10 for a more detailed discussion of the impact of criminal victimization. See Ogilvie and Lynch (2002) for a more detailed discussion of gender and criminal/traumatic victimization.

As we would expect, there is a strong statistical association between age and victimization, given that the older the respondent, the more time/opportunity there will be to experience a traumatic event. The data reveal a very clear age progression in the proportion of respondents reporting having had such an experience. Only 10 per cent of the 11–13 year old group reports a traumatic event during their lifetime, compared with 23 per cent of the 14–15 year old group and 35 per cent of the oldest group.

The Relationship Between Age and Crime in a Multivariate Context

In this chapter we have been concerned with two major issues. First, the nature of age differences with respect to reported offending, and, second, the impact of selected variables—cohort, gender, family structure and support, neighbourhood characteristics and victimization—on the relationship between age and self-reported offending. We were interested to determine whether the causal factors were the same for those in early, middle, and late adolescence. The data has already provided some indication that different factors may be involved at different age levels.

To explore this issue more thoroughly in a multivariate context, we carried out three ordinary least squares regression analyses predicting youth offending levels (as measured by the 31-item ASRD additive scale) for the three age groups. Table 3.11 presents the results of these analyses using the independent variables described previously, which are presented in dummy variable format. What we observe are, in general, differences in the 'reach' of particular variables in the different age groups. That is to say, the data suggest differences in the extent of the influence of statistically significant independent variables in the three different age groups.

For the youngest group, there are six significant independent variables (Table 3.11). These are:

- the absence of a parent in the household (compared with two parents in the household)
- no high level of emotional support from either parent[7]
- being male
- being victimized
- member of the Offender or Vulnerable cohort, in contrast to the School cohort.

For the middle age group, there are seven significant independent variables (Table 3.11). These are:

---

7   This variable only approaches significance (p = 0.07).

- the absence of a parent in the household (compared with two parents in the household)
- the presence of one (rather than two) parents in the household
- no high level emotional support from any parent
- being victimized
- being male
- member of the Offender or Vulnerable cohort, in contrast to the School cohort.

For the oldest group, there are seven significant independent variables (Table 3.11). These are:

- no high level emotional support from any parent
- the neighbourhood perceived as unfriendly
- being male
- being victimized
- level '2' of the Index of Relative Disadvantage[8]
- member of the Offender or Vulnerable cohort, in contrast to the School cohort.

There are interesting similarities and differences in the importance of these predictors. It is clear that in each of the age groups, those from the Offender and Vulnerable cohorts are more likely to report offending behaviour than are those from the School cohort. As well, a lack of a high level of emotional support from any parent, having experienced victimization, and being male are important predictors of reported offending in each age group. A summary of these trends is provided in Table 3.12.

---

8   The fact that only this level of the Index emerges as statistically significant suggests that the association is actually a statistical artifact deriving from an uneven distribution of Offenders across the various neighbourhood 'levels'. That is, it would seem likely that all this significant probability calculation is revealing is a 'lumpy' spread of Offenders.

Table 3.11 OLS regression model for the three age groups: precursor structural factors/variables as predictors of self-reported offending

Independent Variables	Parameter Estimates		
	11–13 yrs	14–15 yrs	16–19 yrs
No High Level of Emotional Support from Either Parent (*support from two parents is the excluded dummy variable*)	2.17*	3.46***	2.78**
High Level of Emotional Support from One Parent	0.31	0.35	1.84
No Working Parent (*two working parents is the excluded dummy variable*)[1]	1.44	0.09	−0.11
One Working Parent	−0.06	−1.13	−1.52
No Parent in Household (*two parents in household is the excluded dummy variable*)	6.92****	4.50***	0.13
One Parent in Household	1.61	2.19**	2.53
Least Advantaged Neighbourhood Level 1 (*most advantaged neighbourhood – level 5 – is the excluded dummy variable*)	0.65	−0.17	−1.13
Neighbourhood Advantage Level 2	1.08	0.13	−2.99**
Neighbourhood Advantage Level 3	−0.40	0.11	−1.67
Neighbourhood Advantage Level 4	0.30	0.01	−1.17
Unfriendly Neighbourhood (*fairly/very friendly neighbourhood is the excluded dummy variable*)	0.78	0.60	2.87*
Wish to Move from Neighbourhood (*not sure or would rather stay is the excluded dummy variable*)	1.38	0.73	0.86
Male (*female is the excluded dummy variable*)	1.98***	2.09***	3.30***

Independent Variables	Parameter Estimates		
	11–13 yrs	14–15 yrs	16–19 yrs
Victimization (*not having been victimized is the excluded dummy variable*)	2.41**	2.37***	2.28**
Offender Cohort (*the School cohort is the excluded dummy variable*)	2.67**	5.69***	6.98***
Vulnerable Cohort (*the School cohort is the excluded dummy variable*)	2.56**	4.90***	4.97***
Intercept	0.44	1.97	2.90
Adjusted R^2 for Model	0.22	0.40	0.41

*p < .05; **p < .01; ***p < .001; ****p < .0001

[1] The 'no parent in household' category is also excluded because it is included as a family structure variable.

Table 3.12 Summary of the significant independent predictors of self-reported offending for the three age groups

Independent Variable	Parameter Estimates		
	11–13 yrs	14–15 yrs	16–19 yrs
Offender Cohort	2.67*	5.69**	6.98***
Vulnerable Cohort	2.56*	4.90***	4.97***
Male	1.98**	2.09***	3.30***
No Parent in Household	6.92***	4.50***	NS
No High Level of Emotional Support	2.17*	3.46***	2.78**
Victimization	2.41*	2.37***	2.28**
Unfriendly Neighbourhood	NS	NS	2.87*

*p<.05; **p<.01; ***p<.001

While many of the same predictors are important for each of the age groups, the results also show differential influence of predictors by age. Differences in the likelihood of self-reported offending between the Offender and Vulnerable groups on the one hand, and the School cohort on the other, are greater among the two older groups. With increasing age, opportunities for offending are doubtless greater, and this is reflected in the greater disparity in offending behaviour in older respondents from the School cohort and the two other cohorts, who exist in a more fertile environment for offending behaviour.

Having no parents in the household makes self-reported delinquency more likely if the young people are less than 16; it is not a significant factor for the oldest group. Being male is not as important for the 11–13 year olds as it is for the older respondents. Lacking a high level of emotional support from parents while growing up is not as important for the youngest group as it is for the two older groups. Being victimized or experiencing a traumatic event is again less important for the youngest group, compared to the two older groups. And, finally, viewing the neighbourhood as unfriendly increases the likelihood of offending behaviour amongst the oldest group, but is not important for the two younger groups. It is clear that while many, but not all, of the factors just discussed are significantly related to self-reported delinquency, there are discernible differences by age for a number of the factors.

The gender differences emerge more sharply with increasing age, as boys and girls differ less in propensity for criminal behaviour in the younger age groups. Lacking parents in the household has a greater impact on the younger groups when parental support is likely to be more important. The absence of high levels of emotional support from parents while growing up impacts more on the older respondents; perhaps the impact takes time to have its effects observed. Victimization, too, is a more important cause of reported offending among the older groups, compared to the 11–13 year old group. Once again, victimization may need time for its effects to be observed. Finally, the importance of an unfriendly neighbourhood environment, and presumably associated peer relations, is significantly greater for the oldest group. Clearly, criminal behaviour is made more or less likely by different factors in different age groups.

So, for the very young, those under age 14, coming from households in which no parents are present can be seen as a significant marker for self-reported delinquency. It is important also, but not as important, for the 14-15 year old group, but not important for those 16 or older. Being victimized and lacking a high level of emotional support from parents are the most important predictors for the 14 to 15 year old group, and being male and living in an unfriendly neighbourhood environment the most important for those over 16. Situational factors, it would seem then, are most important for the youngest group, experiential factors for those in the middle group, and structural and environmental factors for the oldest group. While there are clearly age differences in the significance of causal factors, we need also to remember that these differences occur in an environment characterized by a range of significant factors impacting on all age groups.

Conclusion

There are two messages that can be drawn from this discussion. First, and consistent with literature concerned with the age/offending relationship, the offending of the Sibling Study respondents changes in terms of both prevalence and frequency as they increase in age. And second, the data show that different factors impact differently on the offending of different age groups. While we would have expected some factors to get weaker and some to get stronger as respondents age, we also observe indications of the way some factors are particularly important at different stages in adolescence. It was unexpected (for example) that the emotional support variable exerts the greatest influence (as measured by the magnitude and significance of the parameter estimates) upon those in mid-adolescence, or the 14–15 year old group. The fact that the data are consistent with typical examinations of adolescent offending (i.e. 'boys do more' and 'older boys do most') encourages us to take seriously the more interesting second message contained in the data reported. If we think of offending as an 'output,' the data are telling us that the 'inputs' are rather different at different stages of adolescence. The implications of this fact in terms of both theory and practice are important. The major theories of juvenile offending are in a very real sense sets of 'input specifications'. So, for example, the input of most interest to control theorists is that of self-control. In contrast, the input of most interest to differential association theorists is peer networks.

The Sibling Study data represent something of a challenge to these 'one size fits all' specifications of particular 'magic bullets'. What these analyses demonstrate is that different theoretical orientations may be more or less important at different points in the movement from childhood towards adulthood. It is not that approaches such as control theory or differential association are in any sense 'wrong', but rather that each is only tapping an aspect of a larger process. As a result, we need theories of adolescent socialization that can draw upon a range of theoretical perspectives and provide a guide as to where and when particular foci are most important. In thinking about this issue, we need to recognize that it is not just a case of 'getting our theory right' because we dislike 'disruptive' data or 'straggly' theory, but rather that there are critical issues at hand in terms of real-world responses by the state to adolescent offending.

If inputs are differentially important at different stages of adolescence, then the leverage points available for interventions aimed at encouraging desistance are equally subject to change. This means that arms of the state, such as the juvenile criminal justice system and protective services, need to embody the recognition of shifting leverage points in the 'policies and procedures' guidelines that frame their interventions into the lives of young people. Such a recognition runs counter to the understandable desire of government departments to develop intervention guidelines that are consistent rather than discretionary. If it is to be seriously suggested that we need to be much more sensitive and flexible about the way the state responds to adolescent offending, we need a much clearer picture of precisely what leverage points are available at what points in adolescence. This is a major challenge for both researchers and practitioners, but fortunately, one that is increasingly being undertaken, particularly by developmental criminologists (see for example, Catalano and Hawkins 1996, Farrington 1995, Herrenkohl *et al* 2000, Laub and Lauritsen 1993, National Crime Prevention 1999, Silva and Stanton 1997, U.S. Department of Health and Human Services 2001a).

Chapter 4

Gender and Offending Behaviours: Opportunity, Motivations and Manifestations

Emma Ogilvie and John S. Western

Introduction

The literature on gender and criminality is now reasonably substantial (Heidensohn 1996), with differences in the frequency of female and male adolescent offending a well-established fact (Chesney-Lind 1997). Official statistics routinely document a 5:1 (male to female) ratio in offending, while self-report data reveal smaller, yet equally consistent differences of approximately 2.5:1 (see Ageton 1983, Cernkonovich and Giordano 1979, Elliott and Ageton 1980, Kratoscki and Kratoscki 1975, Mak 1993, Ogilvie 1996, Short and Nye 1958, Simpson 1991, Triplett and Myers 1995, Williams and Gold 1972). This chapter examines the issue of sex differences and sex similarities in the self-reported offending of the Australian young people who participated in the Sibling Study research project. The chapter begins with a focus upon opportunities and motivations for offending. This is followed by a consideration of the particular types of offences committed by young females and males, and the emotional responses of respondents to their offending behaviours.

A wide variety of theoretical perspectives has been used by researchers interested in understanding the relationship between gender and criminality (see Alder 1997, Daly 1998, Naffine 1996). Interestingly however, current research increasingly appears to be revisiting traditional criminological explanations of male criminality. Much of the current interest in causes of gender differences in crime is thus drawing upon power control theory (McCarthy, Hagan and Woodward 1999), social disorganization (Wilcox-Rountree and Warner 1999), differential association (Heimer and DeCoster 1999), strain theory (Broidy and Agnew 1997), and low self-control and opportunity (LaGrange and Silverman 1999). Other theorists have however adopted more feminist frameworks, in the belief that such approaches are better able to explain the complexities of women and crime than are traditional approaches characterized by a primary interest in males (Bottcher 1995, Daly 1994, Hahn-Rafter and Heidensohn 1995, Maher 1997).

Irrespective of the particular theoretical orientation used to guide the research, one of the first factors that needs to be considered when attempting to identify the precursors to persistent offending is that of access to 'criminal' environments. Ever since Sutherland (1979), the issue of opportunity to learn criminality has been acknowledged as a crucial factor in offending. With respect to gender, theorists such as Gottfredson and Hirschi (1990) argue that females have similar levels of opportunity as males to commit crime and that therefore gender differences in criminal behaviour result from females having higher levels of self-control. In contrast to this view, feminist theorists such as Maher (1997) and Miller (1998) argue that the gendered contexts women find themselves within severely restrict the opportunities of females to engage in criminal activities, forcing them to enact crime in a distinctly different manner from men (see Miller 1998:60).

In addition to exploring the gendered nature of opportunities for crime, theorists have examined females' and males' motivations and experiences of offending. Some researchers argue that females engage in crime for qualitatively different reasons than men do (Campbell 1993, Denno 1994, Wilson and Daly 1998), and that the female experience of criminality is qualitatively different from that of males (Messerschmidt 1994, Miller 1998). Alternatively, other theorists argue that while both the experience and act of offending may be different for young females and males, the underlying causes for engaging in crime are essentially the same (Box 1983). Gender differences are thus not so much in the underlying causes of behaviour, but rather in the consequences of being a criminal female as opposed to a criminal male—with females reporting greater experiences of humiliation, shame and disgrace (Braithwaite and Daly 1994, Broidy and Agnew 1997, Worrall 1990). In Australia, however, while there has been a great deal of theoretical debate devoted to these issues (Alder 1997, Daly and Chesney-Lind 1988, Naffine 1996), rather less empirical research has been undertaken that might point towards the strengths and weaknesses of the various approaches. While a detailed consideration of the relative merits of different theoretical perspectives in explaining gender differences is beyond the scope of this chapter, using the Sibling Study data to explore gender differences in opportunity, motivation, engagement and the experience of crime is a useful contribution to the ongoing debates about the most appropriate theoretical orientation.

Opportunity for Offending

As was noted in Chapter 2, respondents in the Sibling Study were asked whether they had ever had a chance to do something against the law or thought was probably against the law. A perhaps surprisingly high 60 per cent of the total sample indicated that they had had this opportunity. Gender differences were observed, with 67 per cent of the 543 boys and 57 per cent of the 476 girls answering in the affirmative. Overall, then, only 10 per cent more boys than girls reported having the opportunity to commit a criminal act (or a probable criminal act), a difference in opportunity which quite clearly cannot account for the 5:1 ratio in officially recorded offending.

We might hypothesize, however, that while the gender difference overall is small, there may be cohort effects, such that gender differences in opportunities will be more apparent in the School group than the Offender cohort. By this we mean that because the girls in the Offender cohort are in this group because of their offending, they are likely to have had as many opportunities for crime as the boys, and we would expect small or no gender differences in this cohort. Alternatively, we could argue that because both boys and girls in the School cohort offend less often than respondents (of both sexes) in the other cohorts, the opportunities to offend must be equally constrained, and gender differences in this cohort will not be great. It is the second hypothesis that garners greater support in the Sibling Study data. Not only was offending within the School cohort significantly less than in the other two cohorts, but gender differences in terms of perceived opportunities for offending did not exist. In contrast, for the Offender and Vulnerable cohorts, boys were far more likely than girls to report offending opportunities (see Table 4.1). In addition, as just noted, the opportunities for offending were significantly greater for both sexes in these cohorts.

Table 4.1 Sex differences in the percentage of respondents with the opportunity to do something against the law, by cohort

Cohort	Male	Female
School	52 (313)	54 (333)
Vulnerable	76 (76)	61 (82)
Offender	92 (154)	71 (61)

Note: Bracketed numbers are the frequencies upon which the percentages are based.

How might we explain these differences in opportunity for offending? It may be that while females from the Offender cohort have greater opportunities for criminality than females (or males) from the School cohort, these opportunities are structured with respect to their immediate environments, so that their perceived level of opportunity is still less than that of males. For example, we might suspect that females have less access to partake in property offences, not because of diminished material opportunities, but rather because of constrained cultural opportunities, i.e. what Miller (1998) refers to as a 'gender stratified' situational context. That is, a situational context that imposes particular norms and behaviours that serve to reinforce particular gendered, raced and classed beliefs (see also Maher 1997, Sommers and Baskin 1993, Triplett and Myers 1995).

To further illustrate this point, we can draw upon qualitative data from those in the Offender cohort. The qualitative data suggest that property offences are indeed a 'given' aspect of criminality for the Offender boys in a way that is not so frequently observed amongst the Offender girls. Where the boys report actually planning and 'creating' opportunities for this offence, the property offences of the girls appear to perhaps be slightly more opportunistic, and arise out of specific circumstances rather than a more established commitment to forward-planning of offending. As Brooke outlined:

It's more if you can, you know, I mean, I don't set out in the morning and say 'I think I'll knock over a shopping centre'. It's more like you'll be sitting at home, and someone will want to, you know, buy some food, or some drugs or whatever, and no-one will have any money. So you think, well how are going to get this stuff, and then you go, well let's do a quick B and E.

Leon, on the other hand, was far more explicit about the organization involved:

You got to be smart, I mean, there's these kids yeah, that are whacked over arse (drug induced) who'll just wander into places you know, put on a CD or something, grab themselves a drink, I don't know. Then they get picked up by the police and come in here talking like they're these long-term crims. It's true! You do that sort of shit you deserve to get caught. I mean, what you got to do is know your locations, know what you're after – you know, you're either doing straight money or goods or whatever, and different places are going to have different stuff. You got to have sense.

These qualitative data cannot of course be taken as conclusive, but they do point to important gender differences that should be examined with respect to our understandings of what 'opportunity' actually means to young females and males.

Motivations and Offending

While there are differences in opportunity for offending between boys and girls, the reasons they each give for their offending are very similar. A list of 12 potential reasons was posited (Table 4.2), and respondents were asked to rate the importance of each on a five-point scale, from 'very important' to 'not at all important'. The top six reasons—'it was easy to do', 'it was just something I did', 'it was fun', 'I was curious', 'it was too good a chance to miss' and 'it just seemed like a good idea'—were the same for both groups. Four of the reasons—'I was bored', 'it was a challenge', 'I wanted to prove I could do it' and 'it's something I can do well'—were more important to boys than to girls, while the remaining two reasons—'my friends wanted me to' and 'I wanted to get back at someone'—were not important to either group. These data shed further light on the comments by Brooke and Leon. For both females and males, issues of ease and fun appear to be important (i.e. opportunistic acts), but for the boys, there is some evidence of a slightly greater concern with less opportunistic factors such as having a challenge and doing something well.

Table 4.2 Sex and cohort differences in the percentage of respondents reporting listed statements as very important reasons for breaking the law

	School		Cohort Vulnerable		Offender	
	Male	Female	Male	Female	Male	Female
It was easy to do	21	30	46	39	35	40
It was just something I did	24	22	35	36	42	36
It was fun	27	20	49	28	24	25
I was curious	22	26	16	27	18	17
It was too good a chance to miss	16	17	39	28	16	28
It just seemed like a good idea	14	16	29	37	26	27
I was bored	7	17	39	39	22	28
It was a challenge	10	16	12	29	24	31
I wanted to prove I could do it	9	16	8	25	12	16
It's something I can do well	4	13	25	34	8	23
I wanted to get back at someone	7	7	10	17	8	15
My friends wanted me to	2	5	6	8	10	8
n	135	152	50	65	50	145

It is particularly interesting that the somewhat lackadaisical motives (it was easy/just something I did/it just seemed a good idea) are not motives one would consider specifically gendered, either as masculine or feminine. Nonetheless, they do accord with adolescents' descriptions of how they found themselves engaging in a variety of different crimes, from property crime, to violence, to simple drug use. Leon's comments notwithstanding, what we see is once again the significance of opportunistic exercises in taking advantage of particular situations as they arise.

For example, Jim's practice of 'tillies' came about through 'just having a good idea'. Jim described having entered a shop 'down on the coast' and viewing a cash register heavily stocked with money. Given that the bench was wide it was impossible to simply reach over and take the money, but he noticed that the cash register was sitting on the bench (as opposed to being bolted) and was connected only by an electrical cord to a power point. As Jim put it:

> I just reached out and grabbed it, the whole thing, and then me and Angus were
> running down Luton Street with this bloody till, the cord flapping out about my
> legs, must have looked hilarious. Nobody stopped us but hey. We must have run
> about ten blocks with that fucking thing. That's how you do a tilly.

The girls' accounts of how they became involved in offending seemed equally
marked by an appreciation of the experiential aspects of offending (i.e. the fun and
excitement involved). For example, Natasha first started getting involved in crime
when a male friend showed her how to break into a car. Natasha loved both the act of
stealing and the 'freedom' the activity represented (or imparted). In describing why
she engages in car theft, Natasha describes a mode of transport far easier than that
available in her neighbourhood, stating:

> I can't stand the just sitting around you know. I mean I live out at W...., you
> decide you want to go somewhere, you're on your arse in a bus-stop for up to an
> hour, just watching these cars go by. Then you see one that's just sitting there
> and you watch it for a bit, you know, checking out its make and that, and then
> you just say fuck it – I need to be somewhere. Doesn't much matter where most
> of the time, just need to be out of there.

Brooke gave a similar account that again shows how the offending can derive from
a particular conjunction of an interest in fun and a concern with the practical
realities of day-to-day life:

> It's transport, I mean you got to go places, you got no car yourself, what're you
> going to do? Walk? I don't think so.

It needs to be understood here that issues of fun and ease are not representative of
the girls' and boys' indifference to, or rejection of, the prevailing moral codes.
Rather they appear to tie into lives characterized by lack of access to infrastructure
(see Lynch and Ogilvie 1999) and levels of familiarity with violent contexts and
criminal opportunities (see Somers and Baskin, 1993). What is particularly
interesting, however, is that whereas opportunities for engagement in criminality
were distinctly gendered amongst offenders, the motivations for actually engaging
in criminal acts were substantially the same for the females and males. The next
question, given different opportunities and similar motivations, is, what are the
actual levels of engagement in criminal behaviour for young males and females?

Engagement in Offending

We have already seen that almost two-thirds of the sample (60 per cent) reported at
least the opportunity to engage in behaviour that was against the law or probably
against the law. What have they done, and does offending behaviour differ for
girls and boys? To answer these questions, we employed the Australian Self-
Reported Delinquency Scale (ASRD Scale). As described in Chapter 2, this scale

asks the young people to report whether or not they had committed a variety of delinquent acts within the last twelve months. Gender differences in responses to all items (with the exception of four 'lie' items) were reported in Table 2.4. In Table 4.3 below, these differences are presented as odds ratios. As can be seen, and consistent with previous literature, boys reported engaging in more crimes than girls, for every type of offence. However, as is also consistent with other research, there is a decreasing gender difference in offending, with the greatest differences being for the more serious offences such as assault, and the greatest similarities being for the more minor offences such as drug use (see Ageton 1983, Junger-Tas, Terlouw and Klein 1994, Steffensmeier and Steffensmeier 1980, Triplett and Myers 1995).

Regarding more serious offences, the largest gender difference observed is for using a weapon in a fight, with boys over five times more likely than girls to have done so. The next largest difference relates to vehicles and bikes, with males between four and five times more likely than females to have raced cars or bikes, driven a car after drinking alcohol, stolen a bicycle or parts thereof, and stolen things or parts from a car or motorbike. Next, males are between three and four times more likely than females to have committed theft or property crimes, including having broken into a house or building to steal things, driven a car or motorbike without a license, deliberately damaged other people's property, taken someone's car or motorbike without permission, stolen money of more than ten dollars, stolen food from dispenser machines, or deliberately damaged property by starting a fire. We also have a slight anomaly in terms of type of offence, with males being three times more likely than females to have deliberately hurt or beaten somebody up (more of an offence against the person than a property offence). Males are more than twice as likely as females to report a variety of other property offences and offences against the person, including having forced someone to do sexual things with them when they didn't want to, deliberately damaged things like telephone boxes, street signs and street lights, taken part in a fight between two or more groups, forced someone to give them things and shoplifted.

The smallest difference between females and males appears with respect to drug offences and more general delinquency. Males were only slightly more likely than females to have gone to see an R-rated movie, used ecstasy, acid or speed, deliberately damaged school property, used marijuana or hash, drunk alcohol in a public place like a bar or club, runaway from home at least overnight, or bought beer wine, spirits or other kinds of alcohol. However, differences between males and females are virtually non-existent for having stolen money of less than $10, put graffiti on walls, toilet doors, bus panels or other public places, and used pills, puffers or medicine for fun.

Table 4.3   Sex differences in self-reported offences

	Male:Female Odds Ratio	Probability
Driven an unregistered car	3.6: 1	0.001
Driven a car or motorbike without a license	3.5: 1	0.001
Driven a car or a motorbike after drinking alcohol	4.7: 1	0.001
Raced cars or motorbikes	4.9: 1	0.001
Taken someone else's car or motorbike without permission	3.3: 1	0.001
Stolen things or parts from a car or motorbike	4.4: 1	0.001
Stolen a bicycle or parts of a bicycle	4.5: 1	0.001
Gone to see an R-rated film at the cinema	1.8: 1	0.001
Bought beer, wine, spirits or other kinds of alcohol	1.4: 1	0.012
Drunk alcohol in a public place like a pub or nightclub	1.5: 1	0.003
Not paid the entrance fee for something like a swimming pool or movie	2.3: 1	0.001
Runaway from home, at least overnight	1.5: 1	0.020
Shoplifted	2.1: 1	0.001
Stolen money of less than $10	1.3: 1	0.053
Stolen money of more than $10	3.1: 1	0.001
Broken into a house or building to steal things	3.9: 1	0.001
Cheated or stolen food from dispenser machines	3.1: 1	0.001
Deliberately damaged other people's property	3.4: 1	0.001
Deliberately damaged property by starting a fire	3.0: 1	0.001
Deliberately damaged things like telephone boxes, street signs and street lights	2.4: 1	0.001
Deliberately damaged school desks, windows or other school property	1.6: 1	0.003
Put graffiti on walls, toilet doors, bus panels or other public places	1.3: 1	0.093
Taken part in a fight between two or more groups	2.2: 1	0.001
Deliberately hurt or beat somebody up	3.4: 1	0.001
Used anything as a weapon in a fight	5.5: 1	0.001

	Male:Female Odds Ratio	Probability
Forced someone to give you things	2.1: 1	0.001
Used marijuana or hashish	1.6: 1	0.001
Used ecstasy, acid or speed	1.7: 1	0.005
Used pills, puffers or medicine for fun when you were not sick	1.3: 1	0.100
Forced someone to do sexual things with you when they didn't want to	2.6: 1	0.018
Used the telephone to play tricks on people	1.3: 1	0.041
Made nasty phone calls to people for fun	1.5: 1	0.009

While there are clearly gender differences in the likelihood of offending, earlier in this chapter we saw that differences in opportunity were more pronounced in the Offender and Vulnerable cohorts. Do we observe similar differences when we look in more detail at frequency of offending, as assessed by the ASRDS? For this analysis, we focus on vehicles, violence, drug use and property offences.[1]

The extent to which young people in the three cohorts report engaging in at least one of the offences in each of these four categories is shown in Figure 4.1. Inspection of the figures reveals that both boys and girls in the Offender cohort are more likely than those in the other cohorts to report offences in all four categories. With the exception of property offences reported by girls, 60 per cent or more of both boys and girls in this cohort report offences in the different categories. The Vulnerable sample is a little less likely to report offences, and the School-based sample is least likely. Not surprisingly, gender differences in offending are also found in each of the three cohorts, with boys more likely to offend than girls, but with smaller differences for drug use.

Gender differences in offending in absolute terms are greatest in the Vulnerable cohort. If we exclude drug use (in which few gender differences exist), we see that for this cohort, the percentage difference between girls and boys is 19 per cent for vehicle offences, 22 per cent for property offences and 23 per cent for violence offences. For the School cohort, while overall percentages in the listed activities

---

1 Vehicle offences include driving an unregistered car, driving a car or motorbike without a license, driving a car or motorbike after drinking alcohol and racing other cars or motorbikes. Violent offences include taking part in a fight between two or more groups, deliberately hurting or beating somebody up, using anything as a weapon in a fight and forcing someone to give you things. Drug use offences include drinking alcohol in a public place like a pub or nightclub, using marijuana or hashish, using ecstasy, acid or speed and using pills, puffers or medicine for fun when not sick. Property offences include stealing money of 10 or more dollars, breaking into a house or building to steal things, deliberately damaging other people's property, and deliberately damaging property by starting a fire.

are lower, gender differences in absolute terms (ranging between 14 per cent for violence, 15 per cent for property and 16 per cent for vehicle offences) are not much different. For the Offender cohort, gender differences vary according to the actual offence. Among this group, percentage differences are negligible for vehicle offences at one per cent, larger for violence offences at 18 per cent, and greatest for property offences at 30 per cent.

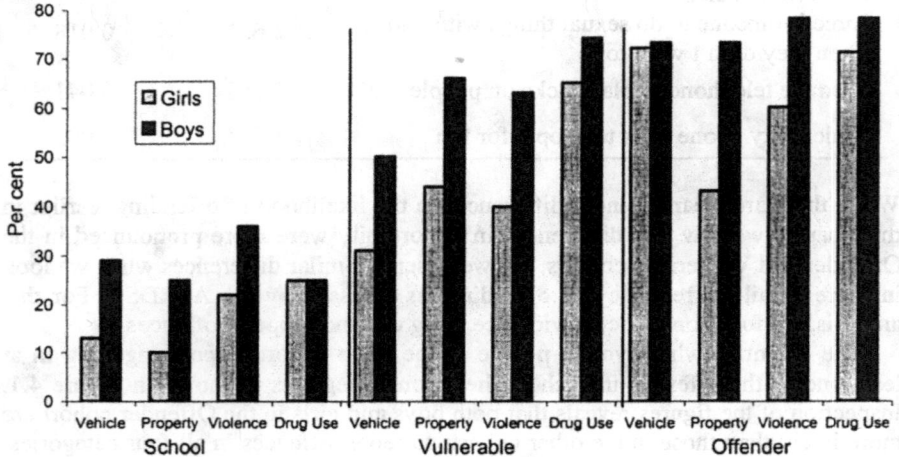

Figure 4.1   Sex and cohort differences in particular offence categories (percentage reporting at least one offence in each category)

As before, we can usefully draw upon the qualitative data in order to more fully elaborate and/or explain the trends just discussed. We will focus on three offence categories—vehicle, violence and drug use offences—as property offences were discussed earlier.

Vehicle Offences

It has been noted that Australian youth are extremely mobile, the localized gang phenomena of the United States not being the experience of Australian young people (Perrone and White 2000). In contrast, Australian young people may routinely travel relatively large distances in order to meet in established places for contact, usually within the city. Thus, trains and cars are frequently utilized for transport. This phenomenon is evident for females and males, and may explain why the gender differences in vehicle crimes are small for the Offender cohort. As explained by the girls and boys in the qualitative component of the Sibling Study:

> You don't need a car much—most times you're just hanging about, you know. If you want to go into the city, you skip the train, and if you really need to get somewhere fast, you take (steal) yourself some transport (Dylan).

> If I want to get somewhere, I'll just steal a car. I mean, it's usually just being bored stupid and wanting some fun, and it's not like you can just ask your mother, can you drive out to Southbank so I can go some gooneys (casks of wine?) (Letitia).

> Nah, you got to understand, it's not like we *steal* them, I'm serious, we *borrow* them. We don't sell them or anything, you just need to get to the Mall, and so you need to get yourself some transport, but then you got to get back home again don't you. So you *return* it... You know, if people were that little bit more willing to share and trust, well shit you know, there'd be no such thing as crime, we'd just all be giving and receiving (Stuart).

There is another shared experience of car theft that is not exclusive to either sex, and that is the importance of the 'rush' associated with car theft. For example, females and males gave almost identical accounts of the excitement associated with this activity:

> I love the driving, you know, the radio up, your mates in the back, passing some yandi. I mean, that's just happiness yeah? (Melanie).

> I love it, all of it, there's a rush you know, coming back from a party, and what are you gonna do? No cabbies gonna pick up some pissed young black fellas, no bus is going stop for you at that time of morning, and so you just, you know, take a car! (Stuart).

It could be argued then, that one factor which needs to be taken into account when attempting to explain gender and vehicle offences, is the apparently shared importance of the freedom offered by vehicles, particularly for those from marginalized backgrounds.

Violent Offences

The quantitative data revealed more differences between girls' and boys' level of involvement in offences against the person. While one possible explanation for this difference is offered below, it is also important to note that violent acts were not particularly unusual for the girls.[2] In addition, violence was often enacted in similar

---

2 It needs to be remembered that the qualitative sample was drawn from two detention centres, and hence the offences for which the group was incarcerated may be as much a result of juvenile justice decisions as they are of the offences of adolescents.

ways and for similar reasons for girls and boys. For example, such acts were often spontaneous, resulting from frustration and anger. Melanie and Ralph gave similar accounts of separate offences involving grievous bodily injury:

> I was just pissed and angry—it wasn't the guy's fault, he was just in the way (Melanie).

> I just lost it I guess, he pissed me off, and I had the tools to do the same (Ralph).

Similarly, Tori justified destroying her mother's property in the following manner:

> She kicked me out. I'd been really irate and shit, you know, just wasn't handling being back home, so I lost it one day when she was at work. Just destroyed everything. Smashed up her video and the TV, busted some windows, tipped everything over and that. She came home to it and just said I had to leave, just she couldn't control me and that ... I mean, she didn't even ask me why I'd done it, or what was going on in my head or anything, just told me to fuck off basically.

Alternatively, violence was sometimes explicitly positioned as a defence, either of themselves or others, by both girls and boys:

> Like, if anyone gives Shen any grief, I'll kill them. There was this time when one of the McAlly sisters called her a black slut, and it was, I mean Shen's still a virgin, she's never even been with a guy, and them calling in the whole race thing ... So I just lost it, went for their throats. Didn't have anything on me but I was pushing my fingers in, hard as any knife (Deborah).

> I was watching on the verandah like, and this guy king hit a mate of mine from behind. I mean Hanson never saw it coming and he went straight down, concussion and all. So I went into it and I found the guy, I mean I was really out of it, and I just pulled a knife and I stabbed him. But like, I was never meaning to kill him or anything, just wanted to, you know, get him back for being so furtive ... turns out in court that he was like this star cricketer, played for state or some shit, so that's basically what I got done for, not for stabbing him like, but because he's this big fucking star that could've played for Australia ... and the thing is he never got sentenced or nothing for knocking out Hanson, and anyway, he can't play cricket for shit (Roger).

To return to the point first made in the discussion of opportunities for offending, when differences between sexes occur, they appear to be related to the cultural and/or gendered opportunities open to violence for young men, particularly young Aboriginal and Torres Strait Islander men, but also Tongan and Maori men. Such occasions can be seen during interactions with the police, although it is not suggested that youth and police were in constant conflict (a high percentage of Offenders actually indicated high levels of respect for police—see Ogilvie 1999). In some cases, however, occasions did arise that were quite specifically open for aggression. For example, differences in treatment by the police were described by respondents, with respect to what it meant to be an Indigenous female as opposed to an Indigenous male. In many cases, males were treated in a more aggressive manner and, in turn, were likely to respond with aggression. For example, Indigenous boys report:

> He just pushed me too far, you know, knocked me into the wire, called me an alcho. I was a dickhead to respond but sometimes you just got to (Lionel).

> They wanted it hey, we wasn't doing nothing, just hanging out, having a bit of Bean, wasn't harming no-one, but it's like 'move on mate, no-one wants to have to deal with your ugly face' ... It's like fuck, who are you calling ugly mate. After that it was all on (Stuart).

The gendered dimensions of these interactions were most explicitly stated by Brooke:

> It's like, the police really harass the black guys, there's no question, they pick 'em up off the street when they're not doing nothing. Give 'em shit to their face and that, just to get them aggro. But the guys they know that, and it's usually only the volatile ones that get into trouble, cause they lose it and that, but most guys just push it far enough that they can't get taken but they still maintain staunch. With girls but, I don't know, it's like they make you feel like, I can't describe it. It's like you're not a person but it's still sleazy in some way, you know?

> *(Interviewer)* I think so but keep on going...

> *(Jennifer, interrupting)* I know what you mean—they'll call you a black slut... I got that one once. So they don't really want to lock you up. They just want you to feel fucked.

Drug Use

The gender differences in regard to the immediate situational context are again apparent with respect to drug use, although the relationship in this case appears to be an inverse one. For example, in discussing drug use, many of the boys explained how they had tried, but rejected, particular types of drugs:

> It just makes you sick man (amphetamines), none of that stuff is any good for you. Like, me and Iain, we did some eccy yeah, didn't get nothing, no rush, no nothing. We sat in this flat with these girls, all keyed up, sitting together on the couches and everything, cosy like. We had Marley on in the background and everything yeah, I mean, we were organized. And then we're just sitting there, waiting for this, you know, ultimate sex drug to work. In the end, we're bored, they're bored. Man! We went and got pissed (Ralph).

> That's evil shit (acid), that sends you crazy. I had a mate that just lost it, ran out of the house and was just screaming down the front street. I'd never do that sort of shit, leave it for the freaks (Graham).

> They'll kill you (cigarettes). You shouldn't be taking any chemicals, any. Me, I don't do alcohol, I don't do the durries, I don't do any of that other shit. The only thing you need is yandi, some rollies and a relaxed attitude. Doesn't matter what anyone does to you, you're not going to get aggro, you're not going to lose it, you just going to smile and think 'well, you're a right fuck aren't ya' ... It's all natural yeah, it makes sense, you eat bad food, you get fat, you take bad drugs, you get fucked (Brendon).

Interestingly, the girls seemed far less hierarchical with respect to their drug use. Thus Brooke, who used heroin, also freely confided her love of the 'whippy' bottle.[3] Similarly, Tori, whose preference was for acid, couldn't imagine her identity if she were to go 'straight'. As she stated:

> My life revolves around them, I mean all my friends, what I do, everything about me, I'm just an old druggo. It's all about losing control, about letting things happen, I love that ... It's one thing to go straight in here (detention centre), you get healthy and fat and everything, but I mean, it's not your life is it. I mean, I know it is for some ... but that's not me. My life's outside of here.

Thus it would appear that the *experience* of drug use is qualitatively different for boys and girls from the Offender sample, with females becoming more enmeshed in the general lifestyle aspects of active use of illicit substances, while the males appear to be somewhat more interested in the particular effects of particular drugs.

The Experience of Offending

Thus far, the reasons young people give for committing crime and the nature of crime they do commit have been examined. In this, the final section of the chapter, the issue of experience is explored. Experience is understood in the present context as the ways in which respondents felt after they had broken the law. As noted in Chapter 1, it has been argued that while the causes of crime are similar for males and females, the experience of criminality is qualitatively different, with females being more likely to feel shame and guilt (Broidy and Agnew 1997), while the dominant social definitions of masculinity protect young males from any 'ignominious disgrace' (Braithwaite and Daly 1994).

To gauge feelings associated with law-breaking, participants were given a list of nine emotions listed in Table 4.4 and asked to report whether they felt these emotions 'a lot', 'a little' or 'not at all', just after having broken the law. The top five emotions that girls reported feeling a lot were 'excited', 'satisfied' and 'guilty', each reported by 26 per cent of females, 'nothing' (reported by 20 per cent), and 'relieved' (18 per cent). The top five responses for boys were remarkably similar, although the ranking was somewhat different: 'excited' (reported by 33 per cent of males), 'guilty' (29 per cent), 'satisfied' (26 per cent), 'relieved' (24 per cent) and 'nothing' (18 per cent).

---

3 Disposable canisters of compressed gas used for producing whipped cream.

Table 4.4   Sex differences in the percentage of respondents reporting the emotion felt a lot just after doing something against the law

Emotion	Male	Female
Relieved	24	18
Excited	33	26
Guilty	29	26
Embarrassed	12	10
Satisfied	26	26
Nothing	18	20
Scared	17	17
Sick	9	15
Annoyed	12	9
n	135	152

As with motivations, cohort differences were not marked, and the top five emotions felt by respondents were the same across the three cohorts (Table 4.5). However, feeling guilty ranked first for the girls in the School cohort, while feeling satisfied was highest for the girls in the other two cohorts. For the boys in the School cohort, feeling excited and guilty were tied for first, while for boys in the Vulnerable cohort, feeling satisfied was the commonest emotion, and feeling excited was reported most often by boys in the Offender cohort.

Table 4.5   Sex and cohort differences in the most common emotion felt just after doing something against the law (percentage indicating the emotion was felt a lot)

			Cohort			
	School		Vulnerable		Offender	
Emotion	Male	Female	Male	Female	Male	Female
Excited	29	24	31	33	38	29
Guilty	29	30	24	16	31	22
Relieved	20	14	24	25	28	20
Nothing	18	18	21	25	17	22
Satisfied	18	17	37	44	30	30

It can be seen then that experience of excitement is not exclusive to males, nor is guilt exclusive to females. Instead, both responses are reported by young female and male offenders, in very similar order.

Conclusion

It is clear from the data that there are important differences in the patterns of offending reported by the young men and women in the Sibling Study, with women consistently reporting lower levels of offending, particularly for violent offences. Perhaps more interestingly, however, is the high level of similarity between the two groups, both in terms of their motivations for offending and their experiences of that offending. Both girls and boys commit criminal acts predominantly because doing so is easy and fun and often 'seems like a good idea'. Experiences of offending are also similar, with girls and boys reporting similar emotions just after offending, including both guilt and excitement, although girls are slightly more likely than boys to feel guilty. The opportunities for engaging in criminality, however, are different. Consistent with other literature, girls in the Sibling Study report somewhat lower opportunities to offend compared with boys. Our findings provide some support for theorists currently examining situational contexts in order to explain gender and criminality, and it may well be that context or opportunity impacts upon both the likelihood of engaging in offending, as well as the style of offending engaged in (Gottfredson and Hirschi 1990, Kennedy and Forde 1995, LaGrange and Silverman 1999, Miller 1998).

However, if there is a central message coming from the data reported in this chapter, it is that we do not seem to be able to explain gender differences in offending on the basis of either opportunity or motivation. Despite some differences between the young females and males in the ways in which they plan, engage in and experience crime, these differences shed remarkably little light upon why it is that males are officially recorded as offending at so much greater a rate than females. In the chapter that follows, we focus very much more directly upon the issue of gender itself in an effort to go some way towards explaining these differences between female and male offending.

Chapter 5

Gender and Offending Attitudes: Criminality, Compliance and Complexity

Emma Ogilvie

Introduction

As was noted in the previous chapter, one of the most consistent findings in criminology concerns sex differences in adolescent offending. Two questions can be posed concerning this phenomenon. First, why do males commit more crime than females, and, second, why do females commit any crime? In addressing these questions, this chapter 'changes tack' with respect to examining criminality and conformity of adolescent females and males, and instead of examining the manner in which traditional criminology explains crime, looks instead at the way in which *gender itself* is explained. In the previous chapter we saw that there were some distinct differences between young females and males offending behaviours, but we did not examine in any detail the importance of gender in explaining this phenomena. It is this issue which is the particular subject of this chapter.

When we examine the dominant approaches to understanding female criminality as an articulation of gender, we see three distinct (albeit related) orientations. The first of these approaches explains males' higher propensity (and, conversely, females' lower propensity) to engage in criminality as a consequence of the nature of the social controls characterizing patriarchal societies. These social controls are said to simultaneously constrain women's opportunity to engage in risky, 'masculine' activities (such as crime), and instill a sense of the importance of passivity and 'feminine' conformity. The second approach is closely related to the first, and draws upon the notion of a female propensity to conform to norms and male propensity to break norms (via criminality) to explain both male and female criminality. The third approach focuses more directly upon the pertinence of different expressions of gender as an aspect of particular social, cultural and historical contexts. That is, instead of norms being the focus as in the first approach, or the influence norms exert as in the second approach, it is the different ways in which gender is expressed in different social contexts by females and males which is the focus. It is this final approach that is most useful in terms of understanding the empirical complexities of gender and criminality as revealed by the Sibling Study data. Before addressing the data, however, it is useful to consider these three different theoretical orientations in more detail.

The First Approach: The Norms Say 'No' and the Girls Say 'OK'

In terms of explaining why males are more likely to offend than females, a frequently advanced line of argument is that of social control. This approach is also utilized in order to explain why females are apparently more conformist (law-abiding). One of the first criminologists to argue the importance of this approach in explaining female conformity was Heidensohn (1985), who argues that what is of most significance in female criminality is the extent of their adherence to social norms. This conformity to law-abiding behaviours is purportedly due to the efficacy of social controls. Similarly, Braithwaite (1989) explains women's lesser involvement in crime as due to a state of dependency upon either the family of orientation or that of procreation. Women are deemed by Braithwaite to be more socially integrated and 'never quite as free to make deviant choices as the male' (1989:92). Similarly, White (1990) argues that the 5:1 gender ratio in crime can be explained by the fact that the options open to women to gain a 'gender identity' are a reflection of their more traditional place in the private domestic sphere of social life (White, 1990:122). Females are thus less likely to enter the masculine arena of the street because society has positioned them as needing 'greater parental protection and guidance as buffers against the outside world' (White, 1990:125). Broidy and Agnew (1997) utilize this concept when discussing gendered strain, whereby the types of strain experienced by women involve 'high levels of social control, and a restriction of criminal opportunities' (Broidy and Agnew 1997:297). Gender differences in crime are, in turn, explained (in part) through different, gendered, emotional reactions to strain, with the anger of females being more likely to be accompanied by depression, guilt, anxiety and shame (Broidy and Agnew 1997:297).

The Second Approach: The Norms Say 'No' and the Girls Say 'OK, Only a bit Then'

There is, however, another stream of theorists who utilize the same general set of understandings drawn upon in the first approach but use them to explain female criminality, rather than female conformity. For example, activities of the kind accommodated and encouraged within delinquent subcultures are regarded by Cohen as 'positively inappropriate' for young girls, given that delinquent activities threaten the feminine sex role because of their 'strongly masculine symbolic function' (Cohen 1955:143–144). If women do become delinquent, their misconduct consists 'overwhelmingly of sexual delinquency' (Cohen 1955:144) because this is the only logical response to the central problem of the female sex role, i.e. how to be attractive to men. Similarly, Katz (1988) contrasts 'masculine' crimes such as stick-ups, which he claims are about celebrating risk, heart and balls, to 'feminine' crimes like prostitution, which are about minimizing risk. For Katz, male pimps control prostitution, while the female prostitute is depicted as 'tied to the home, envious and feeling incompetent to risk entry into a bigger, classier world without the security of her pimp guide' (Katz 1988:244).

Worrall describes female criminals as resigned to being found guilty 'partly because of their low self-esteem and generalized sense of guilt about being a woman and thus "always and already" failing, but partly as a result of being treated as though they were always and already guilty' (Worrall 1990:137). Hudson argues that the 45 delinquent girls she interviewed appear as women who 'failed to meet the criterion of "proper" deviants because their actions appeared to be incomprehensible, irrational and symptomatic of individual pathology rather than conscious rebellion and resistance to social injustice or convention' (Hudson 1990:117). For women, 'aggression is the first step on the slippery slope to selfishness and chaos', whereas for men, aggression is about 'coercive power' (Campbell 1993:11). Campbell argues that girls in gangs may utilize instrumental aggression, but it develops from fear and vulnerability. These putative experiences are not advanced with respect to young boys living in similar neighbourhoods with similar experiences of violence, but instead we are told that 'boys in gangs eagerly exploit the full range of their instrumental aggression' (Campbell 1993:140). More recently Miller (1998) argues that while men and women may express similar motives for engaging in robbery, the immediate context that women find themselves in, the 'gender-stratified street setting', forces them to enact crime in a distinctly different manner. Thus, females and males have similar motives for engaging in robbery, primarily material gain, which stem from similar structural and cultural contexts. However, in order to 'accomplish robberies successfully, women must take into account the gendered nature of their environment' (Miller 1998:60). They do this through such strategies as deliberately targeting other women (because they are perceived as easier targets), or playing up their sexuality in order to manipulate male targets into being vulnerable. In comparison, men 'accomplish street robberies in a strikingly uniform manner', i.e. through confrontation (Miller 1998). The extent to which these arguments parallel those noted in the first approach is clearly substantial and both these approaches are markedly different from the third major theoretical orientation.

The Third Approach: The Norms for Both Boys and Girls Say 'Maybe Yes, Maybe No'

The third approach to gender argues that it is the social context of an individual that defines and creates a gender, criminal, or indeed race, class or sexual identity. People do not simply acquire one identity. They play out multiple identities as a function of circumstances and contexts (see Daly and Maher 1998, Schwartz and Milovanovic 1996, Ogilvie and Lynch 2002). These contexts represent nodes, or points, at which a myriad of imperatives intersect. The basis of this intersectionality thesis was developed by Crenshaw (1991), who sought to develop more sociologically sophisticated explanations of the reality of the lives of women of color. Crenshaw argues that women of color are positioned in a location that denies their specific experiences. She argues that 'because of their intersectional identity as both women and of color, within discourses that are shaped to respond to one or the other, women of color are marginalized within both' (Crenshaw

1991:1241). For Crenshaw, racism and sexism intersect in black women's lives in a manner which cannot be explained by viewing black women as either black or female. More recently, Maher (1997) has used the concept of intersectionality to examine gender and the drug market economy, focusing upon how race and gender intersect in constructing social positions, market place opportunities and personal identities. In doing so, Maher criticizes those theoretical approaches which privilege class as the crucial variable in explaining pathways to poverty, arguing that they 'fail to elucidate relations among people who ostensibly share a class position' (Maher 1997:170). Instead, Maher offers a framework for understanding how not only socio-economic disadvantage, but also gender and ethnicity 'underpin the organization of labor markets in the street-level drug economy' (Maher 1997:171). Finally, Messerschmidt (1994, 1995) asserts that these links may also be utilized when attempting to understand the variability between different femininities and masculinities. He argues that differences between masculinities and femininities are constructed through the different class, race and ethnic context of individuals and groups, as well as through intervening factors such as school, peers, family and work places. These variations in gender need to be understood if we are to understand the links between gender and criminality (Messerschmidt 1993, 1994).

In briefly considering these three theoretical orientations, three issues come to the fore when considering the relationship between gender and crime. Firstly, much criminological theory (regardless of perspective) has to date been ostensibly directed towards explaining why 'five boys do' and 'four girls don't'. These explanations have invariably utilized, intentionally or otherwise, stereotypical understandings of gender, whereby males embody attitudes of instrumental aggression and defiance and females are left as passive, slightly pathetic conformists to the status quo. Secondly, criminologists have proceeded to utilize these explanations (of the four girls who don't) in explaining why the one girl who is, in fact, engaging in criminal activity is (engaging in crime). That is, the very same gender characteristics used to explain why girls don't offend are then mobilized to explain why girls do offend.

What we have then, in terms of criminological theorizing, is not the typical 'add girls and stir' attitude so frequently bemoaned by feminists. The practice of constructing a theory which explains male behaviour, and simply assuming it will work equally well for females does not appear to be the pattern observed when it comes to criminology. Instead, what appears to be occurring is the application of an overarching theory of gender and gender relations. Males are positioned as risk taking, ruthless and dominant, whilst females are positioned as passive and subservient, and these representations and relations are then applied to the social phenomenon of crime. Crime becomes simply the canvas upon which a standard portrait of gender relations is painted, or, staying true to the original metaphor, criminality is simply the two minutes of hot water necessary for the ready mixed girls (and boys) to stir in.

There is, however, the increasingly prominent third approach to gender and criminality that begins with recognition of multiple femininities and masculinities. This approach accepts gendered differences in criminality but incorporates an understanding of the complexity of the nature of gender into its theoretical paradigm. That is, gendered identities and attitudes are not assumed to be dichotomous and oppositional, but rather more varied and more complicated.[1] It is this more complex approach that will be drawn upon in this chapter to examine gendered attitudes and offending as reported by the Sibling Study respondents. As a first step in this process, we examine a range of attitudinal items that 'tap' the sorts of gender characteristics routinely focused upon by criminologists seeking to explain female/male offending as just another articulation of traditional gender roles.

Attitudinal Factors

A range of attitudes assumed to be associated with both offending and femininity/masculinity were included in the Sibling Study instrument. In this chapter, eight attitudes are described: self-obsession, orientation to others, attitude towards authority, peer alignment, risk-seeking, self-interest, willingness to break norms, and self-esteem. These attitudes were chosen for two reasons. First, they are all based upon established measures, and second, they can all be matched to specific arguments regarding the usefulness of sex-role stereotypes. While it has to be noted that such an exercise was not the intended purpose of these measures when they were originally developed, they nonetheless provide an assessment of many of the attitudes regarded as gendered by the theorists discussed earlier. For example, attitudes such as risk-taking (Cohen 1955, Hagan *et al* 1979, White 1990) and negative attitudes to authority (Cohen 1955, White 1990) are almost routinely seen as consistent with masculinity (as well as male involvement in crime), while low self-esteem (Hudson 1990, Broidy and Agnew 1997, Worrall 1990), lack of willingness to break norms (Hagan 1979, Heidensohn 1985) and positive orientation to others (Worrall 1990) are equally routinely seen as representative of femininity (and female involvement in crime).

With the exception of the peer alignment measure (described later in the chapter), the measures used to represent the nine attitudes were developed in the same manner. Each measure was originally comprised of a set of questions coded on a four-point Likert scale (from 'agree a lot' to 'disagree a lot'). Where necessary, scores were reversed in order to ensure a consistent direction for all items. Items within each measure were then summed and trichotomized into low, moderate or high levels of agreement.

The following sections describe the ways in which each attitude varies by gender and cohort. The last section of the chapter then summarizes the general findings, to demonstrate that the relationship between gender and crime may be

---

1   It should be noted that these perspectives are not limited to those feminists or pro-feminists who identify themselves as interested in intersectionality or multiple masculinities and femininities. Many criminologists from different orientations are incorporating the recognition of complexity into their analyses of gender and crime (see Sommers and Baskin 1993, Triplett and Myers 1995).

more complex than allowed for under traditional approaches, providing support for the phenomena of multiple femininities and masculinities.

Self-Obsession

> You know what they got me up for in court? 'Not showing suitable remorse', like not feeling sorry and guilty for what I done. And I was just thinking shit, you know. They had me on theft, yeah, which I admitted to, I mean, it was only Fairmont but it obviously wasn't mine. So I've admitted to it and all but they want me to be sorry as well. It wasn't even the guy's car it was a fucking company car, but somehow it had upset him so much that I've got to show 'suitable remorse', I mean if I killed the guy's wife and kids, then yeah, I'd be remorseful, but it was just a Fairmont! (Cassie, 14 year old female*).*

The measure of self-obsession was developed from the Attitudes to Self and Others Scale (Feeney and Noller 1996, Feeney, Noller and Hanrahan 1994), which was designed to measure young people's affective relationships, including those with little or no experience of romantic relationships. A factor analysis of the scale was conducted and resulted in two factors: self-obsession and orientation to others. Self-obsession, considered first, is based upon five questions:

> If I upset people it is their problem not mine
> I try and get what I want even if it causes problems for other people
> You sometimes have to play dirty to win
> I look after myself first even if it makes things hard for other people
> I'm not much interested in other people's problems

The data presented in Table 5.1 clearly demonstrate significant differences in self-obsession between the girls and boys in both the Vulnerable and School cohorts, and between the girls in different cohorts and the boys in different cohorts. Overall, boys appear more likely than girls to have high self-obsession, and the differences are quite regular across the cohorts.

In absolute terms, however, high self-obsession is more common in the Offender and Vulnerable groups. If we turn our attention to examining the differences between females and males across the cohorts, we also find consistent differences. Girls in the School cohort are much less likely than girls in the other two cohorts to report high levels of self-obsession, and a similar pattern holds for boys.

It is important to keep in mind that the issue at hand is not so much the presence or absence of a cohort effect, but rather indications (or lack thereof) of multiple femininities/masculinities. It is for this reason that both differences within and across cohorts are examined.

The presence or absence of these differences suggests the extent to which sex-stereotyped behaviours are apparently undermined by different articulations of femininity and masculinity. Put another way, if multiple femininities and masculinities exist, we would expect to find that girls from different cohorts vary from one another as much as they do from boys (in their own and other cohorts).[2]

Table 5.1   Sex and cohort differences in self-obsession (column percentages)

Self-Obsession	Cohort					
	School		Vulnerable		Offender	
	Female	Male	Female	Male	Female	Male
Low	75	47	51	30	49	34
Moderate	9	16	5	9	12	8
High	17	37	44	61	39	58
n	304	301	74	66	51	137

Orientation to Others

> You just don't do it. I mean they're just trying to earn a living and their insurance will cover a couple of one-offs but after that the [insurance] premiums won't make it worth staying in shop. I mean you don't want to send people broke, you just want a bit of money. You got to have some respect [Serge, 15 year old male, describing break and enters of small businesses].

The second attitudinal factor derived from the Attitudes to Self and Others Scale (Feeney and Nolley 1996, Feeney, Noller and Hanrahan 1994) is orientation to others. As implied by its name, this attitude represents the extent to which the respondent is other-oriented, or comfortable engaging and interacting with others. This scale is comprised of the following items:

> I can get on with people pretty easily
> I'm sure people will be there when I need them
> I don't mind depending on other people
> I like to know what other people are thinking before I make up my mind

In analyzing the effects of orientation to others, we observe a somewhat similar pattern to that apparent when the self-obsession measure was examined. As shown in Table 5.2, there are marked differences between the sexes in the School cohort with 47 per cent of the girls and 31 per cent of the boys recording a high orientation to others, but not in the other two cohorts. Within the Vulnerable cohort, 34 per cent of both the girls and boys record a high orientation to others, while 51 per cent of the girls and 41 per cent of the boys in the Offender cohort record similar levels. With respect to gender differences, then, girls are much more likely than boys to have a high orientation to others within the School cohort, but these differences are less marked within both the Vulnerable and the Offender cohorts. There are also marked sex differences *across* the cohorts. Among the girls,

2   See Rowe, Vazsonyi and Flannery (1995) for an examination of the importance of considering inter- and intra-group differences when looking at gender and offending.

47 per cent of the School cohort record a high other-orientation compared with 34 per cent in the Vulnerable cohort and 51 per cent in the Offender cohort. The differences between the boys are somewhat less marked, with 31 per cent of the School boys, 34 per cent of the Vulnerable boys, and 41 per cent of the Offender boys recording a high other-orientation.

Table 5.2   Sex and cohort differences in orientation to others (column percentages)

Orientation to Others	Cohort					
	School		Vulnerable		Offender	
	Female	Male	Female	Male	Female	Male
Low	26	39	48	46	36	43
Moderate	27	30	18	19	13	16
High	47	31	34	34	51	41
n	318	298	74	68	55	143

In summary, we can see that while the measures of both self-obsession and orientation to others are associated with gender differences, the differences are greater for the self-obsession measure. Girls from all three cohorts are much more likely than boys to display low self-obsession scores, while only for the School cohort are girls more likely than boys to show high orientation to others. Moreover, and critically, there are gender differences across the cohorts, for both girls and boys. Low self-obsession scores are more likely among girls from the School cohort than girls from the other two cohorts, while low orientation to others scores are more likely among the girls from the Vulnerable cohort, compared to girls from the other two cohorts. Among boys, those from the School cohort display lower levels of self-obsession than those from the other two cohorts, while high scores on orientation to others are more likely among the Offender boys. These latter findings are a first indication of the possible presence of multiple masculinities and femininities.

Attitude Towards Authority

> They're [police] just doing their job, just like we're doing ours. I mean, if you've nicked a car pissed out of your brain, tooling down the Pacific [highway] at 110 an hour, and a cop picks you up, you've just got no space for attitude (Jeremy, 16 year old male).

The next attitudinal factor to be examined is that of attitude towards authority, derived from five items from the Attitude to Authority Scale (Rigby and Schofield, 1985):

> We would be better off without the police
> It's OK to break the law if you can get away with it
> The law usually treats people fairly

> You can respect a police officer
> Laws are necessary in our society

When we examine differences with respect to attitude towards authority between the sexes, we find a number of significant differences (Table 5.3). Girls are more likely to have a positive attitude towards authority than are boys in the School cohort, at 38 per cent and 30 per cent respectively. Interestingly, there are slightly greater differences within the Vulnerable cohort, with 21 per cent of girls displaying a positive attitude towards authority, compared with only 14 per cent of boys. Within the Offender cohort, however, the differences between the sexes are negligible, with 10 per cent of girls and eight per cent of boys demonstrating a positive attitude towards authority. Marked differences for both boys and girls across the cohorts can also be seen. For both sexes, respect for authority decreases as we move from the School to the Vulnerable to the Offender cohort.

Table 5.3   Sex and cohort differences in attitude towards authority (column percentages)

Attitude Towards Authority	Cohort					
	School		Vulnerable		Offender	
	Female	Male	Female	Male	Female	Male
Low	22	30	47	68	67	67
Moderate	40	41	32	18	24	25
High	38	30	21	14	10	8
n	299	298	74	68	56	140

Peer Alignment

> I'd do anything for a true friend, anything. If a friend of mine was in trouble there isn't anything I wouldn't do to help them and there isn't anything I wouldn't do to anyone who hurt them (Melanie, 16 year-old female).

The Sibling Study instrument contains items designed to tap the importance the adolescents place upon peer networks. For this chapter, nine questions have been used to measure peer alignment, or the extent to which respondents promote their peers over norms and are willing to join in the criminal activities of their friends. Participants were asked to respond to nine questions:

> If you had a friend who started shoplifting what would you do?
> If you had a friend who started breaking into houses what would you do?
> If you had a friend who started stealing cars what would you do?
> If you had a friend who started bullying other people what would you do?
> If you had a friend and they started vandalizing things what would you do?
> If you had a friend who started doing graffiti or tagging what would you do?
> If you had a friend and they started getting drunk a lot what would you do?

If you had a friend who started using drugs what would you do?
If you had a friend and they started getting into fights what would you do?

To which they could answer:

I would join in
I would try to stop them
I would do nothing
I don't know what I would do
I would report them
I would walk away

If respondents said they would join in with friends, they were coded as '1' (friends prioritized); if they would try to stop or report their friends, they were coded as '–1' (norms prioritized); if they would do nothing, didn't know what they would do or would walk away, they were coded as '0' (passive/undecided). High peer alignment represents the likelihood of joining in with delinquent friends, while low peer alignment represents those who are more likely to try to stop or report their friends.

With respect to peer alignment, Table 5.4 indicates marked differences between the sexes in all cohorts, with girls noticeably more likely to prioritize norms over friends (low peer alignment). In the School sample, virtually all females priortize norms, while in the other two groups, around two-thirds do so. Boys are much less likely to prioritize norms over friends, as low peer alignment is reported by 79 per cent of the School cohort and 50 per cent or less of the other two groups (Table 5.4). Sex differences across cohorts are more apparent. Girls from the School cohort are far more likely than those in the other cohorts to have low peer alignment, and the same is true for boys. That is, markedly more girls in the Vulnerable and Offender cohorts, compared to the School cohort, would join in criminal activities if their friends were engaging in such activities. A similar pattern exists for boys, but they are overall more willing to follow their friends.

Table 5.4   Sex and cohort differences in peer alignment (column percentages)

Peer Alignment	Cohort					
	School		Vulnerable		Offender	
	Female	Male	Female	Male	Female	Male
Low	94	79	67	51	63	46
Moderate	2	10	7	8	11	12
High	4	11	26	41	26	42
n	348	330	82	77	66	160

Risk-Taking

> You know when people talk about their heart beating, I swear, mine was busting out. I was scared, really, really fucking scared but, this is the thing, I just couldn't stop smiling. The copper thought I was being a total smart-arse, but it was so intense, such a rush (Natasha, 16 year old female, discussing car theft).

Risk-taking as a precursor to delinquent behaviour has long been a focus of attention (Schalling, Edman and Asberg 1983). In the Sibling Study, risk-taking was measured based on respondents' level of agreement with four items:

> I'm more interested in what's happening now than in the future
> Sometimes it's exciting to do things even if they might get me into trouble
> Sometimes I do things that are a bit risky
> Sometimes I do something risky just for the fun of it

As with the other attitudes, there are both sex and cohort differences with respect to risk-taking. The greatest difference between girls and boys occurs within the School cohort, with the girls far more likely than the boys to report low risk-taking behaviours (Table 5.5). Similar differences exist within the other two cohorts, although they are not as great as those displayed by the School cohort. There are sex differences across the cohorts as well. Risk-taking is more likely among the girls from the Offender and Vulnerable cohorts than it is among the School group. A similar finding exists among the boys, although the differences are less marked.

Table 5.5   Sex and cohort differences in risk-taking (column percentages)

Risk-Taking	School		Cohort Vulnerable		Offender	
	Female	Male	Female	Male	Female	Male
Low	62	35	32	17	28	14
Moderate	18	32	27	29	21	27
High	21	32	40	54	51	58
n	314	301	75	72	57	138

Self-Interest and Willingness to Break Norms

> I'm 14 now, so I figure I've really only got three years to get myself really sorted. I'd really like a house for myself, I'm helping my mum pay off hers at the moment so I'd like enough to be able to, you know, put a decent deposit down. I've already got most of the general stuff I want, you know, bikes and a stereo (Rupert, 14 year old male—discussing the proceeds of theft).

The next two attitudes are taken from the Delinquency Disposition Scale (Paternoster and Mazerolle 1994), which was originally designed to test low self-control. A factor analysis conducted for the total scale resulted in two distinct factors, self-interest and a willingness to break norms. Unlike the earlier measure of self-obsession, which was concerned with egocentricity, self-interest reflects the extent to which respondents prioritize themselves over others and is based on five items:

> You sometimes have to play dirty to win
> You sometimes have to lie to stay out of trouble
> It's OK to lie if it keeps your friends out of trouble
> You have to be willing to break rules if you want people to be your friends
> Making a good impression is more important than telling the truth.

The second factor comprises four questions related to a willingness to break social norms. The questions drawn upon for this measure include:

> If you have to break rules or the law to keep your friends they are not worth having
> It's important to be honest with your parents even if they get upset and punish you
> You can make it in school without having to cheat at exams
> It's important to do your own work at school or work, even if it means some people won't like you

Considering self-interest first, the data reveal that while cohort differences exist, there are no sex differences within cohorts (Table 5.6). Within the School sample, 33 per cent of both girls and boys report high self-interest, while within the Vulnerable and Offender cohorts, respectively 51 per cent of girls and 57 per cent of boys, and 49 per cent of girls and 44 per cent of boys, report high self-interest. Consistent with the previous trends, cohort differences for both sexes are apparent. Among the girls, approximately half of those in the Vulnerable (51 per cent) and Offender (51 per cent) cohorts report high self-interest, compared to one-third (33 per cent) of those in the School cohort. The pattern for boys is very similar, with 57 per cent of Vulnerable boys, 44 per cent of Offenders, and 33 per cent of the School boys reporting high self-interest.

Table 5.6   Sex and cohort differences in self-interest (column percentages)

| Self-Interest | Cohort | | | | | |
| | School | | Vulnerable | | Offender | |
	Female	Male	Female	Male	Female	Male
Low	27	23	13	12	16	21
Moderate	39	44	36	32	35	35
High	33	33	51	57	49	44
n	298	301	76	73	58	137

Cohort and sex differences in willingness to break norms are shown in Table 5.7. Again, there are virtually no sex differences within cohorts, although boys in the

Vulnerable cohort are a little more likely than girls to report a willingness to break norms. In contrast, there are quite significant cohort differences for both sexes, with the School cohort being the least likely to report a willingness to break norms. Among girls, those in the Offender cohort are most likely to report a willingness to break norms (62 per cent), followed by the Vulnerable (53 per cent) and School (49 per cent) cohorts. For boys, the pattern is somewhat different, with those in the Vulnerable cohort being the most likely to indicate a willingness to break norms (71 per cent), those in the School cohort least likely (50 per cent), and those in the Offender cohort in between (63 per cent).

Table 5.7   Sex and cohort differences in willingness to break norms (column percentages)

| Willingness to Break Norms | Cohort | | | | | |
| | School | | Vulnerable | | Offender | |
	Female	Male	Female	Male	Female	Male
Low	10	15	19	9	17	14
Moderate	41	35	28	21	21	22
High	49	50	53	71	62	63
n	309	304	75	73	61	139

The preceding sections have yielded some fascinating results regarding the ways in which attitudes vary by gender both within and across the three cohorts. Table 5.8 summarizes these results and details whether or not such differences are statistically significant. In the first column of the table, we see that orientation to others, peer alignment, and risk-taking have statistically significant (p<0.05) sex differences for the School cohort only, but there are significant cohort differences for both females and males. For these three attitudes, the only *within*-cohort sex differences are for the School cohort, while there are significant differences *across* the cohorts for both boys and girls. For example, girls in the School cohort have a lower level of peer alignment compared to girls in the Vulnerable and Offender cohorts, and the same is true for boys. Self-obsession and attitude towards authority have sex differences within the School and Vulnerable cohorts, and, again, cohort differences exist for both females and males. For self-interest and willingness to break norms, there are no statistically significant sex differences within any of the cohorts, but there are cohort differences for both sexes. Finally, significant sex effects emerged for females and males for self-esteem, but a cohort effect is found only for males.

Table 5.8   **Summary of sex and cohort differences in attitudes relating to offending**

Sex effect – School Cohort effect – both sexes	Sex effect – School and Vulnerable Cohort effect – both sexes	Sex effect – none Cohort effect – both sexes	Sex effect – School and Offender Cohort effect – males
ORIENTATION TO OTHERS	**SELF-OBSESSION**	**SELF-INTEREST**	**SELF-ESTEEM**
Sex Effect	**Sex Effect**	**Sex Effect**	**Sex Effect**
School p = 0.001	School p = 0.001	School p = 0.314	School p = 0.013
Vulnerable p = 0.96	Vulnerable p = 0.042	Vulnerable p = 0.809	Vulnerable p = 0.933
Offender p = 0.486	Offender p = 0.079	Offender p = 0.666	Offender p = 0.91
Cohort Effect	**Cohort Effect**	**Cohort Effect**	**Cohort Effect**
Females p = 0.001	Females p = 0.001	Females p = 0.005	Females p = 0.313
Males p = 0.015	Males p = 0.001	Males p = 0.004	Males p = 0.047
PEER ALIGNMENT	**ATTITUDE TOWARDS AUTHORITY**	**WILLINGNESS TO BREAK NORMS**	
Sex Effect	**Sex Effect**	**Sex Effect**	
School p = 0.001	School p = 0.047	School p = 0.124	
Vulnerable p = 0.109	Vulnerable p = 0.036	Vulnerable p = 0.073	
Offender p = 0.053	Offender p = 0.938	Offender p = 0.884	
Cohort Effect	**Cohort Effect**	**Cohort Effect**	
Females p = 0.001	Females p = 0.001	Females p = 0.010	
Males p = 0.001	Males p = 0.001	Males p = 0.007	
RISK TAKING			
Sex Effect			
School p = 0.001			
Vulnerable p = 0.096			
Offender p = 0.067			
Cohort Effect			
Females p = 0.001			
Males p = 0.001			

Dimensions of Gender

In order to further explore gender differences and similarities, the seven attitudes were re-grouped into four categories: empathy, instrumentality, propensity to reject norms and risk-seeking. Empathy is indicated by orientation to others and willingness to abide by norms (the original measure of willingness to *break* norms has been reversed). Two measures define instrumentality (self-interest and self-obsession) and propensity to reject norms (attitudes towards authority and peer alignment), and risk-seeking is defined by the risk-taking attitudinal measure. Table 5.9 displays rankings by sex and cohort for each attitude, grouped into the four categories. The group most likely to have a high score on the attitude was coded '1', while the group least likely to have a high score was coded '6', and all other groups were coded accordingly. For example, girls in the School cohort are the least likely to have a high score for peer alignment (under the propensity to reject norms category), and, consequently, they are designated '1'; boys in the

School cohort are next (designated '2'); girls in the Vulnerable and Offender cohorts score equally on this measure and so have the same ranking (designated '4'); boys in the Vulnerable cohort are the second-most likely to score high on the measure (designated '5'); and boys in the Offender group are the most likely to have a high peer alignment, and are designated by a '6'.

The rank ordering of boys and girls on the various measures shown in Table 5.9 is, in some ways, consistent with traditional accounts of their offending behaviour. At the same time, however, the results provide some interesting challenges to traditional conceptions and, in doing so, draw attention to the importance of examining the complexities of femininity and masculinity. For example, when we examine the propensity to reject norms category, we see that School girls are the least likely to reject norms (as indicated by the lowest scores for rejecting authority and peer alignment), and Offender boys are the most likely, results consistent with traditional theories of crime and gender. But, the School girls more closely resemble the School boys than they do the Vulnerable and Offender girls in their propensity to reject norms. Similarly, the Vulnerable and Offender girls are more like the Vulnerable and Offender boys, compared to the School girls. These similarities and differences between girls and boys in the three cohorts point to the existence of multiple femininities and masculinities. Furthermore, these patterns are not readily accounted for by approaches to gender based upon traditional sex role stereotypes.

As a further example, empathy is traditionally accorded to girls rather than boys (Karniol, Gabay, Ochion and Harari 1998, Sochting, Skoe and Marcia 1994). Therefore, we might expect all three groups of girls to score highly on the orientation to others measure (one of two measures comprising the empathy category). Only the Offender and School girls score highly, however, while girls from the Vulnerable cohort have lower scores compared to the Vulnerable and Offender boys, and the School boys have the lowest scores of all groups. Risk-seeking behaviours, too, show both expected and unexpected results in regards to gender. The School girls are the least likely to indulge in risk-taking, while the Offender and Vulnerable boys are the most likely. More surprisingly, the Vulnerable and Offender girls have a greater appetite for risk than do School boys. Finally, instrumentality, often cited as a defining characteristic of masculinity and used as a counterpoint to the supposed expressive aspects of femininity (see Campbell 1990), also demonstrates the existence of multiple femininities and masculinities. Self-interest and self-obsession are least likely among both girls and boys in the School cohort, compared to any of the other groups. The Vulnerable boys are most likely to indicate high levels of self-interest and self-obsession, but they are closely followed by the Vulnerable girls, as well as the Offender boys (see Table 5.9).

If we focus on the groups with extreme scores listed in Table 5.9 (i.e. groups scoring 1 or 6), we obtain a clearer picture of gender differences and similarities. Immediately obvious is the contrast between School girls and Offender boys, with differences in striking accord with traditional understandings of femininity and masculinity. Girls from the School cohort are least willing to reject authority, least willing to offend with peers and are the least likely to be risk-seekers, all attitudes encouraging conformity. Conversely, boys from the Offender cohort are most willing to reject authority, most willing to offend with peers and have the highest appetite for risk-seeking, attitudes assumed to lead to offending. It is also worth noting that the School girls have the lowest propensity to reject norms and the highest orientation to others, stances that also sit comfortably with traditional sex-role stereotypes. However, if we examine other measures, the challenge to traditional sex-role thinking becomes clear. For example, the School boys score lowest in terms of orientation to others, followed by the Vulnerable girls, suggesting that the attitudes we readily associate with gender are substantially affected by cohort membership, a result underscored by the fact that the Offender girls score highest on this measure. Other findings also demonstrate that gender is not necessarily an overarching attribute, and that differences between groups of boys and groups of girls may occur as often as differences between the sexes.

Table 5.9   Sex and cohort differences in four derived categories: empathy, instrumentality, the propensity to reject norms and risk-seeking*

Derived Categories	Attitudes	Cohort					
		School		Vulnerable		Offender	
		Female	Male	Female	Male	Female	Male
Empathy	Orientation to Others	5	1	2	3	6	4
	Abides by Norms	6	5	4	1	3	2
Instru-mentality	Self-Interest	1	1	5	6	4	3
	Self-Obsession	1	2	4	6	3	5
Propensity to Reject Norms	Rejects Authority	1	2	3	4	5	6
	Peer Alignment	1	2	4	5	4	6
Risk-Seeking	Risk-Taking	1	2	3	5	4	6

* The numbers in the table are relative rankings of each of the six groups on each of seven attitudes. A '6' means that the specified group has the greatest proportion of those scoring high on the attitudinal measure, while a '1' means that the specified group has the smallest proportion of those scoring high on the attitude.

Conclusion

Overall, these results suggest very distinct gender differences at least between boys in the Offender cohort and girls in the School cohort, which provide a substantial measure of support for explanations of criminality based on traditional understandings of sex-roles. This consistency with traditional male-stream approaches is a welcome indication of validity, given that it could never reasonably be suggested that somehow criminologists had got everything wrong for the past 40 years. However, this validity comes at a cost, for in comparing low-offending girls with high-offending boys, we omit from consideration more than half the population we are presumably interested in. In addition, the results provide a welcome legitimation for challenging traditional approaches. In many ways, the attitudes of girls and boys in the Offending cohort are far closer to each other than they are to the attitudes of the same sexes in the School cohort.

It is not the case that gender is made invisible or explained away by the cohort effect. The data do not allow us to replace one overarching notion (gender) with an alternative overarching notion (such as disadvantage), based upon the socio-demographic factors associated with the three cohorts. Despite the differences in background characteristics which undoubtedly define and influence members of the three cohorts, gender remains resistant to being explained away, and simultaneously, resists interpretation solely in terms of traditional sex-role understandings. Given this situation, it is important to remember that the dominant theoretical approach based on sex-roles does appear to work for the 'four girls who do not offend'. The crucial issue, however, is the use of these stereotypes to then explain the behaviour of the 'one girl who does offend'.[3] The data reported here lead us to a re-consideration of the very nature of gender, and specifically femininity. If we are saying that traditional approaches to female offending actually explain conformity rather than offending, and that the explanations for male offending are not applicable to female offending, then we cannot address female offending without giving serious attention to the special (and gendered) configuration of factors underpinning criminality among young females. At the risk of belabouring the point, it will not prove possible to satisfactorily explain the behaviour of criminal girls until our criminological understandings of femininity advance beyond the stereotypes so routinely employed by criminologists from both conservative and (perhaps more surprisingly) radical feminist ends of the spectrum.

---

3   I am not suggesting that the same explanation(s) of male offending can be applied to female offending. For some, this would be an obvious and reasonably appealing option. If (for example) risk seeking is associated with offending, and boys are greater risk-seekers than girls, then perhaps the offending girls are simply risk-seekers on a par with young males. There is a complex issue at hand here, in that risk-seeking may well be (indeed is) associated with offending, but it is open to question as to whether or not the enjoyment of risk is both experienced and articulated in exactly the same way across the sexes. Qualitative data certainly provide indications that risk-seeking is experienced differently by young females and males (Maher 2000, Miller 1998, Ogilvie 1996), depending upon their situation. However, for the moment, it is enough to note that in criticizing the logic so frequently employed when explaining female offending, we need to take care to avoid utilizing an equally flawed logic. That is, to over-simplify the issue, we need to avoid the suggestion that female offenders are effectively equivalent to male offenders. The unsatisfactory nature of this logic is immediately obvious if we replace gender with race/ethnicity. In the Australian context, Indigenous youth are grossly over-represented in every area of the criminal justice system. This is never used, however, as the basis to argue that white offenders engage in crime because in crucial respects they are Indigenous.

Chapter 6

Social Inequality, Alienation and Socio-Economic Position

John S. Western

Introduction

A feature of all societies is the presence of socially defined scarce and valued resources to which access is limited. To the extent that access to such resources is determined in a structurally patterned way, then to that extent social inequality can be said to exist. Let me be a little more concrete. By scarce and valued resources I mean such things as paid employment, income, education, health, security and leisure time. Access to these resources is not equally available to all social groupings in the society, and social inequality is a corollary of this fact.

I have argued elsewhere (Dwan and Western 2003) for the presence of four major structural sources of social inequality in the Australian context. These include social class, gender, ethnicity and aboriginality. We have already had a great deal to say about gender, and offending by Indigenous respondents is the focus of Chapter 9. In the current chapter, we will consider class-based inequalities, and the implications of these inequalities for the involvement of young people in the criminal justice system. For our purposes, social class indexes the economic structure of society. It can be seen in terms of the social relations of production and in market power; that is, in the social relationships that are established between people involved in the production and distribution of goods and services.

What of the class/crime link? Writing in 1979, John Braithwaite, after reviewing a vast array of data, suggested the following conclusions:

- lower-class adults commit those types of crime which are usually handled by the police at a higher rate than middle-class adults
- adults living in lower-class areas commit those types of crime which are usually handled by the police at a higher rate than adults living in middle-class areas
- lower-class juveniles commit crime at a higher rate than middle-class juveniles
- juveniles living in lower-class areas commit crime at a higher rate than juveniles living in middle-class areas (Braithwaite 1979:179).

Not all support Braithwaite's view. Writing a decade later, Tittle and Meier (1990:271) comment that the relationship between class and crime 'is said to be positive (direct), negative (inverse), *conditional* or some combination of the three'. Hagan (1992) has suggested that the different findings may be due to methodological differences, in that the measures employed in different studies are not the same. In a slightly different context, Simpson and Ellis (1994) have suggested that there may be gender differences in class effects, with the class/crime relationship stronger for women than for men.

It is also instructive to look at the relationship between social inequality and crime from a slightly different perspective. To illustrate, the rapid growth of cities has given rise to a new form of social inequality emerging from increasing social polarization. Social polarization refers to a growing division between a large and expanding group, the new urban poor, who are located at the disadvantaged end of the socio-economic continuum, and another large and expanding group, those in affluent and socially-secure households, who are at the advantaged end. Social polarization has been measured in a number of ways. Raskill and Urquhart (1995) have shown a growing income polarization in the major Australian cities during the 1980s. In addition, changes to class and occupational structure have been noted. At one end of the spectrum, there has been a marked growth in professionals and managers, or, in Erik Wright's (1985) terms, expert managers and expert non-managers. At the other end, there has been a sharp decline in the industrial working class following de-industrialization, as well as an equally sharp increase in both an insecure service working class employed in support activities (ranging from retail to clerical work, as well as from entertainment to cleaning) and a diverse collection of unskilled, insecure low-paid workers, identified by some as an 'underclass' (Wilson 1987) and by others as the 'new urban poor' (Gans 1993, Mingione 1993).

Increasing social polarization, it has been held, is likely to be accompanied by increasing crime rates, rising levels of anomie and alienation, increasing drug dependence and other indicators of social disorganization (Wilson 1987). South East Queensland, and particularly the City of Brisbane, are characterised by increasing social polarization. Recent Australian Bureau of Statistics data have revealed somewhat higher levels of unemployment in Queensland than in either New South Wales or Victoria and slightly lower levels of income. In addition, levels of personal anomie or alienation have been found to be higher among the young unemployed and those with unstable social relationships (Western and Lanyon 1999). It is in this context of inequality, due to traditional social class processes and to the changing nature of urban life, that we examine the impact of class and related processes on the involvement of young people in the criminal justice system.

Class-Based Measures of Social Inequality

There are two perspectives from which we can view the class arena of the young people in the Sibling study. The first is a contextual perspective and is based on the characteristics of the suburb in which the adolescents live. The second is more immediate and concerns the socio-economic standing of the households in which they are growing up.

Contextual Measure

As previously discussed in Chapter 2, the Queensland Government Statistician's Office has developed an Index of Relative Disadvantage, based on information from suburbs in South East Queensland. More specifically, the statistical local areas (SLAs) comprising each suburb were classified according to the following criteria:

- percentage of individuals with low income
- percentage of individuals with low levels of education (educational levels not exceeding primary school)
- percentage employed in unskilled occupations
- percentage of persons unemployed.

A low score on the index suggested an area with a high proportion of persons with low incomes, widespread low levels of education and employment in unskilled jobs, and a high proportion of unemployed persons. On this basis, suburbs were ranked from '1' (most disadvantaged) to '5' (least disadvantaged). Based on their home address, respondents in the Sibling Study were coded for socio-economic disadvantage. As we saw earlier (Table 1.4), those from the School-based sample are disproportionately from the least disadvantaged suburbs, while those from the Vulnerable cohort are disproportionately from the most disadvantaged. The Offender cohort falls between these extremes, but is closest to the Vulnerable group.

Household Measures

Six household measures of social class or socio-economic standing were included in the questionnaire. The first concerned the number of employed parents in the household, classified as no employed parents, one or both parents employed or no parents in the household. The distribution of the cohorts over these categories is shown in Table 6.1. The differences between groups are substantial. Over half of those from the School cohort have both parents employed, and a further one-third have one parent employed, resulting in nearly 90 per cent of the young people from the School sample coming from homes in which one or both parents are in paid employment. In contrast, less than half of those from the other two groups are from similar backgrounds. Instead, the majority come from households in which no parents are present or, if present, parents are not employed.

The next two household measures of social class are based on father's and mother's occupation. Open-ended questions were provided which asked respondents whether or not their parents worked and, if so, in what types of jobs.

**Table 6.1   Family measures of socio-economic standing
(column percentages)**

		School n=679	Cohort Offender n=225	Vulnerable n=160
Employment Status of Parents				
Both parents employed		52	18	19
One parent employed		37	28	30
No employed parents		10	21	13
No parents in household		2	33	38
Occupational Status of Parents				
Father	White-collar	40	14	14
	Blue-collar	34	14	22
	Not working	10	12	12
	Not in household	14	59	51
	Other	2	1	1
Mother	White-collar	52	26	19
	Blue-collar	11	8	10
	Not working	31	26	26
	Not in household	5	39	43
	Other	1	1	1
Parental Education				
Father	Left school before grade 12	38	46	56
	Completed grade 12	16	10	10
	Attended TAFE	6	4	3
	Attended uni/college	19	8	14
	Not known	17	30	13
	Other	4	2	4
Mother	Left school before grade 12	41	49	50
	Completed grade 12	20	15	16
	Attended TAFE	5	4	1
	Attended uni/college	19	11	13
	Not known	11	20	18
	Other	4	3	3

Many of the respondents lacked sufficient knowledge about their parents' paid work to provide answers precise enough to enable specific coding to be undertaken; however, enough information was provided to allow for a distinction between white-collar and blue-collar work. As shown in Table 6.1, there were again considerable differences between the three groups. Most strikingly, white-collar jobs predominated amongst the fathers of the School cohort (40 per cent so employed), while over 50 per cent of the fathers in the other two groups did not live in the household. The pattern with respect to mothers was very similar. Over half (52 per cent) of the mothers of the School-based cohort were employed in white-collar jobs, while around one-third (31 per cent) were not working. In the other two cohorts, upwards of one-third of mothers (39 per cent among the Offender cohort and 43 per cent among the Vulnerable sample) were not in the household, and a further one-quarter (26 per cent in each case) were not employed.

Next, parental education was measured, as based on respondents' reports of whether their mother or father left school before grade 12, completed grade 12, attended TAFE or attended university or college. The differences between groups for this measure were not as marked as they were for parental occupation. The modal category for both parents in each of the cohorts was having left school before grade 12. Tertiary education was a little more common among both parents for the school cohort, but there were few other persistent differences (Table 6.1).

The final measure of socio-economic standing was based on household possessions, and was, in essence, a proxy measure of wealth. Respondents were presented with a list of 12 items and asked to indicate which of them 'you have in the place where you usually live'. The list included: television, video recorder, computer games, personal computer, CD player, microwave oven, telephone answering machine, telephone, radio, cassette player, one car, and more than one car. The most common items were radios and cassette players, with over 90 per cent of the full sample reporting access to them. Other common items included televisions (87 per cent), telephones (78 per cent), video recorders (73 per cent) and CD players (68 per cent). Least prevalent were answering machines, reported by only 18 per cent of the sample. Interestingly, more respondents had access to two cars (39 per cent) than one car (35 per cent). Aggregating the number of items the young people had access to, for each cohort, produced the distribution shown in Table 6.2.

There is little difference between the Offender and Vulnerable cohorts, as around 50 per cent of each group report no more than seven items, and approximately the same proportion report eight or more; in contrast, there is quite a difference between these groups and the School-based sample, where around 70 per cent of youth report eight or more items.

Table 6.2   Availability of household possessions, by cohort
(column percentages)

Number of Goods	School $n=661$	Cohort Offender $n=219$	Vulnerable $n=153$
Less than 5	15	12	24
5–7	14	33	29
8–9	38	38	31
More than 9	33	16	15

This initial exploration of class origins of the sample reveals striking differences. The School cohort members are, by and large, from relatively affluent backgrounds and generally live with both parents, who, at a minimum, have completed grade 12 and are employed in white-collar jobs. They also have available significant numbers of valued consumer durables. In contrast, the young people from the other two cohorts are more commonly from disadvantaged schools and are significantly less likely to be living with their parents. Parents who are present have typically not completed grade 12, are more likely to be unemployed and, if working, are typically in blue-collar jobs. Access to valued consumer durables is markedly less. Though young people from the Offender and Vulnerable cohorts come from significantly disadvantaged backgrounds, it remains to be seen whether or not this disadvantage contributes to their propensity for engaging in crime.

Self-Esteem and Social Integration

As stated earlier in this chapter, increasing social polarization and the consequent rise in social inequality has recently been argued to result in increased anomie, a lowering of self-esteem and a decline in social integration (Atteslander, Gransow and Western 1999), the necessary preconditions perhaps for a rise in delinquent and criminal behaviour. To determine the extent to which anomie and self-esteem are experienced by the young people in our study, and the impact of these states on self-reported delinquency, a self-esteem scale was constructed using an essentially exploratory procedure. Twenty-eight items bearing on self-esteem ('sometimes I think I'm no good at all') and feelings of social integration ('I worry about people getting to know me too well') were subject to a factor analysis. Following a varimax rotation, three factors were identified. The first was defined by five items, the second and third by four items each. As the content of all items was remarkably similar, we investigated the possibility of constructing a single scale from all items, or from a subset which cut across the factors. Successive sets of corrected item total correlations and Cronbach alphas were calculated while omitting items with low correlations and those that impacted negatively on alpha measures. This exploratory analysis resulted in a seven-item scale is described in Table 6.3.

Table 6.3   Items comprising the self-esteem scale

Item	Corrected Item Total Correlation
I worry that I'm not the same as others	0.679
I worry that I'm not as good as others	0.673
I wonder why people want to know me	0.627
I sometimes think I am no good at all	0.629
I worry about people knowing me well	0.626
I find it hard to depend on others	0.594
I find it hard to trust others	0.582
Cronbach's alpha	0.783

These items were presented in the questionnaire in Likert format, with four response categories ranging from 'agree a lot' (scored 1) to 'disagree a lot' (scored 4). With seven items, raw scores could range from 7 to 28, with low scores indicating low self-esteem and low levels of social integration. Four respondents obtained the minimum score of seven and six the maximum score of 28. Around 30 per cent of the total sample has low or moderately low self-esteem (scores of 7 to 15). A further 38 per cent are in the middle range (scores of 16 to 19), while 31 per cent are in the moderately high or high range (scores of 20 or more). In the bivariate analyses to follow, we will be focusing on these three levels of self-esteem.

As shown in Table 6.4, there are differences between the three cohorts. High self-esteem is most likely for the School cohort, while the Offender and (particularly) Vulnerable cohorts are more likely to report low self-esteem.

Table 6.4   Cohort differences in self-esteem (column percentages)

	Cohort		
Self-Esteem Level	School	Offender	Vulnerable
	n=595	*n*=181	*n*=141
Low	28	32	43
Medium	37	43	30
High	34	24	26

The Impact of Age, Gender and Socio-Economic Status on Self-Esteem

Age and Gender

Based on previous research (Western and Lanyon 1999), one might expect to find levels of self-esteem linked to age, gender and socio-economic status. While the age and gender links will probably not be terribly strong in the Sibling Study, as it contains a restricted age range, and age and gender were linked in their effects on self-esteem in the earlier research, we might reasonably expect to find some socio-economic differences. It is to these matters we now turn before examining the impact of socio-economic factors and self-esteem on levels of self-reported delinquency.

While there are, of course, cohort differences in self-esteem, differences within cohorts between boys and girls and those of different ages are not marked. Indeed, there are virtually no gender differences, whereas age has different effects in the three cohorts. Self-esteem increases with increasing age among young people in the School cohort, but decreases in the other two groups: low self-esteem is reported more commonly as age goes up.

Socio-Economic Status

The socio-economic status of the neighbourhood in which the sample members reside has no discernible impact on levels of self-esteem. No systematic differences in self-esteem displayed by cohort members living in suburbs which differ in socio-economic standing were observed. If there is an 'ecological effect', then more sensitive analyses will be necessary to identify it. We will return to this issue later in the chapter.

The significance of employment status, that is, whether parents work or not, for self-esteem is marked. For the School cohort, parental employment status makes virtually no difference to levels of self-esteem; however, for the Offender sample, having both parents working makes low self-esteem less likely, and for the Vulnerable sample, the absence of parents or having no parents working makes low self-esteem more likely. Occupation and education of parents as measures of socio-economic standing make little difference to self-esteem. There are no differences in levels of self-esteem reported by those from white-collar as compared with blue-collar families across all three cohorts; however, while parental education is not related to levels of self-esteem in either the School or Offender samples, in the Vulnerable sample, low levels of self-esteem are least likely in families in which parents had undertaken tertiary education.

The proxy measure of household wealth (i.e. the number of possessions in the respondent's household) on self-esteem is a little more promising. For the School sample, there is a systematic relationship between household possessions and self-esteem. As the number of household possessions increases, the incidence of low self-esteem declines, suggesting a relationship between family affluence and self-esteem. The relationship is not as marked in the Offender group, however, and is even weaker in the Vulnerable sample, suggesting perhaps that family affluence may have a somewhat different connotation in more socially disadvantaged groups.

In summary, there are few consistent patterns in the material just discussed. There are cohort differences in levels of self-esteem, with high levels more likely in the School cohort and less likely in the other two, and particularly in the Vulnerable group. But, differences in socio-economic standing within the cohorts do not have systematic effects on levels of self-esteem. In the School cohort, coming from a family in which the father is unemployed makes low self-esteem more likely, while in the Vulnerable cohort, coming from a parentless household or a family in which the mother is not working makes low-self esteem more likely. In the Offender cohort, low self-esteem is also more likely when the mother is not working. However, there are not strong and consistent links between self-esteem, age, gender, workforce participation and socio-economic standing. We turn now to delinquent behaviour.

Crime and the Social Order

As we have seen, the three cohorts of young people in the Sibling Study come from very different social backgrounds, they have different levels of self-esteem, and they report very different levels of delinquent behaviour. The School sample live in relatively privileged suburbs, their parents are generally employed and are typically in middle-class jobs. They have relatively high levels of self-esteem and self-reported delinquency is low. In contrast, the Offender and Vulnerable sample live in poorer suburbs; when parents do live with their children (which is less common than in the School group), they are often unemployed or working in blue-collar positions. In addition, the young people display lower levels of self-esteem and higher levels of self-reported delinquency. Do these essentially ecological associations translate into individual effects? That is to say, is the propensity to engage in delinquent acts at the individual level affected by the socio-economic and subjective factors that distinguish between the cohorts at the aggregate level?

Socio-Economic Status and Generalized Delinquency

The practice adopted in the first stage of the analysis was to cross-tabulate each of the SES measures (including the social status of neighbourhood, employment status of parents, occupation and education of father and mother, and household wealth), and the measure of self-esteem with the generalized self-reported measure of delinquency, as well as each of the subscales, including illegal vehicle use, theft, assault, disorderly behaviour, drugs and alcohol use and vandalism. At this time, we will comment only on those relationships found to be significant, although in the multivariate analyses to follow, we will revisit all relationships to determine whether, in the context of controlling for effects, a somewhat different pattern emerges.[1]

Among the class-based measures of social inequality, employment status and occupation of father and mother all provided significant relationships with the aggregate measure of self-reported delinquency (Table 6.5), although, paradoxically perhaps, it was not always class differences that proved significant. Looking first at employment status, among the School cohort, the only significant difference is between parental households and non-parental households, with reported delinquency significantly more likely in non-parental households than parental households. Level of parental employment does not make a difference to reported delinquency. A similar pattern exists in the Vulnerable cohort, while, in the Offender cohort, self-reported delinquency is least likely when both parents are employed.

As also shown in Table 6.5, occupational status of fathers *per se* makes very little difference to delinquency. In each of the three cohorts, having an unemployed father or a father in a blue-collar or white-collar job makes little difference to self-reported delinquency, but living in a household in which the father is not present does. In these latter households, self-reported delinquency is systematically greater. True class effects are more likely when we consider the mother's occupational status. In all three cohorts, young people with mothers in white-collar occupations

---

1   For ease of presentation and discussion, the full results of the bivariate and multivariate regression models are not presented. However, the detailed results are available from the author upon request.

are less likely to report high levels of delinquency than are young people with mothers from blue-collar backgrounds. Overall, this data seems to suggest firstly that social disorganization, or a lack of social integration, as represented by living in households in which no parents are employed or present, increases the likelihood of self-reported delinquency, as does coming from a household where the mother is in blue-collar rather than white-collar employment.

Table 6.5   Self-reported delinquency and socio-economic standing (percentage of respondents with four or more offences in past 12 months)

Employment Status of Parents	No Parent Employed	One Parent Employed	Both Parents Employed	No Parents in Household
School Cohort	28	32	33	60
n	(57)	(216)	(306)	(10)
Offender Cohort	93	85	71	91
n	(41)	(54)	(35)	(67)
Vulnerable Cohort	50	62	63	86
n	(20)	(42)	(30)	(52)

Occupational Status of Father	Blue-Collar	White-Collar	Unemployed	Not in Household
School Cohort	31	32	21	48
n	(197)	(237)	(62)	(82)
Offender Cohort	77	75	83	92
n	(26)	(28)	(24)	(117)
Vulnerable Cohort	62	57	44	86
n	(34)	(23)	(18)	(69)

Occupational Status of Mother	Blue-Collar	White-Collar	Unemployed	Not in Household
School Cohort	41	32	28	44
n	(70)	(308)	(181)	(25)
Offender Cohort	94	73	92	90
n	(16)	(52)	(52)	(77)
Vulnerable Cohort	73	62	51	86
n	(15)	(29)	(41)	(58)

The absence of systematic class effects is perhaps not surprising. As noted earlier, the literature is equivocal regarding this issue: some studies report class effects, others do not. The suggestion that class differences, when they do exist, are linked to the mother's occupational status is noteworthy. Such a finding has not been reported elsewhere and clearly warrants further investigation, which will be undertaken in the multivariate analysis later in this chapter. The impact of being in a household in which neither parent is employed, or indeed in which neither parent is present, also draws attention to the significance perhaps of a less structured or anomic environment, or one lacking social integration for delinquent behaviour.

Self-Esteem and Generalized Delinquency

While the relationships were admittedly not strong, earlier analyses suggested, particularly for the Offender and Vulnerable cohorts, that low self-esteem was more likely to be experienced by young people from households in which parents were not working or not present—perhaps indirect evidence for their anomic environment.

Households that are lacking in social integration are households in which young people report lower levels of self-esteem and higher levels of delinquent behaviour. How, then, are self-esteem and delinquent behaviour related? The data are reported in Table 6.6. In general, higher levels of self-esteem mean lower levels of reported delinquency. Among the School cohort, self-reported delinquency is at a minimum; nonetheless, those with high self-esteem are less likely than those with low self-esteem to report four or more offences in the year preceding the interviews. The differences are even more pronounced in the Offender and Vulnerable cohorts, as between one-half and one-third of those with low self-esteem report four or more offences, compared with one-quarter of those with high self-esteem. Low self-esteem, whether or not it is a consequence of households lacking social integration, clearly is associated with higher levels of self-reported delinquency.

Table 6.6   Self-reported delinquency and self-esteem (percentage of respondents with four or more offences in past 12 months)

	Cohort					
Self-esteem Level	School		Offender		Vulnerable	
Low	4	(148)	46	(54)	32	(56)
Medium	3	(196)	36	(70)	28	(40)
High	1	(190)	29	(42)	23	(35)

Note: The bracketed numbers refer to the totals on which the percentages are based.

Socio-Economic Status and the Delinquency Sub-Scales

In examining the delinquency sub-scales, similar patterns to that observed for the overall measure were apparent (Table 6.7). Neighbourhood social disadvantage was not significant in any of the analyses; neither were the measures of parental education or household wealth. The variables describing the employment status of parents and occupation of fathers and mothers were significantly related to all the self-reported measures but, as indicated in Table 6.7, this was likely due to differences between those with no parents in the household, compared with other households. For example, in all three cohorts, illegal vehicle use was more likely among those from households in which no parents were present. Similar results were found for theft and burglary, assault, drug and alcohol use and vandalism. For disorderly behaviour, the pattern held only for the Vulnerable cohort.

In summary, there were not socio-economic differences in offending, so much as differences stemming from relative stability of household structures. A lack of household social integration rather than social stratification appears to be contributing to delinquent behaviour.

Table 6.7   Significant household factors and the self-reported delinquency sub-scales

		Cohort	
	School	Offender	Vulnerable
Illegal Vehicle Use			
Parent employment	No parents*	No parents	No parents
Father's occupation	Not in household	Not in household Unemployed	Not in household
Mother's occupation	Not in household	Not in household Unemployed	Not in household
Theft and Burglary			
Parent employment	No parents	No parents	No parents
Father's occupation	Not in household	Not in household Unemployed	Not in household
Mother's occupation	Not in household	Not in household Unemployed	Not in household
Assault			
Parent employment	No parents	No parents No employed parent	No parents
Father's occupation	NS	Not in household Unemployed	Not in household
Mother's occupation	Not in household	Not in household Unemployed	Not in household
Disorderly Behaviour			
Parent employment	NS	NS	No parents
Father's occupation	NS	NS	Not in household
Mother's occupation	NS	NS	Not in household
Drug and Alcohol Use			
Parent employment	No parents	No parents	No parents
Father's occupation	Not in household	Not in household	Not in household
Mother's occupation	NS	Not in household	Not in household

Vandalism			
Parent employment	No parents	No parents No employed parent	No parents
Father's occupation	Not in household	Not in household	Not in household
Mother's occupation	NS	NS	Not in household

* No parents = No parents in household.

Self-Esteem and the Delinquency Sub-Scales

Table 6.8 presents data regarding self-esteem and the percentage of respondents with two or more offences in the last 12 months, by cohort and sub-scale of delinquency behaviour. In 17 of the 18 models (three cohorts x six delinquency sub-scales), those with low self-esteem reported more illegal acts than those with high self-esteem. As can be seen, the differences were greater with respect to certain sub-scales than others, and with respect to particular cohorts. Nevertheless, the findings indicate that self-esteem significantly contributes to delinquency.

This brings this section of our analysis to a close. To summarize, class effects on delinquent behaviour are not great, but family instability, as measured by the absence of parents or parents not in the workforce, appears to make self-reported delinquency more likely. A lack of self-esteem, related to family instability particularly in the Offender and Vulnerable cohorts, also appears to increase the likelihood of self-reported delinquency. Indeed, of all the factors we have examined, the effects of self-esteem appear the strongest and most consistent across the different measures of delinquency. Based on this evidence, and particularly for the Vulnerable cohort, it is possible that family instability leads to low self-esteem, which, in turn, leads to increased propensity for delinquent behaviours. We could represent this situation diagrammatically as shown in Figure 6.1:

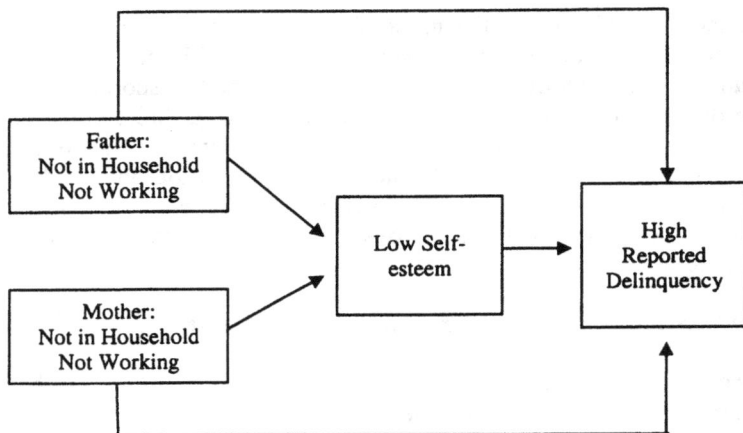

Figure 6.1   Links between family instability, self-esteem and delinquency

Table 6.8   Self-esteem and the self-reported delinquency sub-scales (percentage of respondents with two or more offences)

	School		Cohort Offender		Vulnerable	
Illegal Vehicle Use						
Low	12	(163)	64	(58)	32	(60)
Medium	8	(215)	53	(74)	31	(42)
High	5	(202)	42	(18)	31	(36)
Theft and Burglary						
Low	16	(156)	65	(57)	53	(60)
Medium	14	(208)	62	(74)	49	(41)
High	11	(197)	58	(45)	34	(35)
Assault						
Low	16	(165)	66	(58)	39	(62)
Medium	14	(217)	52	(77)	40	(43)
High	9	(202)	39	(46)	19	(36)
Disorderly Behaviour						
Low	21	(160)	68	(57)	56	(59)
Medium	20	(215)	55	(74)	48	(42)
High	17	(202)	58	(43)	36	(36)
Drug and Alcohol Use						
Low	23	(162)	81	(57)	54	(61)
Medium	16	(210)	78	(76)	68	(41)
High	15	(201)	53	(45)	56	(36)
Vandalism						
Low	14	(165)	49	(57)	48	(61)
Medium	14	(217)	43	(76)	43	(42)
High	8	(201)	33	(45)	28	(36)

In the language of the statistician, the absence of parents or parents not working has direct effects on delinquent behaviour, represented by the long arrows in the diagram, as well as indirect effects, represented by the two short arrows on the left of the diagram, through self-esteem, which itself has a direct effect on reported delinquent behaviour, as represented by the short arrow at the right of the diagram. This is, of course, a very general statement of the relationships. It does not take account of differences between the cohorts, or the possible effects of other variables. The analysis that follows uses multiple regression techniques to address these important issues.

The Antecedents of Self-Esteem in a Multivariate Context

We know already that the three cohorts differ in self-esteem, but we have not yet determined whether these cohort effects will remain when examined in the context of socio-economic and family stability factors. So, for the first analysis, we will aggregate the three cohorts and examine the way in which self-esteem is affected by cohort membership as well as the socio-economic and family stability factors. Next, we will look at the three cohorts separately.

The technical details of the multiple regression analysis need not delay us here, except to say that the analysis reveals the 'independent' effect of each independent variable, controlling for the effects of all other variables in the analysis. By doing so, this analysis provides a more precise account of how the different factors affect the dependent variable, in this instance self-esteem, and later, self-reported delinquency (see footnote 1).

Table 6.9 provides a summary of the significant effects of four analyses undertaken on the aggregate sample and the three cohorts. Four predictor variables—cohort, level of schooling, father's occupation and mother's occupation—were found to be significant in the aggregate analysis and are listed down the left side of the table. They are presented in dummy variable format. Thus, cohort is defined as School, Offender and Vulnerable, with School as the excluded category, against which the other two are compared. Schooling is defined as less than grade 12 and greater than grade 12, with less than grade 12 being the excluded category. Father's and mother's occupations are defined as white-collar, blue-collar, not working and not in household, with white-collar being the excluded category against which the other categories are compared.

The parameter estimates (i.e. the figures in Table 6.9) are a measure of the strength of the listed factors in explaining variability in self-esteem. To summarise the results, we can interpret the parameter estimate of −1.081 as meaning that the Vulnerable cohort is significantly more likely than the School cohort, the excluded category, to display low self-esteem. The fact that the parameter estimate for the Offender cohort is not significant means that the School and Offender cohorts do not differ significantly in self-esteem when all socio-economic and family factors are controlled. Therefore, it is probably legitimate to infer that members of the Vulnerable cohort display significantly less self-esteem than either the Offender or School cohort. The significant parameter estimates for father not working and mother not working mean that, across all cohorts, those from families in which mothers and fathers are not engaged in paid work are more likely to report low self-esteem than those from families in which parents are working, irrespective of whether they are in blue- or white-collar jobs. Finally, education makes a difference. Again, across all samples, those with more than grade 12 schooling are likely to report greater self-esteem than those with 12 years of schooling or less.

These results demonstrate that self-esteem is enhanced by family stability, father and mother in paid work, and a dose of human capital, more rather than less education. These findings hold up across all cohorts, despite the fact that the Vulnerable cohort has a lower level of self-esteem than the other two.

What of self-esteem within the three cohorts? The data are also provided in Table 6.9. As with the aggregate analysis, the models included all the socio-economic variables we have been considering. No variables other than the four already identified proved to be significant. In the School cohort, self-esteem is adversely affected by the father not working; in the Offender cohort, schooling makes a difference, with those whose parents have more than 12 years schooling exhibiting greater self-esteem; while in the Vulnerable sample, a mother not working makes self-esteem less likely.

While these three variables are clearly related to self-esteem in the three cohorts, the overall effects are not strong. Socio-economic factors are not directly related to self-esteem. Coming from a home in which the parents are employed in white-collar jobs and have higher levels of education does not make high levels of self-esteem more likely, nor does coming from a relatively wealthy family or an advantaged neighbourhood. But, having parents in paid employment does seem to make a difference, as does having more rather than less schooling. In general, these results are consistent with those obtained earlier. While clearly self-esteem varies in its strength in the three cohorts, it is not strongly linked to the socio-economic environment in which the young people live.

Table 6.9   Predictors of self-esteem (significant parameter estimates)

Predictors	Total Sample	School	Offender	Vulnerable
Cohort				
Vulnerable	−1.081[a]	–	–	–
Schooling				
> Grade 12 schooling	0.517[c]	–	1.268[c]	–
Father's Occupation				
Not working	−1.593[b]	−2.001[c]	–	–
Mother's Occupation				
Not working	−1.066[c]	–	–	−3.879[b]

[a]$p < 0.01$; [b]$p=0.01–0.05$; [c]$p=0.05–0.10$.

Self-Reported Delinquency, Self-Esteem and the Socio-Economic Environment

As with self-esteem, the cohorts differ in self-reported delinquency, although the differences in this instance are substantially larger. To examine the cohort differences in the context of self-esteem and the designated socio-economic factors, we adopt similar procedures just used. The results are shown in Table 6.10.

The results for the aggregate sample are given in the first column. Five predictor variables—cohort, self-esteem, employment status of parents, and father's and mother's occupation—were significant. While self-esteem is a continuous variable, the other four are in the dummy variable format used earlier. Not surprisingly, being a member of the Offender or Vulnerable cohort makes self-reported delinquency far more likely than being a member of the School cohort. But, self-esteem also has an independent effect, such that low self-esteem is a strong predictor of higher levels of self-reported delinquency. Family instability is again important. Living in a household in which there are no parents or coming from families in which no parents are in the workforce or where the father is not working all increase the likelihood of reported delinquency.

The patterns are quite similar for each of the three cohorts. As shown in columns 2, 3 and 4, low self-esteem makes delinquency more likely in each cohort, as does coming from a family in which neither parent is in the workforce. Having a father or mother unemployed makes delinquency more likely for the School and Vulnerable cohorts, but not for the Offenders. Finally, consistent with the finding from the aggregate sample, living in a household without parents makes delinquency more likely among the Vulnerable cohort.

Table 6.10   Predictors of self-reported delinquency (significant parameter estimates)

Predictors	Total Sample	School	Offender	Vulnerable
Cohort				
Offender	7.005[a]	–	–	–
Vulnerable	4.710[a]	–	–	–
Self-Esteem	–0.175[b]	–0.067[e]	–0.497[c]	–0.238[e]
Employment Status of Parents				
No parents	4.065[c]	–	–	5.685[e]
No parents working	5.760[b]	3.188[e]	6.402[e]	11.512[d]
Father's Occupation				
Father not working	–4.229[a]	–2.751[d]	–	–8.334[e]
Mother's Occupation				
Mother not working	–2.076[d]	–1.457[e]	–	–6.434[e]

[a]$p < 0.0001$; [b]$p=0.0002–0.0004$; [c]$p=0.001–0.005$; [d]$p=0.01–0.05$; [e]$p=0.05–0.10$.

Quite clearly, family stability and self-esteem make a difference to reported delinquency. When family stability is high, as indexed by parents being in the paid workforce in contrast to unemployed, and as present rather than absent from the family situation, self-reported delinquency is, in relative terms, low, both in the overall sample and in each of the three cohorts. When self-esteem is high, in both the overall sample and the three cohorts, reported delinquency is less likely than when self-esteem is low. But, again, socio-economic factors as such are not important. Coming from a white-collar background or from a family in which parents have a high level of education does not make self-reported delinquency less common. Neither does coming from a relatively wealthy family or an advantaged neighbourhood.

These patterns are maintained across the delinquency sub-scales. Significant predictors of illegal vehicle use, theft and burglary, disorderly behaviour, drug and alcohol use, vandalism and assault from the aggregate sample are shown in Table 6.11.

Table 6.11   Predictors of self-reported delinquency sub-scales for the total sample (significant parameter estimates)

Predictors	Illegal Vehicle Use	Theft and Burglary	Disorderly Behaviour	Drug and Alcohol Use	Vandalism	Physical Assault
Cohort						
Offenders	1.43[a]	1.47[a]	1.08[a]	1.51[a]	0.76[a]	1.11[a]
Vulnerable	0.50[a]	1.03[a]	0.57[a]	1.13[a]	0.83[a]	0.53[a]
Self-Esteem	−0.35[a]	−0.04[a]	−0.03[b]	−0.03[b]	−0.03[a]	−0.04[b]
Schooling						
Greater than grade 12	—	—	—	−0.20[c]	—	—
Employment Status of Parents						
No parents	0.93[a]	0.87[b]	0.67[b]	0.86[c]	0.44[d]	0.70[a]
No employed parents	1.30[a]	1.55[a]	1.37[a]	0.85[b]	0.81[c]	0.88[b]
Father's occupation						
Not working	−0.73[a]	−0.05[a]	−0.85[a]	−0.61[c]	−0.66[b]	−0.61[a]
Mother's occupation						
Not working	−0.47[b]	−0.52[c]	−0.61[a]	−0.37[c]	—	—

[a] p=0.0001–0.0010; [b] p=0.001–0.01; [c] p=0.01–0.05; [d] p=0.05–0.1.

It comes as no surprise that there are cohort effects, with the Offenders and the Vulnerable group significantly more likely than the School-based sample to report higher levels of delinquent behaviour in each of the areas of criminal endeavor. Self-esteem makes a difference in each area as well, with low self-esteem associated with higher delinquency levels. Family instability, indicated as we know by absence of parents or parents not employed and specifically by father and mother not in the workforce, again quite consistently means greater likelihood of reported delinquency. It is worth remembering that these effects are independent of cohort. That is to say, while both the Offender and Vulnerable groups report more delinquent behaviour than the School sample, coming from an unstable family background or lacking self-esteem makes delinquent behaviour more likely whether one is a member of a 'low' delinquency group such as the School sample or a 'high' delinquency group such as those from the Offender and Vulnerable groups. The only minor class effect we were able to uncover had to do with the impact of schooling on drug and alcohol use; more schooling makes use less likely.

Finally, what of the within cohort effects? What makes a difference to reported offending in the areas defined by the six sub-scales among each of the three groups of young people?

To answer these questions, we carried out separate analyses for each cohort on each of the six sub-scales, a total of 18 analyses in all. A summary of the main results is provided in Table 6.12. It will be noted that the actual parameter estimates have not been included in the table. Rather, to make the findings a little more digestible, only the significance levels of the listed factors have been shown (see footnote 1).

As can be seen by reading across the rows, self-esteem predicts offending in 14 out of the 18 analyses; specifically, in all three cohorts for theft and burglary, vandalism and physical assault, and in two cohorts for illegal vehicle use (School and Offender) and disorderly behaviour (Offender and Vulnerable). Coming from a family in which the father was unemployed predicts offending behaviour in 13 analyses: in all three cohorts for disorderly behaviour, the same two cohorts (School and Vulnerable) for illegal vehicle use, theft and burglary and vandalism, and the same two cohorts (Offender and Vulnerable) for drug and alcohol use and physical assault.

Coming from a family in which no parents were in the workforce predicts offending behaviour in 11 analyses: in all three cohorts for theft and burglary and disorderly behaviour, and in two cohorts for illegal vehicle use (Offender and Vulnerable) and drugs and alcohol use (School and Vulnerable). Coming from a parentless household predicts offending behaviour in eight analyses: disorderly behaviour and physical assault (School and Offender), illegal vehicle use (School and Vulnerable) and vandalism (Offender and Vulnerable). Finally, coming from a home in which the mother was unemployed also predicts offending behaviour in eight analyses: disorderly behaviour and drug and alcohol use (School and Vulnerable), vandalism (Offender and Vulnerable), disorderly behaviour (School) and illegal vehicle use (Vulnerable).

Table 6.12 Predictors of self-reported delinquency sub-scales for the three cohorts*

Predictors	Illegal Vehicle Use			Theft and Burglary			Disorderly Behavior			Drug and Alcohol Use			Vandalism			Physical Assault		
	a	b	c	a	b	c	a	b	c	a	b	c	a	b	c	a	b	c
Self-esteem	4	3	—	1	2	3	—	3	4	—	1	—	4	3	3	4	3	3
Schooling																		
Greater than grade 12	—	—	—	—	—	—	—	—	—	—	—	3	—	—	—	—	—	—
Parental Employment Status																		
No parents	3	—	3	—	—	—	3	4	—	—	—	—	—	2	3	4	3	—
No employed parents	—	4	2	1	1	4	3	4	3	4	—	3	—	—	—	—	3	—
Father's occupation																		
Not working	3	—	4	2	—	3	3	4	3	—	4	3	4	—	4	—	4	4
Mother's occupation																		
Not working	—	—	2	2	—	—	4	—	3	4	—	3	—	3	3	—	—	—

*Cohort: a = School; b = Offender; c = Vulnerable.

Significance of parameter estimates: [a]p < 0.0001–0.001; [b]p=0.001–0.01; [c]p=0.01–0.05; [d]p=0.05–0.1.

Conclusion

These findings reinforce our earlier conclusions that a lack of self-esteem and factors contributing to family instability are important determinants of delinquent behaviour among young people. To a degree, these conclusions have arisen serendipitously from the analyses undertaken in this chapter. The chapter began with a discussion of the possible effects of social class and socio-economic status on delinquent and criminal behaviour. We noted that the literature was equivocal regarding these relationships. Some studies reported noticeable class effects, while others failed to find them. A somewhat different take on class, it was noted, comes from the social polarization literature. This literature suggests that urban growth is accompanied by increased disparities in wealth and access to other scarce and valued resources. Consequences of this growing social polarization of the population include decreases in self-esteem, as well as increases in personal estrangement, delinquent or criminal behaviour, and a range of other social pathologies.

These issues provided the conceptual underpinnings for the analyses undertaken in this chapter. Some of these underpinnings fared less well than others. Overall, self-esteem has clearly emerged as a significant factor. In both the bivariate and multivariate analyses and for both the overall measure of reported delinquency as well as the sub-scales, self-esteem has been found to be a significant predictor. In contrast, social class or socio-economic status has little explanatory value. Whether the measure is based on community characteristics, or the occupation, education or wealth of the family or household of the young people in the study, it does not make a difference. Those from lower socio-economic backgrounds are no more likely than those from higher backgrounds to show a greater propensity for delinquency. But, growing up in a parentless household or one in which parents are not in the workforce does affect involvement in crime. This was our serendipitous finding. It emerged because, when constructing our socio-economic measures based on parental workforce involvement, we were confronted by the fact that significant numbers of parents were either absent from families or not in the workforce. Initially these were thought to be residual categories in our analyses. After the analyses had been undertaken, it became clear that they were far from residual; indeed, they became central to our understandings of the factors making delinquency more likely.

Chapter 7

Family Influences and Delinquency

Lisa Kennedy, Ian O'Connor and John S. Western

Introduction

The assumption that inadequate parenting practices increase a young person's propensity to commit delinquent acts is widespread in both the criminological and wider community. This chapter looks at a range of parenting practices, including parental support and supervision, in the context of their impact on self-reported delinquent behaviour among two of the cohorts of the study.

From Control to Strain: Parenting as Inductive and/or Coercive Supervision

The assertion that inadequate parenting practices increase a child's propensity to commit delinquent acts derives mainly from social control theory. As described in Chapter 1, a fundamental tenet of control theory is that all human beings have the potential to be delinquent or criminal, and these propensities can only be suppressed by some external expression (or imposition) of control. Control theory posits two general types of control systems: personal and social. Explicating personal control systems requires the use of psychoanalytic concepts, while explicating social control systems requires a focus on levels of attachment to institutions such as school and the family (Shoemaker 1990). Hirschi defines four basic elements of the 'social bond', which draws upon elements of both personal and social control:

- attachment to conventional others, such as parents and teachers
- commitment to conventional activities, such as school
- involvement in conventional activities, such as sport, and
- belief in conventional norms, such as disapproval of criminal activities.

The purpose (or at least result) of these control systems is the management of desires and needs. Desires or needs can be satisfied by either legitimate or illegitimate means. Because these needs and desires are assumed to be evenly distributed throughout the population, the difference between a person who breaks the law and one who does not is that the law-abiding person, when faced with an opportunity to profit through illegitimate means, chooses not to do so. In contrast, people who have relatively low levels of social control are more inclined to satisfy their desires through illegitimate means because these are typically expedient and involve a lesser degree of conflict with systems of control. These differences in the extent to which needs and desires are managed are central to control theory. As Hirschi argues, 'the important differences between delinquents and non-delinquents are not differences in motivation; they are, rather, differences in the extent to which natural motives are controlled' (Hirschi 1969:329).

However, the concept of control is highly complex. Children are subject to the will of their parents as much as they are to more explicit and direct expressions of control. For Hirschi, the 'important consideration is whether the parent is psychologically present when temptation to commit a crime occurs' (Hirschi, 1969:88). This psychological presence, or attachment, to a parent consists of three elements:

- virtual supervision: a measure of the extent to which a child perceives that his/her parents are aware of their activities and associates
- intimacy of communication: a measure of the reciprocal exchange between parent and child of feelings and thoughts
- affectional identification: a measure of the love, respect and care that a child has for his/her parents (Hirschi 1969).

For control theorists in general, and Hirschi in particular, three elements interact so that a child is 'less likely to commit delinquent acts not because his [sic] parents actually restrict his activities, but because he shares his activities with them; not because his parents actually know where he is, but because he perceives them as aware of his location' (Hirschi 1969:89–90). Social bonds thus impede criminality (and promote conformity) through young people's internalization of self-control. Hirschi argues that families who teach their children self-control (by monitoring behaviour and punishing deviance), who limit the opportunities for risky behaviour, and who command love and respect are the most likely to raise children who embrace conformism (Hirschi 1994:55–58). Once individual patterns of ideation/behaviour with regard to self-control are established via intra-family socialization processes, they are highly resistant to change. However, if these practices are not inculcated, individuals will pursue pleasure via criminality as readily as via conformity.

There is a considerable body of research supporting the link between lack of supervision and the development of delinquent behaviours (Barnes and Farrell 1992, Mak 1990 1991, Loeber and Stouthamer-Loeber 1986, McCord 1979). Parents who fail to supervise their children are often unaware of how their children spend their leisure time or the identities of their children's peers. Lack of awareness of a child's activities diminishes the opportunities of parents to discipline their child for antisocial or deviant behaviour. For example, Mak's (1990) research demonstrated that high levels of parental attachment were inversely related to self-reported delinquency among both girls and boys for some of the more serious offences contained in the Australian Self-Report Delinquency

Scale. In a second study, she also found that parental bonding was significantly lower among delinquents compared with non-delinquents (Mak 1991). Similarly, Loeber and Loeber-Stouthamer's (1986) review of the literature found that delinquency and aggression were most often associated with a lack of parental involvement, poor supervision and discipline, and parental rejection. The relationship between parental care and delinquency was also discussed by Barnes and Farrell (1992), who found that monitoring of children's behaviour was significantly related to lower rates of delinquency and problem behaviour, leading the authors to conclude that lack of monitoring was the most powerful predictor of delinquency. However, they also found a linear relationship that was highly significant for maternal coercive control, with more coercive control associated with higher rates of delinquency. The authors ultimately suggested that 'coercion may be the negative aspect of the support construct' (Barnes and Farrell 1992:769).

Although the evidence that the bond between parent and child is a crucial precursor of criminality is persuasive, it is much less clear how the processes of social bonding actually work. Moreover, control theory's ability to fully explain this relationship has been questioned. For example, the assumption that needs and desires are evenly distributed at individual and population levels has been extensively critiqued, especially by strain theorists, and while proponents of strain theory, particularly those advocating Agnew's General Strain Theory, agree with control theorists that variables such as parental attachment are important in predicting juvenile delinquency, they suggest an alternate explanation of the way in which it may lead to involvement in crime. Simply put, strain theorists suggest that attachment may result in deviance because it provokes a sense of strain among adolescents (Agnew and Broidy 1993:249). For example, if children are not treated in a manner that is agreeable to them, frustration, as well as an impoverished adolescent/parent relationship, may develop, and these processes may result in children's deviance. Understood in this way, low levels of parental attachment may lead to deviance not simply because adolescents are free of the social bonds that restrict delinquency, but because they are also frustrated by a lack of, or unsatisfactory experience of, parental attachment.

Another area of disagreement between control and strain theorists is the degree to which parental supervision is inductive or coercive. While Hirschi describes parent supervision as existing on a continuum, with 'virtual' supervision at one pole and 'discipline' at the other, control theory focuses on the importance of virtual supervision in reducing the likelihood of delinquency. According to Hirschi (1969), virtual supervision involves children believing that their parents know, or at least care, where they are and what they are doing. This perception of parental interest and involvement results in the self-imposition of supervision. In situations where the child is conscious that transgressions will cause aggravation and distress to parents, as well as friction in the parent-child relationship, virtual supervision endures. This form of supervision can be understood as inductive in character. In contrast, parental discipline is an altogether more coercive form of supervision. And, according to strain theorists, it may be that coercive types of parental supervision are more important in leading to crime, as they may result in strain for the child, which, in turn, increases the likelihood of criminal involvement.

In summary, there is an enduring lack of agreement between strain and control theories regarding the nature of parental supervision, as well as the extent to which supervision is positively or negatively correlated with delinquency. While inductive supervision can readily be seen as an extension of parental care and therefore related to control theory, the possibility that coercive supervision is related to criminal outcomes, as posited by strain theorists, has been much less examined. This chapter uses data from the Sibling Study to examine these competing theories in more detail.

Family Structure

The relationship between family structure and delinquency has also been the subject of considerable research and debate, particularly due to the increasing instability of marital relationships throughout the Western World. While the relationship between marital breakdown and delinquency is complex, especially due to the wide range of correlates associated with family disruption (including lowered family income, marital conflict and parental absence), most major longitudinal studies have found at least a link between delinquency and broken homes (Juby and Farrington 2001). Amato and Keith (1991) suggest that this link is primarily a function of the marital conflict that may precede separation. In addition, Farrington (1994) noted that family breakdown was associated with a range of factors, including marital conflict, lowered income, parental absence, and juvenile delinquency, although the most important predictor of delinquency was marital conflict.

The notion that delinquency is a consequence of marital conflict is consistent with strain theory, as strain is the consequence of a young person living with such conflict. It is also consistent with control theory because, as noted earlier in this chapter, attachment to parents is a function of virtual supervision, intimacy of communication, and affectional identification. These forms of attachment are usually disrupted for at least one parent when separation and divorce occur.

While recognizing the potential consequences of marital conflict, it is also important to note that single-parent families do not necessarily provide lower levels of care than dual-carer families. Indeed, where a high level of care is provided by a sole parent, it has been suggested that there are no deleterious effects on the children. McCord's (1990) research indicated that the incidence of delinquency among boys from intact families was generally low, as was the case in single-parent families headed by an affectionate mother. Thus, McCord (1990) suggested that it was parental conflict associated with the break-up of the family that heightened the probability of delinquency. Further support for this hypothesis comes from several studies which found that where the loss of a father was due to death rather than marital breakdown, boys were no more at risk of delinquency than were boys from intact families (Amato and Keith 1991, McCord 1990, Wadsworth 1979). Farrington (1996) provides further evidence with data from the Cambridge Youth Study. In this project, boys from families in which a marital separation occurred before age five were 'not usually criminogenic' (1996:11).

Family Characteristics, Age and Sex

As noted elsewhere and in other chapters in this book, age and sex are central to all major theories of juvenile delinquency. Adolescence is (rightly) recognizd as a time when young people engage in risky behaviour as a 'rite of passage' typical of the transition between childhood and adulthood. While there are some variations in terms of the age of onset of delinquency and the peak age for committing particular types of crimes, there is little doubt that age is an important predictor of delinquent activity. In general, the peak age in terms of the prevalence and frequency of offending is around 17 (Farrington 1995). Similarly, sex is consistently identified as an important determinant of crime and delinquency. Both self-reported delinquency and officially detected crime clearly document that males are more likely than femalesto engage in criminal behaviours (for example, see Criminal Justice Commission 1995, Mukherjee 1997).

Not surprisingly, age and sex have also been shown to impact significantly on parenting practices. For example, Sokol-Katz, Dunham and Zimmerman (1997) found that sex differences in delinquency were associated with differences in parents' levels of control over their sons and daughters. As would be expected, parents typically imposed greater control over girls than boys. Hill and Atkinson also argue that 'while both males and females report considerable parental support (from mothers and fathers alike) ... the relative strengths of maternal and paternal support are significantly different for female and male children. Girls are more affected by maternal support and boys more by support from the father' (Hill and Atkinson 1986:144). Adding age to this relationship, Seydlitz suggests that 'the effect of age on delinquency depends on gender, that the effect of parental attachment on delinquency depends on age, and that the effect of parental attachment on delinquency depends on gender' (Seydlitz 1990:211).

Parental Care and Supervision in the Sibling Study

This chapter investigates the effects of parenting practices on adolescents' self-reported offending. More specifically, the analyses reported focus on the ways in which parental care and supervision influence involvement in crime, and whether these relationships are affected by respondents' age, sex and family structure. The analyses begin by discussing the ways in which parental care and supervision have been measured in the Sibling Study, and whether or not these characteristics vary by cohort type. It should be noted that the sample frame used in this chapter comprises respondents from the School and Offender cohorts only, and the analyses will focus on differences between these two groups.[1]

---

1   This decision was made based on the fact that a significant proportion (23 per cent) of respondents in the Vulnerable cohort reported that they were not living with their parents at the time the Sibling Study was conducted.

Maternal and Paternal Care

Measures of maternal and paternal care were derived from eight items from the Parental Bonding Instrument (Parker, Tupling and Brown 1979) care sub-scale, assessing (separately for mothers and fathers) how often the respondents' parents:

- spoke to me in a warm and friendly voice
- gave me as much help as I needed
- seemed to understand my frustrations and worries
- were affectionate to me
- liked talking things over with me
- understood what I needed
- made me feel I was wanted
- gave me praise.

Four response categories, ranging from 'very often' to 'hardly ever' were provided.

To determine whether these items adequately captured the constructs of maternal and paternal care, they were subjected to a principal components analysis and varimax rotation. The principal components analysis produced two factors with eigen values greater than one, accounting for 79.5 per cent of the variance. The varimax rotation resulted in the paternal items all loading heavily on the first factor, while the maternal items loaded equally heavily on the second. Thus, the conclusion appeared justified that maternal and paternal care could each be represented by these eight items. With scores on each item ranging from one to four, scale scores could potentially range from eight to 32.

Substantial differences in the two cohorts in maternal and paternal care are shown in Table 7.1. High levels of maternal and paternal care are more likely in the School cohort than in the Offender cohort. However, for both cohorts, high levels of maternal care are more likely than high levels of paternal care. Clearly, in contrast to those in the Offender cohort, young people in the School cohort report warm and close relationships with both parents, but particularly with mothers.

Table 7.1   Cohort differences in levels of maternal and paternal care (column percentages)

	Cohort	
Maternal Care	School	Offender
Low (8–15)	4	20
Medium (16–23)	19	31
High (24–32)	77	49
Paternal Care		
Low (8–15)	13	38
Medium (16–23)	18	29
High (24–32)	60	33
n	600	186

Parental Supervision

Parental supervision is measured by four questions. The first asked respondents about the number of rules they had to follow in their household. The responses were assessed on a four-point scale, from 'a lot of rules' to 'no rules'. The second question asked respondents how hard their parents tried to get them to do things their way, measured on a three-point scale from 'trying quite hard' to 'didn't try much'. The third question asked respondents how much interest their parents took in them, as assessed on a three-point scale, ranging from 'a lot of interest' to 'no real interest'. The final question asked whether the respondents were allowed to go out at night, either alone or with friends. Total responses to each item were dichotomized as close to the median as possible, and scores indicating a positive interest or active supervision were scored as '2' while responses indicating less interest or a more laissez faire approach to supervision were scored as '1'. Scores on the supervision scale could therefore range from 4 to 8.

Levels of parental supervision are shown in Table 7.2. Again, the differences between the cohorts are marked, with those in the Offender cohort having lower levels of supervision. Specifically, very low supervision is reported by more than one-third (37 per cent) of the Offender cohort, compared to 14 per cent of the School group. Similarly, moderate to high supervision is reported by more than half the School cohort (55 per cent), but less than one-third (30 per cent) of the Offender cohort.

Table 7.2   Cohort differences in levels of parental supervision (column percentages)

Level of	Cohort	
Supervision	School	Offender
Very Low (4–5)	14	37
Low (6)	31	33
Moderate (7)	39	23
High (8)	16	6
n	637	164

Age, Sex and Cohort Differences in Family Influences

It is clear from the data already examined that there are marked differences in the two cohorts in terms of family influences, but the questions that are central to this chapter—how are differences in family influences to be understood, and how do family influences affect offending behaviour?—have yet to be addressed. We turn to these issues now.

These questions will be investigated by first examining gender, age and family structure differences in maternal and paternal care and parental supervision, and then exploring the manner in which these variables are related to self-reported delinquency. Bivariate analyses are presented first, followed by more complex

Understanding Youth Crime: An Australian Study

multivariate procedures, in which the independent effects of the three family measures on crime are examined while controlling for the effects of gender, age and family structure. This analysis will enable us to determine the importance of family factors in accounting for differences in levels of self-reported delinquency, when the effects of other important factors (i.e. gender, age and family structure) are included in the analysis. To begin, the impact of gender, age and family structure on maternal and paternal care and parental supervision is reviewed.

Interestingly, there are virtually no gender differences, with boys and girls reporting very similar levels of both maternal and paternal care, although the relative cohort differences observed in Table 7.1 are maintained and, for both cohorts, higher levels of maternal care are reported.

Table 7.3   Age and cohort differences in levels of maternal and paternal care (column percentages)

| | Cohort | | | | | |
| | School | | | Offender | | |
	11–14	15	15+	11–14	15	16+
Maternal Care						
Low	2	4	2	8	24	19
Medium	30	38	39	37	43	45
High	68	58	58	55	43	36
n^1	330	147	152	38	44	120
Paternal Care						
Low	10	9	15	27	26	45
Medium	39	46	46	46	55	34
High	51	45	39	27	18	21
n^1	327	142	152	37	38	112

[1] The small differences in *n*s for maternal and paternal care result from missing data.

Not surprisingly, age makes a difference to levels of maternal and paternal care, as shown in Table 7.3. As can be seen, younger boys and girls are more likely to report higher levels of maternal and paternal care, compared to older respondents. In fact, over two-thirds (68 per cent) of the School sample aged 14 and younger report high levels of maternal care, compared with 58 per cent of those aged 16 or over. The same relationship holds for the Offender cohort, although the overall levels of care reported are not as great. These differences are similar when examining paternal care, but, again, the overall levels of care are less. To summarize, mothers are more likely than fathers to be seen as providing care, and the younger respondents are more likely to report caring behaviour than older respondents.

Are there differences in levels of maternal and paternal care reported by those in households with two carers, in contrast to one carer? The answer is 'yes' and 'no', with differences depending on the care-giver (i.e. mother versus father) and cohort membership. The data are provided in Table 7.4.

Table 7.4   Family structure and cohort differences in levels of maternal and paternal care (column percentages)

	Cohort			
	School		Offender	
	Two-Parent Family	One-Parent Family	Two-Parent Family	One-Parent Family
Maternal Care				
Low	2	2	8	15
Medium	34	37	40	48
High	63	61	52	37
n^1	536	90	73	62
Paternal Care				
Low	8	29	28	47
Medium	43	37	47	34
High	49	34	24	19
n^1	530	86	74	53

[1] The small differences in *n*s for maternal and paternal care result from missing data.

If we look first at maternal care in the School cohort, it is apparent that there is not a great deal of difference in the levels of care reported by young people from two- and single-carer households. Around two-thirds of both groups report high levels of care, and almost no-one reports low levels of care. Among the Offender cohort, however, 52 per cent of those from the two-carer households report high levels of maternal care, compared to only 37 per cent from one-carer families. Thus, low levels of care are apparently more likely among young offenders from single-carer families.

Different levels of paternal care are reported by young people from the School cohort who come from one- and two-carer families; for this cohort, young people from two-carer families are more likely to report high levels of paternal care (see Table 7.4). The same pattern holds for the Offender cohort, although the overall levels of paternal care are lower among this group. Presumably, lower levels of paternal care are more likely among single-carer families, as they are more likely to be mothers than fathers.

As described previously, young people from the School cohort tended to report higher levels of supervision than did those in the Offender cohort. What impact do gender, age and family structure have on these relationships? The data are presented in Table 7.5, with the original measure (shown in Table 7.2) dichotomized, combining the very low and low categories, and the moderate and high categories. In general, and not surprisingly, the differences between the cohorts are maintained. As shown, within each cohort, boys and girls report very similar levels of parental supervision. A little less than half of boys and girls (45 per cent and 44 per cent, respectively) in the School cohort report low levels of supervision, while the remainder report high levels. Among the Offender cohort, approximately 70 per cent of the boys and girls report low levels of supervision, while 30 per cent report high levels.

Age also makes a difference, with the youngest sample members (those under 15 years) in both cohorts being somewhat more likely to report higher levels of supervision than older respondents. Family structure affects levels of supervision in the School cohort, but not for the Offenders. More specifically, lower levels of supervision are more likely among respondents from single-parent families in the School cohort, while there are no differences in supervision levels among those from single-parent and intact families among the Offenders (see Table 7.5).

Table 7.5   Sex, age and family structure differences in levels of parental supervision among the School and Offender cohorts

	Cohort					
	School			Offender		
	Parental Supervision					
	Low	High	*n*	Low	High	*n*
Sex						
Male	45	55	329	70	30	49
Female	44	56	308	71	29	115
Age						
11–14 years	42	58	330	51	49	37
15 years	51	49	153	78	22	36
16+ years	50	50	149	77	23	88
Family Structure						
Single-parent	53	47	92	66	34	59
Two-parent	44	56	534	67	33	69

To summarize the overall findings at this point, the analyses suggest a more prominent role for mothers in contrast to fathers as carers. In addition, levels of parental care vary by age, cohort and family structure. More specifically, the data suggest that younger children, as well as members of the School cohort, are more likely to experience a nurturing environment, compared to older respondents and Offenders. In addition, mothers in single- and two-parent families provide the same levels of care for youth in the School sample, but not in the Offender sample, where those from single-parent families receive less care. Finally, no gender differences were found, suggesting that boys and girls have similar nurturing experiences.

Regarding parental supervision, similar findings emerge. Specifically, structured supervision and interest in activities by parents are reported more commonly by those in the School cohort, compared to the Offender group, as well as by younger respondents. In addition, among the School cohort, family structure does not affect levels of supervision, but among the Offender sample, those from single-parent families report less supervision and interest than do those from two-parent families. As with maternal and paternal care, there are no gender differences in supervision: both boys and girls report being treated very similarly.

Overall, then, being caught up in the criminal justice system (i.e. in the Offender cohort) is associated with less care, supervision and interest. In addition, younger children receive more care, supervision and interest. Finally, single-parent status is associated with less care, supervision and interest for the Offenders, but not for the School cohort. There are no gender differences in these experiences.

These family circumstances set the stage for the next phase of our analysis, the relationship between offending and family structure, parental care, and supervision. We will first consider the aggregate measure of offending, then the sub-scales.

Family Influences and Offending Behaviour

The association between family structure and total number of offences in the last 12 months as assessed by the Australian Self Report Delinquency Scale (ASRDS) (Mak 1993) is shown in Table 7.6. Focusing on the last four columns of the table, a cohort difference in the rate of offending is immediately apparent, but family structure also makes a difference for each group. Among the Offender cohort, over one-third (36 per cent) of those from intact families report having committed no more than one offence in the past 12 months, while among those from single-parent families, only 17 per cent report the same level of offending. At the other end of the scale, 44 per cent of those from one-parent families report at least four offences, while less than one-third (30 per cent) from intact families report the same number. The pattern of offending reported by those in the Offender group not living with parents closely resembles the offending behaviour reported by those from single-parent families. For the School cohort, similar patterns emerge, but the differences are not as great. Thus, 69 per cent of those from one-parent families report no more than one offence in the past 12 months, compared with 79 per cent from two-parent families (see Table 7.6).

Table 7.6   Cohort differences in family structure and the number of offences reported in the last 12 months (column percentages)

			Cohort			
Number of		School Cohort			Offender Cohort	
Offences		Family Structure (Parents in Household)				
	None	One	Two	None	One	Two
0–1	40	69	79	12	17	36
2–3	40	25	19	45	40	34
4+	20	6	2	43	44	30
n	5	84	491	58	60	70

No parents = not living with parents or living with relatives.
One parent = mother only or father only in house.
Two parents = mother and father, mother and step-father or father and step-mother in house.

As shown in Table 7.7, both maternal and paternal care influence the number of offences reported by the Offender cohort, but only maternal care is significant for the School cohort. Among those in the Offender group with low levels of maternal care, four per cent report no more than one offence in the past 12 months, compared to one-quarter (29 per cent) among those with high levels of care. Thus, the higher the level of maternal care, the fewer the offences. A similar pattern exists for paternal care. Moving from low to high levels of paternal care, the percentage of those with no more than one offence rises from 10 to 37 per cent. Among the School cohort, a similar pattern exists for maternal care, albeit with lower rates of offences. No more than one offence is reported by 57 per cent of those experiencing low maternal care, compared to 81 per cent of those with high care. Interestingly, paternal care has no impact on offending for this group.

Table 7.7   Cohort differences in maternal and paternal care and the number of offences reported in the last 12 months (column percentages)

	Cohort					
	School			Offender		
Number of Offences	Level of Maternal Care					
	Low	Medium	High	Low	Medium	High
0–1	57	71	81	4	22	29
2–3	36	24	17	53	36	35
4+	7	4	2	43	42	36
n	14	181	358	26	78	76
	Level of Parental Care					
0–1	79	72	81	10	29	37
2–3	20	24	17	40	31	41
4+	2	4	3	51	40	22
n	56	239	253	63	68	36

Cohort differences are also found for parental supervision (Table 7.8). For the School cohort, parental supervision does not have much effect on offending, with those reporting low levels of supervision having only marginally greater levels of offending than those with high levels of supervision. For the Offender cohort, parental supervision has a more consistent effect, with those receiving lower levels of supervision having higher offending rates.

Next, we utilize the ASRDS sub-scales to consider whether family differences impact more markedly on certain types of offending. First, the effects of family structure on offending are considered.

The percentage of respondents with two or more offences in the past 12 months is shown in Table 7.9 for each ASRDS sub-scale. Some interesting differences regarding family structure emerge. Coming from a one-parent or two-parent household seems to make no difference to whether the young people will engage in illegal vehicle use, drug and alcohol use, or vandalism. However, youth living in households in which no parents are present are more likely to report having engaged in these offences, compared to those from one- or two-parent households. For both cohorts, family structure appears to make a difference to theft. Those growing up in single-parent households are more likely than those in two-parent families to have stolen a bicycle, shoplifted, stolen money, or engaged in break and enter. Family structure does not have an impact on the likelihood of engaging in physical assault or public disorder for those in the School sample, but for the Offender cohort, those from two-parent families are less inclined to engage in these behaviours.

Table 7.8   Cohort differences in levels of parental supervision and the number of offences reported in the last 12 months (column percentages)

Number of Offences	Cohort			
	School		Offender	
	Level of Parental Supervision			
	Low	High	Low	High
0–1	72	79	22	38
2–3	23	20	39	38
4+	5	1	39	23
n	245	308	100	42

In summary, family structure appears to influence whether or not young people are likely to engage in relatively minor property crimes, such as stealing a bicycle, shoplifting, or break and entering, with those in single-parent families more likely to engage in these crimes than those in two-parent families. Likewise, those in the Offender cohort who come from single-parent families are more likely to report assaulting others and behaving in disorderly ways, but are no more likely to use drugs or alcohol illegally or to engage in vandalism than their contemporaries from two-parent families. Interestingly, however, those from parentless households are more likely to use drugs and alcohol and engage in vandalism. Among young people who have not come before the courts (i.e. those in the School cohort), whether they come from an intact family or a one-parent family seems to have only marginal significance on their likelihood of engaging in delinquent behaviours of any kind, with the exception of relatively minor property offences.

We have already seen that maternal care makes a difference to overall reported delinquency. But, does the effect of parental care differ for the specific types of delinquency we are considering? Table 7.10 presents data for respondents with two or more offences in each of the sub-scale areas and the levels of maternal care they have reported. Clearly, maternal care is important: in four out of the six sub-scales, there are systematic differences in the proportion of respondents reporting two or more offences, with those with lower levels of care having higher rates of crime than those with higher levels of care. In some areas, the differences are quite small; in others, they are substantial. For example, in the Offender cohort, 89 per cent of those with low levels of maternal care report two or more drug and alcohol offences, compared to 65 per cent of those with high levels of maternal care. In the School cohort, these proportions are 50 and 14 per cent, respectively.

Table 7.9   Cohort differences in family structure and self-reported offending (percentage of respondents with two or more offences in the past 12 months)

	Cohort					
Sub-Scale	School			Offender		
	Family Structure (Parents in Household)					
	None	One	Two	None	One	Two
Illegal Vehicle Use	29	10	9	62	58	57
Theft	29	27	13	67	75	57
Assault	29	20	12	54	76	48
Public Disorder	29	28	19	57	75	60
Drugs and Alcohol	29	25	18	85	76	67
Vandalism	43	19	11	61	53	43
n	7	88	500	61	55	60

Maternal care also has an impact on theft, which is more pronounced in the School cohort than the Offender cohort. For the former, 36 per cent of those with low levels of maternal care report theft offences, compared to 13 per cent of those with high levels of maternal care. For the Offender cohort, the proportions are 70 and 59 per cent, respectively (see Table 7.10). For assault, a similar trend of about the same magnitude for the Offender cohort, but less for the School sample, can be observed. For illegal use of vehicle and disorderly conduct offences, maternal care affects the likelihood of committing offences in the expected direction, particularly for the Offender cohort. Finally, vandalism is not affected by maternal care for the Offender cohort, but it does make a difference for the School cohort.

As shown in Table 7.11, the effects of paternal care on crime are more noticeable for the Offender than the School cohort. Those in the Offender cohort with low levels of paternal care are more likely to commit each type of offence compared to those with high levels of paternal care. Of those who experience low levels of paternal care, 66 per cent report committing illegal vehicle crimes, compared to 32 per cent of those with high care. Similarly, 74 per cent of respondents with low levels of paternal care report theft offences, compared to 50 per cent of respondents with high levels of care. Thus, even while those in the Offender cohort are more likely to be involved in crime, those reporting positive relationships with their fathers are significantly less likely to report offending. Paternal care is not as influential for the School cohort. Those with low levels of paternal care have higher rates of offending for three sub-scales (theft, drugs and alcohol, and vandalism), but similar rates as those with high levels for the other sub-scales.

Table 7.10 Cohort differences in maternal care and self-reported offending (percentage of respondents with two or more offences in the past 12 months)

	Cohort					
	School			Offender		
	Level of Maternal Care					
	Low	Medium	High	Low	Medium	High
Illegal Vehicle Use	14	13	7	65	58	49
Theft	36	15	13	70	62	59
Assault	21	15	11	64	55	52
Public Disorder	14	24	18	67	70	50
Drugs and Alcohol	50	23	14	89	74	65
Vandalism	21	15	10	46	41	46
n	14	204	380	27	84	82

Table 7.11 Cohort differences in paternal care and self-reported offending (percentage of respondents with two or more offences in the past 12 months)

	Cohort					
Sub-Scale	School			Offender		
	Level of Paternal Care					
	Low	Medium	High	Low	Medium	High
Illegal Vehicle Use	9	12	8	66	53	32
Theft	19	16	11	74	56	50
Assault	12	14	11	62	49	51
Public Disorder	19	20	19	73	56	53
Drugs and Alcohol	25	23	12	87	73	45
Vandalism	14	13	11	57	44	36
n	64	250	276	68	73	40

Cohort differences are also found for parental supervision (results are not shown). Among the School cohort, where levels of offending are low, parental supervision has very little effect at all. In fact, those reporting very low or low levels of supervision are no more likely to offend than those reporting moderate or high levels of supervision. Among the Offender sample, the pattern is very different, with those reporting low levels of supervision markedly more likely to offend. For example, where parental supervision is at a minimum, the percentage of respondents reporting two or more offences in the past 12 months ranges from 83 per cent for illegal drug and alcohol use to 71 per cent for theft, 65 per cent for disorderly behaviour, and 52 per cent for vandalism, while at the highest levels of supervision the corresponding percentages are 20 per cent for drugs and alcohol, 30 per cent for theft and disorderly behaviour, and 10 per cent for vandalism.

It is clear that maternal and paternal care and parental supervision are related to reported offending behaviour. Paternal care and parental supervision appear to have stronger and more systematic effects in the Offender cohort, while maternal care appears to have consistent effects across both cohorts. While these bivariate relationships provide a broad picture of how family matters affect reported delinquent behaviour, the fact that these influences are themselves related still needs to be addressed. Thus, multivariate analyses will be conducted to identify the so-called 'independent effects' of each family variable on crime.

In addition, we already know that there are age and gender differences in reported delinquent behaviour, so the analyses will also control for their effects. In this way, we will advance our understanding of how family influences affect delinquency in the context of the age and gender of the young people involved. We must also bear in mind that we have two groups of very different young people. A group who, at the time of our data collection, was quite intimately involved with the juvenile justice system, the Offender cohort, and a second group whose involvement was, on the basis. of the information available to us, substantially less, the School cohort. Do families operate similarly in these two situations? The answer we have been able to provide to date is yes and no. We hope that this next and final step in our analysis will enable us to be a little more precise.

Multivariate Analyses of the Relationship Between Family Influences and Offending

In this final section of the chapter, two models of offending behaviour are presented. The first is a baseline model, predicting offending behaviour as a function of the three core family factors we have been principally concerned with; namely, maternal care, paternal care and parental supervision. We then add to this baseline model the control variables of age, sex, and family structure. We will focus on both the generalised measure of offending and the six sub-scales relating to assault, illegal vehicle use, public disorder, drug and alcohol use, theft and vandalism. In total, 14 analyses are performed. A summary of the results is provided in Table 7.12, which identifies the significant predictor variables in each model and their levels of significance.[2]

As shown in Table 7.12, the results suggest that family characteristics have somewhat different effects in the two cohorts. First, for the School cohort, several family characteristics emerge as significant predictors of crime. Maternal care (including having a mother who spoke in a warm and friendly voice, who provided as much help as was needed, who seemed to understand frustrations and worries, was affectionate, liked talking things over, understood what was needed, made the person feel wanted and gave them praise) is an important predictor of self-reported delinquent behaviour. It is related to lower levels of self-reported delinquency, for the generalized measure of offending as well as every sub-scale except illegal vehicle use. In addition, it is significant in the first model, when its effects are

---

2   The detailed results of the multivariate regression analyses are available from the primary author upon request.

compared with those of paternal care and parental supervision, and it is equally important in the second model, which controls for age, sex and family structure.

Less influential for the School cohort, but still important, is parental supervision. In seven of the 14 analyses, supervision is significant, with higher levels of parental supervision associated with lower levels of reported delinquency. Parental supervision, it will be remembered, is assessed in terms of whether or not rules had to be followed, whether or not parents tried to get young people to do things their way, how much interest parents took in their children, and whether or not they were allowed to go out either alone or with friends at night. For the generalized crime measure, parental supervision is significant in both the first model, and the second, when age, gender and family structure were introduced. It is also significant in both models for the public disorder and drug and alcohol use sub-scales, but is only significant in the first model for illegal vehicle use, suggesting that when age and gender are also considered, the effect of parental supervision becomes less pronounced. Finally, parental supervision is not related to theft, vandalism or assault.

Age and gender are both significant in five of the seven analyses. More specifically, older respondents in the School cohort are more likely to report generalized crime, illegal vehicle use, theft, drugs and alcohol use and vandalism, and this trend occurs independently of the effects of maternal care and parental supervision. Regarding gender, boys are more likely than girls to engage in activities included in the generalized measure, illegal vehicle use, theft, vandalism and assault, but not illegal drug and alcohol use, or public disorder crimes (i.e. relatively trivial offences as having gone to see an R-rated film, not paid an entrance fee, not attended class or 'wagged' school). Family structure was significant in some models, with young people from single-parent families more likely than their peers from two-parent families to engage in theft, public disorder crimes, and vandalism (see Table 7.12).

What is striking about the analyses of the School group is the robustness of the maternal care and, perhaps to a lesser extent, the parental supervision factors. While boys may be more prone to report delinquent behaviours than girls, and while older respondents report more delinquent behaviour than younger respondents, those experiencing high levels of maternal care and structured parental supervision may have developed internalized controls in much the way that Hirschi (1969) has described, so that these family factors have minimized the likelihood of transgressing the law.

In the Offender cohort, the picture is different. As shown in Table 7.12, maternal care is not significant in any of the analyses. Earlier, we saw that the levels of maternal care were lower in the Offender cohort than they were in the School cohort, but, nevertheless, almost half of the former reported high levels of care. Despite this finding, maternal care does not affect the likelihood of offending according to the multivariate analyses. Similarly, there is limited support for the effect of paternal care on offending, as it is significant only in the first model for the generalized measure of crime, and in both models for drug and alcohol use.

Parental supervision, however, does have pronounced effects for those in the Offender cohort, in eight of the 14 analyses. It is significant (in the expected direction) in both models for theft, public disorder, and drugs and alcohol use. It is significant in the first model for generalized delinquency and illegal vehicle use, but once gender is introduced into the analyses, parental supervision is no longer significant. This result suggests that there may be an interaction effect between parental supervision and gender, with parental supervision impacting on the likelihood of delinquent behaviour among girls (as they commit fewer crime), but more analysis is needed to confirm this hypothesis.

Regarding other predictors of criminal involvement, gender is an important predictor of the same types of reported delinquency as was found for the School cohort. Thus, boys are more likely than girls to report offending in the generalized measure, as well as for illegal vehicle use, theft and burglary, vandalism, and physical assault. Perhaps these behaviours are more likely to be gendered than those comprising the public disorder and drugs and alcohol sub-scales, and the observed gender effect overrides, as it were, any differences between the cohorts. Age is not an important consideration for the Offender cohort, with the exception of drug and alcohol use, which is likely to increase with increasing age.

Table 7.12   Predictors of self-reported offending–summary table

	Maternal Care	Paternal Care	Parent Support	Age	Male	No Parent	Single-Parent	Two-Parent
	School Cohort							
Generalized Delinquency								
Model 1	*		**					
Model 2	*		*	***	***			
Illegal Vehicle Use								
Model 1				*				
Model 2				***	***			
Theft								
Model 1	*							
Model 2	*			***	***		**	
Public Disorder								
Model 1	*		***					
Model 2	*		**				**	
Drug and Alcohol Use								
Model 1	*		***					
Model 2	*		***	*				

	Maternal Care	Paternal Care	Parent Support	Age	Male	No Parent	Single-Parent	Two-Parent
School Cohort								
Vandalism								
Model 1	**							
Model 2	**			**	**		**	
Assault								
Model 1	*							
Model 2	*				***			
Offender Cohort								
Generalized Delinquency								
Model 1		*	*					
Model 2					***			
Illegal Vehicle Use								
Model 1			*					
Model 2					**			
Theft								
Model 1			*					
Model 2			**		***			
Public Disorder								
Model 1			*					
Model 2			*					
Drug and Alcohol Use								
Model 1		**	***					
Model 2		**	*	***				
Vandalism								
Model 1								
Model 2					*			
Assault								
Model 1					***			
Model 2								

*p< 0.05; ** p< 0.01; ***p< 0.001

Note: Model 1 is the baseline model, assessing the effects of parental care and supervision on offending. Model 2 controls for age, sex, and family structure.

Conclusion

The multivariate analyses reinforce and help clarify issues suggested by the bivariate analyses, as well as by the strain and control theories discussed earlier. To summarize, the results indicate the importance of maternal care and parental supervision in the School cohort, as well as the importance of parental supervision in the Offender sample. It is noteworthy that maternal care, perhaps the more 'affective' of the two measures, has no impact on reported delinquency among the Offender cohort, while parental supervision, the more 'structured' of the two measures, has the same impact on reported delinquency in both groups.

The results also reveal somewhat more support for control theory than for strain theory. First, the multivariate analyses demonstrate that high levels of maternal care result in lower rates of offending (for the School cohort), which is consistent with control theory, as it indicates that bonding to parents reduces delinquency. In contrast, the results do not suggest that low levels of care increase offending, which would be predicted by strain theory. Similarly, the analyses indicate that high levels of supervision also reduce offending, as posited by control theorists, but do not support strain theory's hypothesis that increased supervision leads to higher levels of offending. However, it is important to note that the items comprising the supervision scale in the Sibling Study are more consistent with Hirschi's conception of supervision as 'inductive,' in that they measure the extent to which parents set rules and take an interest in their children. In contrast, the supervision scale does not reflect whether discipline is coercive or unduly harsh, which is the focus of strain theory. Thus, further analyses are needed to better assess the ways in which parental support and supervision influence involvement in crime, and whether or not these processes can best be explained by control or strain theory.

Interestingly, family structure does not appear to be related to most criminal outcomes for either cohort. For the Offenders, coming from a single-parent or two-parent family, or even households in which no parents are present, makes no difference to the level of reported delinquency. For the School sample, coming from single-parent families makes theft, public disorder and vandalism more likely, but has no impact on the generalized measure, illegal vehicle use, the use of drugs and alcohol or assault. While surprising, these results are consistent with previous research which suggests that the link between family breakdown and delinquency may be better explained by other processes occurring in families, such as parental conflict (Juby and Farrington 2001).

Overall, this chapter has shown that, in coming to an understanding of the factors predisposing young people to delinquent behaviour, the family matters. Important for young people growing up in a relatively stable environment, if we can so describe the School cohort, are levels of appropriate care that mothers provide, as well as more structured forms of supervision provided by both parents. The latter is also important among the young Offenders, for whom maternal care does not appear to have the same impact, but for whom paternal care appears important, albeit to a lesser extent. It is also important to realize that gender and age also affect criminal involvement, and that these effects are independent of those attributed to the family.

Chapter 8

The Influence of Siblings on Substance Use and Delinquency

Denise A. Durrington, Abigail A. Fagan and David Chant

Introduction

As described in Chapter 1, an innovative feature of the Sibling Study is its purposive sampling of opposite-sex sibling pairs. In fact, this type of research design is rarely used in criminology, even though it is very well suited to testing criminological theories and identifying risk and protective factors influencing crime and conformity. For instance, to the extent that siblings do not resemble one another in their propensity for offending, these differences in propensity for offending can be used to identify differences in each sibling's experiences which may influence crime, such as personality characteristics and interactions with others. In contrast, if similarities in rates of offending by siblings are found, these similarities can be further explored to determine the shared experiences that influence involvement in crime, such as family background.

This chapter provides a preliminary examination of the relationship between siblings in the Sibling Study. After reviewing the literature and describing the sample design, the chapter explores the resemblance in siblings' self-reported rates of delinquency and drug use using bivariate and multivariate analyses.

Literature Review

Although criminologists have long been concerned with identifying familial influences on crime, they tend to focus upon the role of parents and general family characteristics, rather than upon sibling influences. For example, parents' criminal histories and favorable attitudes towards deviance, as well as the extent and quality of their monitoring, supervision, and affection towards children, have been extensively studied. Research has also focused upon the ways in which background characteristics of the family, such as family structure, size, socioeconomic status, family crises, and area of residence, affect children's criminality (see Chapter 7 for further information regarding family influences on delinquency). Comparatively, there has been little attention to the potentially vital role of siblings in influencing offending behaviour. This oversight is rather surprising, given the fact that siblings spend as much time (if not more) with one another as they do with their parents.

Similarly, although delinquent peers are considered one of the most important predictors of adolescent involvement in crime, criminologists have largely failed to acknowledge that siblings may also act as deviant peers. In fact, given the amount of time siblings spend with each other, as well as the long-lasting and inescapable nature of their relationship, one would expect that the role siblings play in influencing crime would be as large (if not larger) than that of the peer group (Robins 1966, Sampson and Laub 1993).

Although there has been a lack of direct attention to the role of siblings in fostering crime, there is compelling evidence that crime tends to be concentrated in a small number of families, suggesting a corresponding concentration of delinquent siblings (Farrington, Barnes and Lambert 1996, Farrington, Joliffe, Loeber, Stouthamer-Loeber and Kalb 2001, Lauritsen 1993, Loeber and Stouthamer-Loeber 1986). For example, Lauritsen (1993) reports that 10 per cent of the households participating in the National Youth Survey account for 76 per cent of the total number of delinquent incidents reported by adolescents, with even larger proportions for more serious crimes (for example, accounting for 100 per cent of robberies and 94 per cent of felony theft offences).

Siblings also tend to resemble one another in their propensity to offend. Studies utilizing a variety of research designs and sample characteristics have demonstrated sibling similarity in a variety of problem outcomes, including externalizing and internalizing behaviours, aggression, delinquency, and drug/alcohol use (Brook, Whiteman, Gordon, and Brook 1998, Edelbrock, Rende, and Plomin 1995, Farrington *et al* 1996, Lauritsen 1993, Rowe 1985 1986, Rowe and Britt 1991, Slomkowski, Rende, Conger, Simons and Conger 2001, Stormshak, Bellanti and Bierman 1996, West and Farrington 1979). West and Farrington (1979) report that 19 per cent of the male respondents in the Cambridge Study who did not have a criminal brother were arrested at least once by age 20, compared to 50 per cent of those with a criminal brother. In a recent report of sibling similarity in delinquency, Rowe and his colleagues (1996) document a mean correlation for sibling delinquency of 0.35 (with a range from 0.32 to 0.49), which they indicate is greater than that of other non-intellectual traits (which have an average correlation of 0.1 to 0.2). Moreover, Bank and his colleagues (1996) speculate that sibling resemblance may be even greater for young children. When assessing within-family problem behaviour, they report a covariation of 0.69 in 'coercive exchanges' between family members (Bank *et al* 1996). Even more convincingly, several studies have shown that the delinquency of one sibling significantly predicts the other's offending behaviour(s), controlling for a variety of risk factors, including shared family experiences (Brownfield and Sorenson 1994, Farrington *et al* 1996, Lauritsen 1993, Rowe and Gulley 1992, Rowe, Rodgers and Meseck-Bushey 1992, Slomkowski *et al* 2001).

Although the evidence for an effect of sibling influence on crime is persuasive, it is far from conclusive and is in need of further clarification. In fact, some investigations have found little support for an effect of sibling influence on crime (Robins 1966, Sampson and Laub 1993). While other studies report a significant correlation in sibling delinquency rates, the correlation is generally small (0.30 or less). Moreover, the strength of the sibling effect often varies according to family, sibling, or individual characteristics. For example, some studies (McGue, Sharma, and Benson 1996, Rowe and Britt 1991, Rowe and Gulley 1992, Slomkowski *et al* 2001, Wilkinson *et al* 1982) demonstrate weak or non-significant sibling effects on adolescent delinquency for opposite-sex pairs, while others report that the number of male siblings, but not female siblings, increases offending rates (Jones *et al* 1980, Lauritsen 1993, Reiss and Farrington 1991). Likewise, the similarity between sibling pairs for adolescent drug use and delinquency has been found to vary by age difference, with more resemblance when the age spacing is close, rather than distant (McGue *et al* 1996, Reiss and Farrington 1991).

What accounts for sibling similarity in offending behaviour? While many researchers profess that sibling resemblance may be attributed to shared genetic factors, empirical evidence does not always support this view. Twin and adoption studies find some support for genetic influences on aggression, delinquency, and crime (Carey 1992, Edelbrock *et al* 1995, Rowe 1986, Rowe and Osgood 1984)[1] but these investigations also reveal that only part of the sibling resemblance can be explained by genetics (Rowe 1986, Rowe *et al* 1996, Rowe and Plomin 1981). It is perhaps more tempting to conclude that shared family influences are responsible for siblings' similarity in offending, given that family factors have been demonstrated to be important determinants of crime. In fact, Sampson and Laub (1993) report that family size, socio-economic status and parent criminality are related to boys' offending, while attachment to deviant siblings is not. Likewise, Rowe and his colleagues (1992) demonstrate that shared characteristics are important in explaining sisters' and mixed siblings' involvement in crime, although this finding is not evident for brothers. In contrast, other investigations find that family factors cannot account for the sibling effect (Lauritsen 1993, Rowe and Gulley 1992). For example, Rowe and Gulley (1992) report that parental drug use, child-rearing styles, socio-economic status and family size do not reduce the sibling effect on adolescent delinquency or drug use.

This chapter examines sibling effects by investigating the extent to which siblings engage in similar levels of offending and drug use, and exploring whether or not this similarity is affected by individual or sibling characteristics, or shared family factors. This project moves beyond prior work in several ways. First, it focuses on the sibling relationship of opposite-sex pairs, which has not been extensively explored. Likewise, the majority of studies have been conducted in the United States (with the exception of the Cambridge Development Study, in London), and there have been no large-scale studies in Australia. Finally, prior research has utilized general population samples of youth, but has not investigated the direction and strength of the sibling effect with the offender and at-risk populations included in the Sibling Study. Thus, this investigation compares the effects of sibling influences on crime among three distinct cohorts who vary in their levels of offending: the School, Vulnerable and Offender groups.

---

1   The extensive literature on genetic influences will not be reviewed here, but recent reviews include Rowe and Osgood (1984), and Rowe and Rodgers (1989).

Method

Sample

As described in Chapter 1, the Sibling Study sample is comprised of participants from the School, Vulnerable and Offender cohorts. During recruitment to the Study, if the primary participant had a sibling within four years of age, he or she was also asked to complete a self-report questionnaire. In this manner, respondents from 683 families were obtained from the three cohorts, as shown in Table 8.1.

Table 8.1   Structure of the Sibling Study sample, by cohort

No of siblings interviewed per family	Cohort							
	School		Vulnerable		Offender		Total	
	n	%	*n*	%	*n*	%	*n*	%
1	73	20	97	77	152	81	322	47
2	284	77	26	21	35	19	345	51
3	11	3	2	2	1	0	14	2
4	1	0	1	0	0	0	2	0
Total	369	100	126	100	188	100	683	100

Note: *n*s indicate the number of participating families.

Among the 683 families recruited, 322 (47 per cent) had only one adolescent complete a questionnaire, and these individuals were dropped from the current study, resulting in a sub-sample of 740 individuals from 361 families. There was also a small number of families in which more than two siblings completed a questionnaire (see Table 8.1). In these cases, the third and fourth siblings have also been excluded from the analyses, for a final sub-sample of 361 pairs of siblings (722 individuals). As shown in Table 8.1, the School cohort contains the largest proportion of sibling pairs, including 296 families, while the Vulnerable and Offender cohorts have 29 and 36 families, respectively.

The Sibling Study was originally intended to include only opposite-sex sibling pairs. This selection goal was difficult to achieve, however, particularly in the Vulnerable and Offender cohorts and, in some instances, it was necessary to substitute a more available or willing same-sex sibling in the study. As a result, the sibling sub-sample includes 25 (7 per cent) same-sex sibling pairs from the three cohorts, as shown in Table 8.2. While the School sample is comprised of primarily opposite-sex sibling pairs, the Offender cohort contains approximately one-third (36 per cent) same-sex pairs, and the Vulnerable group has about one-fourth (24 per cent) same-sex pairs.

Consistent with the majority of studies assessing sibling effects, this chapter explores the influence of older sibling behaviour on younger sibling delinquency and drug use. As shown in Table 8.3, there is some variation in the three cohorts regarding the age and sex distribution of the sibling pairs. The School cohort includes primarily opposite-sex pairs, with approximately equal numbers of older male/younger female and older female/younger male siblings. The same is true for the Vulnerable cohort, although this sample also includes two pairs of brothers and five pairs of sisters. The Offender cohort, in contrast, contains a large number (10) of brother pairs, 23 opposite-sex pairs, and three pairs of sisters. Age spacing between siblings (not shown in the table) ranges from 0 to 4 years, with a mean of 1.8 years for the School cohort, compared to 2.7 years for the Vulnerable cohort and 2.4 years for the Offender cohort. In addition, older siblings average 15.3 years in the School cohort, compared to 16.5 years in the other cohorts, and younger siblings are somewhat younger in the School cohort (13.5 years), compared to the Vulnerable (13.8) and Offender (14.1) cohorts.

Table 8.2   Sex composition of sibling pairs, by cohort (number of sibling pairs)

Composition	Cohort							
	School		Vulnerable		Offender		Total	
	Pairs	%	Pairs	%	Pairs	%	Pairs	%
Opposite-Sex	291	98	22	76	23	64	336	93
Same-Sex	5	2	7	24	13	36	25	7
Total	296	100	29	100	36	100	361	100

Table 8.3   Age and sex distribution of sibling pairs, by cohort (number of sibling pairs)

Sibling	Cohort					
	School		Vulnerable		Offender	
	Younger Brother	Younger Sister	Younger Brother	Younger Sister	Younger Brother	Younger Sister
Older Brother	1	145	2	13	10	14
Older Sister	146	4	9	5	9	3
Total	147	149	11	18	19	17

Measures

Each sibling completed the large, self-report questionnaire described in Chapter 1. This chapter is specifically interested in items inquiring about participation in delinquent activities, alcohol and drug use, and family characteristics.

The measure of delinquency was created using items adapted from the 37-item Australian Self-Report Delinquency Scale (ASRDS) (Mak 1993) described in Chapter 2. Both older and younger siblings were asked whether they had engaged in a variety of delinquent activities during the previous 12 months. The four lie items, the five drug and alcohol offences, and two items reported by less than five per cent of the sample (forcing someone to do sexual things with you, and starting a fire) were omitted from the current analyses.[2] The total delinquency scale sums the remaining set of delinquent activities, yielding a score ranging from 0 to 25. Analyses are also based on the following sub-scales, as described in Chapter 2: motor vehicle offences (6 items), public disorder (4 items), theft and burglary (6 items), vandalism (5 items), and assault (4 items). Substance use was measured by a five-item summated scale. Participants were asked to report whether or not they had bought alcohol, drunk alcohol in a public place, used marijuana, used hard drugs (for example, ecstasy, acid or speed), or used pills, puffers or medicine for fun in the previous year. The scale sums these reports, yielding a possible score from 0 to 5.

A number of family measures were created to explore the possibility that shared environmental influences may account for any similarities between siblings in delinquent behaviour and substance use. Although both siblings reported family characteristics, analyses are based on responses from the older sibling. If a response was unavailable from the older sibling, the younger sibling's report was used.

These shared family characteristics are presented in Table 8.4. Family disruption is a dichotomous variable. Siblings living in homes in which one or both biological parents are absent because of remarriage, separation, divorce, or other circumstances (for example, desertion or death) are coded '1', and those in intact (i.e. non-divorced) homes are coded '0'. Although prior studies have considered the importance of losing one or both parents, few studies have assessed the importance of the addition of half- or biologically-unrelated siblings into the current family. In this study, the dichotomous 'blended families' variable compares families with all full siblings (coded '1') to those with half- or step-siblings (coded '0'). Father's employment and mother's employment are dichotomous variables. Parents with a paid job are coded '1', and those without a job or who are absent are coded '0'. Mother's educational attainment and father's educational attainment are coded on three-point scales, differentiating between those with less than grade 12 (coded '1'), grade 12 (coded '2'), and post-secondary education (coded '3'). Residential mobility represents the number of times the participant has moved house during the last two years, and ranges from none to more than three times.

---

2 Another item, playing telephone tricks, was also omitted, based on prior analyses indicating that this offence had a very low factor loading on the total delinquency scale.

Table 8.4   Shared family characteristics of sibling pairs, by cohort (row percentages)

Characteristics		Cohort		
		School	Vulnerable	Offender
Family Disruption[1]				
Nondivorced		79	59	47
Remarried/Separated/Divorced/ Other		21	41	53
Blended Families[1]				
Full Biologically-Related Siblings		86	69	78
Other		14	31	22
Employment				
Father[1]	Employed	79	66	50
	Other	21	34	50
Mother	Employed	69	62	69
	Other	31	38	31
Educational Attainment				
Father	< Grade 12	52	46	72
	Grade 12	17	25	12
	TAFE/College	31	29	16
Mother	< Grade 12	52	54	51
	Grade 12	20	25	26
	TAFE/College	28	21	23
Residential Mobility[1]				
None		73	55	42
Once		15	21	19
Twice		8	7	14
Three times		4	3	11
> Three times		0	14	14

[1] Indicates cohort differences (p <0.05).

Although cohort differences in family characteristics are described in more detail in Chapter 7, it is important to note that the cohorts have many different demographic characteristics. As expected, siblings in the School cohort are least likely to experience family risk factors. Most of these respondents live in non-divorced families, have biologically-related brothers and sisters, a working father, and have never moved. In contrast, both the Vulnerable and Offender groups have experienced greater levels of family disruption and paternal unemployment. The cohorts also differ in sibship size (not shown), with the School cohort averaging 3.5 siblings, compared to 3.9 in the other two cohorts. Likewise, respondents from the Offender cohort report more brothers (2.4) compared to the other two cohorts (1.8 each), while those in the Vulnerable group report more sisters (2.3), compared to the School (1.8) and Offender (1.5) cohorts.

Results

Bivariate and multivariate analyses are used to assess sibling effects on delinquency and substance use. First, the magnitude of similarity among sibling pairs for delinquent behaviour and substance use is presented, with Pearson correlation coefficients used to assess the bivariate relations among the older and younger siblings' measures. Ordinary Least Squares (OLS) regression analysis is then used to examine whether or not the sibling effect can be attributed to shared family characteristics (i.e. whether or not the influence of one sibling upon another remains statistically significant after including family variables in the analyses).

How Similar are Siblings in Their Levels of Substance Use and Delinquent Behaviour?

Table 8.5 presents Pearson correlation coefficients between the older and younger siblings' self-reported substance use and delinquency, by cohort. The cohort distinction is of primary importance, as the three groups vary in their levels of offending. The School cohort is most representative of a general population of adolescents, and thus results for this group can be compared to those produced in most other studies, which also tend to be based upon general samples. The other two cohorts represent groups of higher-offending adolescents, and sibling effects among these types of adolescents have not been well established (if examined at all).

Beginning with the School cohort, the older sibling's substance use is strongly associated (0.22) with the younger sibling's own use of substances, as well as with the younger sibling's public disorder, vandalism, and total delinquency measures. These results are similar to other studies indicating sibling influences on drug and alcohol use, even for mixed-sex pairs (for example, Brook *et al* 1988, Conger and Reuter 1996, McGue *et al* 1996). However such work tends to focus on drug use only and does not consider whether or not drug use by an older sibling affects the younger sibling's delinquency. Few other correlations emerge as significant for the largely opposite-sex sibling pairs in the School cohort, indicating little to no resemblance in siblings' levels of delinquency. These findings are also consistent with the literature, which tends to demonstrate very low or insignificant correlations in offending for mixed-sex siblings.

Table 8.5 Sibling correlation coefficients for involvement in substance use and delinquency, by cohort

Older's Behaviour	Younger's Behaviour						
	(1)	(2)	(3)	(4)	(5)	(6)	(7)
School							
(1) Substance Use	0.22***	0.04	-0.00	0.14**	0.08	0.15***	0.12**
(2) Assault	0.09	0.05	-0.03	0.06	0.03	-0.03	0.03
(3) Vehicle	0.02	0.04	-0.06	-0.04	-0.07	-0.03	-0.07
(4) Public Disorder	0.14**	0.02	-0.00	0.16***	0.06	0.01	0.07
(5) Theft and Burglary	0.04	0.04	-0.00	-0.03	0.05	0.05	0.04
(6) Vandalism	0.06	-0.01	-0.08	0.01	-0.01	0.06	-0.00
(7) Total Delinquency	0.10	0.03	-0.05	0.04	0.02	0.02	0.02
Vulnerable							
(1) Substance Use	0.35*	0.26	0.49***	0.22	0.19	0.15	0.31*
(2) Assault	0.08	0.20	0.23	0.28	0.23	0.03	0.25
(3) Vehicle	0.25	0.14	0.53***	0.26	0.18	-0.05	0.25
(4) Public Disorder	0.00	-0.04	0.04	0.03	0.00	0.13	0.04
(5) Theft and Burglary	0.05	0.31	0.34*	0.34*	0.32*	0.27	0.41**
(6) Vandalism	0.08	0.44**	0.28	0.19	0.46***	0.48***	0.50***
(7) Total Delinquency	0.15	0.32*	0.46***	0.34**	0.36**	0.26	0.45**
Offender							
(1) Substance Use	0.11	-0.12	-0.08	0.20	0.01	-0.07	-0.00
(2) Assault	-0.53***	-0.33**	-0.37**	-0.46***	-0.53***	-0.42***	-0.53***
(3) Vehicle	-0.12	-0.11	-0.14	-0.15	-0.09	-0.11	-0.15
(4) Public Disorder	0.06	-0.10	-0.02	-0.04	-0.14	-0.26	-0.13
(5) Theft and Burglary	-0.22	-0.31*	-0.25	-0.32*	-0.24	-0.41**	-0.37**
(6) Vandalism	-0.17	-0.10	-0.10	-0.16	-0.17	-0.23	-0.19
(7) Total Delinquency	-0.23	-0.23	-0.23	-0.26	-0.28	-0.34**	-0.33*

* p <0.10; ** p <0.05; *** p <0.01 based on Pearson correlation coefficients.

As in the School cohort, there is a significant correlation in sibling substance use for respondents in the Vulnerable cohort, indicating that high levels of substance use by older siblings are associated with higher levels of substance use, as well as vehicle offences and total delinquency by younger siblings. Although two of these three relationships only approach significance (p <0.10), the size of the correlations are higher for the Vulnerable cohort, as compared to the School cohort, and the level of significance may be related to the smaller sample size of the Vulnerable group. Unlike the School sample, the results also indicate a strong sibling resemblance in delinquency for the Vulnerable respondents, with a correlation of 0.45 for total delinquency, and moderate to strong effects for vehicle-related offending (0.53), vandalism (0.48), and theft and burglary (0.32).

For the Offender cohort, the results indicate no relationship for sibling substance use, and a negative correlation for total delinquency (–0.33) and assault (–0.33), as well as between various sub-types of delinquent behaviour. The moderately strong negative associations suggest a deterrent effect on offending, whereby higher levels of delinquency for one of the siblings are associated with lower levels of offending by the other. These effects are somewhat unexpected, given that prior research suggests either non-significant, or positively associated, relationships in sibling behaviour. However, such work has focused on offending by the general population of adolescents, and has not considered young people officially identified as offenders.

To summarize, the findings indicate the weakest sibling relationships for members of the School cohort, although older siblings' substance use is positively associated with younger siblings' substance use. Stronger effects are found for the Vulnerable and Offender groups, but the direction of the relationships is different. Higher rates of substance use and delinquency by older siblings are associated with higher rates by younger siblings in the Vulnerable cohort. However, greater levels of offending by older siblings are related to lower rates of offending by younger siblings, and vice versa, in the Offender group (and there is no sibling relationship for substance use). It is important to remember that these cohort differences may be related to the sex composition of the sibling pair, given that the School cohort contains primarily mixed-sex siblings, while the Vulnerable and Offender groups contain a larger proportion of same-sex siblings (24 per cent and 36 per cent, respectively). Others have noted stronger sibling effects for same-sex than mixed-sex pairs.

Correlations between the sub-types of offending are presented in Table 8.5 in order to determine the extent of family specialization in delinquent behaviour. Following Lauritsen (1993), the correlations along the diagonal (indicating specialization) were compared to correlations off the diagonal (indicating a lack of specialization). In general, the findings indicate that siblings from the same family do not tend to engage in the same types of delinquent acts. However, siblings show some specialization in the Vulnerable cohort. With the exception of assault and public disorder, the correlations along the diagonal are statistically significant. The older sibling's report of involvement in vandalism is highly correlated with the younger sibling's report, the older sibling's report of involvement in theft and burglary is correlated with the younger sibling's report, and so on (see Table 8.5).

Do Shared Family Characteristics Account for Sibling Similarity?

This section explores whether or not family characteristics account for the significant correlations between the older and younger sibling's self-reported delinquent behaviour and substance use. Correlations between the family variables (and younger siblings' sex) and younger siblings' outcomes are examined first. As shown in Table 8.6, very few family variables are consistently related to the younger sibling's reports of delinquency and substance use, and the results vary by cohort. Only sex and residential mobility are significant for all three groups, with males and those who report frequent moves generally having higher levels of delinquency and substance use.

Table 8.6   **Correlations among family characteristics, sex of the younger sibling and younger sibling delinquency and substance use, by cohort**

	School (12)	School (13)	Vulnerable (12)	Vulnerable (13)	Offender (12)	Offender (13)
(1) Family Disruption[a]	0.04	0.07	0.23	0.25	0.22	0.06
(2) Blended Families[a]	−0.02	−0.03	0.14	−0.11	−0.15	−0.07
(3) Size of Sibship	0.06	−0.03	−0.19	−0.13	0.32*	0.18
(4) No. of Brothers	0.05	−0.01	−0.14	−0.17	0.36**	0.20
(5) No. of Sisters	0.04	−0.06	−0.22	−0.10	0.01	0.02
(6) Father Employed[a]	−0.04	−0.01	0.15	0.11	−0.09	0.09
(7) Mother Employed[a]	−0.07	0.04	−0.36*	0.04	−0.32*	−0.14
(8) Father's Education	−0.03	−0.05	−0.10	0.00	0.37**	0.36**
(9) Mother's Education	−0.05	−0.10*	−0.04	0.08	0.43***	0.37**
(10) Residential Mobility	0.20***	0.12**	0.54***	0.56***	0.09**	0.13
(11) Younger's Sex[a]	0.23***	0.05	0.55***	0.13	0.37**	0.15
(12) Younger's Delinquency	–	0.61***	–	0.45***	–	0.75***
(13) Younger's Substance Use	–	–	–	–	–	–

* p <0.10; ** p <0.05; *** p <0.01

[a] Indicates point biserial correlation (a dichotomous measure associated with a continuous measure).

Six OLS multiple regression analyses were performed next. These regression analyses correspond to the six significant correlations between older and younger siblings' total delinquency and substance use (as given in Table 8.5). Thus, two models were run for the School cohort, based on the significant associations between older and younger siblings' drug use, and between older siblings' drug use and younger siblings' delinquency; three models were run for the Vulnerable cohort, which showed similar associations as the School cohort, as well as a correlation in siblings' delinquency; and one model was run for the Offender cohort, which demonstrated a significant association between siblings' delinquency. Younger siblings' delinquency and substance use were regressed on the older siblings' reports of the same behaviours. The significant (p <0.10) family characteristics shown in Table 8.6 were also included in the model,[3] to determine whether or not the family factors significantly reduce the older sibling coefficient, thereby accounting for sibling resemblance in offending. The unstandardized coefficients and adjusted variance explained for the six models are shown in Table 8.7.

The findings demonstrate that for both the School and Offender cohorts, older siblings' behaviour is significantly associated with younger siblings' behaviour, even after the family background characteristics and sex of the younger sibling are added to the model. As before, the relationships are in opposite directions. For the School cohort, there is a positive association, with increased substance use and delinquency by older siblings related to increased substance use by younger siblings. For the Offender cohort, increased delinquency by older siblings predicts reduced levels of delinquency by younger siblings. For both cohorts, variability in delinquency between older and younger cannot be attributed to shared family characteristics and is likely due to sibling influences and/or characteristics of the sibling relationship.

For the Vulnerable cohort, however, the inclusion of family background characteristics has a strong impact on the sibling relationship. When family variables are added to the model, the direct effect of older siblings' delinquency and substance use on younger siblings' behaviour is no longer significant. These results indicate that siblings' similar behaviour may be attributed to their shared family characteristics, rather than to the nature of the sibling relationship. Siblings' residential mobility, or number of times their family has moved, has a particularly strong effect on younger siblings' outcomes, which is surprising given that this variable has not been extensively assessed in previous work examining sibling effects.

---

3   Sex of the younger sibling was also included in each model to control for its effects on outcomes.

Table 8.7   Younger siblings' delinquency and substance use regressed on older siblings' delinquency and substance use, by cohort (unstandardized coefficients)

		Cohort	
	School	Vulnerable	Offender[1]
Younger's Delinquency on Older's Delinquency			
Older's Delinquency	–	0.24	−0.42**
Number of Brothers	–	–	1.06
Mother Employed	–	−1.39	−6.40**
Father's Education	–	–	1.55
Mother's Education	–	–	2.25
Residential Mobility	–	1.12**	0.01
Younger's Sex	–	3.23**	0.77
Intercept	–	−0.20	5.86
Adjusted R^2	–	0.47	0.39
F	–	7.18***	3.79***
Younger's Delinquency on Older's Substance Use			
Older's Substance Use	0.27*	0.31	–
Mother Employed	–	−1.23	–
Mother's Education	−0.17	–	–
Residential Mobility	0.65***	1.21**	–
Younger's Sex	1.38***	3.62**	–
Intercept	0.59	−0.27	–
Adjusted R^2	0.09	0.45	–
F	7.81***	6.61***	–
Younger's Substance Use on Older's Substance Use			
Older's Substance Use	0.16***	0.10	–
Mother Employed	–	0.36	–
Mother's Education	−0.11*	–	–
Residential Mobility	0.11	0.46***	–
Younger's Sex	0.08	0.18	–
Intercept	0.29*	−0.61	–
Adjusted R^2	0.06	0.24	–
F	4.92***	3.21**	–

Note: n = 266–267 for School cohort; n = 29 for Vulnerable cohort; n = 31 for Offender cohort.
* p < .10; ** p < .05; *** p < .01.

[1] Size of sibship was not included due to the very small sample size and its strong correlation to the variable assessing number of brothers.

Conclusion

These results add to the growing literature demonstrating sibling influences on adolescent delinquency, and, importantly, extend the research to an Australian sample comprised of adolescents with varying levels of criminal involvement. In fact, the results demonstrated that sibling effects differed depending on the cohort examined. The weakest sibling relationships were found for members of the School cohort, the group most closely resembling the general population of young people. For this group, there was little sibling resemblance in levels of delinquency, although older sibling substance use was positively associated with younger siblings' substance use. Although the size of the correlation (0.22) was somewhat smaller than that found in other studies, it is important to note that the majority of sibling pairs in this cohort are of the opposite sex, and most work tends to find stronger effects for same-sex, rather than opposite-sex sibling pairs. Moreover, the effect remained significant even controlling for shared family factors.

Strong, positive sibling effects were found for the Vulnerable group, comprised of adolescents considered 'at-risk' for delinquent behaviour. Although the majority (76 per cent) of siblings in this group are also of the opposite sex, the Pearson correlations in drug use and overall delinquency were both very strong (0.35 and 0.45, respectively). While the sibling effect lost significance in multivariate analyses controlling for shared family characteristics, this result should be taken with some caution, based on the very small sample size. Thus, additional research with larger samples is needed to better determine the ways in which family factors, particularly residential mobility, may affect sibling relationships.

Perhaps the most surprising finding was the strong, negative relationship in sibling delinquent behaviour for the Offender cohort, a group characterized by high levels of delinquency. Although there was no sibling similarity in drug use, older siblings' delinquency is negatively related to younger siblings' delinquency, even controlling for family factors. While sibling effects are often argued as having a genetic basis, this negative relationship is more likely attributed to social influences. The findings suggest that siblings who are involved in criminal activities have a deterrent effect on the likelihood of another sibling engaging in crime. It may be that when younger siblings watch their older siblings become involved in the criminal justice system, and perhaps spend time in detention centres, they become less likely to break the law themselves. Although deterrent theories have not received much support in criminology generally, the perspective may be more applicable on an individual level, in that youth who directly experience the negative effects of having a family member processed by the criminal justice system are likely to refrain from crime.

The negative sibling relationship found for the Offender group is in some contrast to prior research, which generally indicates either positive or non-significant relationships in sibling delinquency. However, these investigations have also failed to include high-level offenders in their samples, and this difference may account for the disparity in findings. It must also be noted that the Offender group contains a very small number of sibling pairs, and the results must be seen as somewhat preliminary. Clearly, then, more research is needed to confirm and further explore whether or not adolescents who have high levels of self-reported delinquency or official contact with the law tend to have deterrent effects on the offending behaviours of their brothers or sisters.

In general, the findings are important in both confirming prior research and demonstrating that the direction and strength of the sibling effect may vary by sibling levels of drug use and delinquency. However, this research does suffer from some limitations that may affect the results, most notably the small sample size. In fact, relatively large numbers of sibling pairs are required for adequate statistical power. Because there are very small numbers of sibling pairs in the Vulnerable and Offender groups, the results must be taken with some caution, but they are provocative and deserve further exploration. Likewise, future studies may wish to explore whether or not characteristics of the sibling relationship (such as levels of warmth or conflict) may vary by the level of offending of siblings, and how such differences may affect sibling resemblance in adolescent delinquency, substance use, or other outcomes.

Chapter 9

Urban Indigenous Young People: Criminality, Accommodation or Resistance

Mark Lynch, Abigail A. Fagan, Emma Ogilvie and Robyn Lincoln[1]

> It must be acknowledged that non-Indigenous interventions in juvenile justice, both historical and contemporary, have been a dismal failure... Franz Fanon (1967) has written about the way the coloniser creates the 'native' as an inferior and subjected being. It is worth extrapolating to consider the extent to which the mainstream juvenile justice system creates the Indigenous juvenile delinquent (Cunneen and White 1995: 154).

> Juvenile offending is increasingly discussed in terms of socio-economic disadvantage and there is no doubt that Aboriginal youth are massively 'disadvantaged'... [however] the concept of 'oppression' is more suitable than 'disadvantage' because it incorporates both the manifestations of disadvantage such as unemployment and the active dimensions of policing and the criminal justice system which have been used to control Aboriginal people (Cunneen 1994: 153).

> What has been described as delinquency could also be regarded as acts of individual defiance. The scale and nature of Aboriginal children's conflict with authority is reflective of a historical defiance (D'Souza 1990: 5).

Taken together, these three quotes draw attention to an important but often overlooked aspect of Indigenous young people's involvement in crime and experience of the criminal justice system. They remind us that criminality is defined by the colonizing culture and is used by both dominant and subordinated cultures: the former, to assert control, and the latter, as a means of resisting that control. The quotes also remind us that non-culturally-specific factors, such as unemployment, may be related to Indigenous offending. However, focusing exclusively on such dimensions may not be productive, as explained by Cunneen:

---

1 This chapter was developed out of research supported by the Criminology Research Council (Lincoln, Lynch and Ogilvie 1998).

The socio-economic or class position of Aboriginal young people may offer some help in understanding their over-representation in police statistics. However, whether Aboriginal young people actually offend more often and more seriously than their non-Aboriginal counterparts is difficult to determine. Policing itself plays such a fundamental role in determining the extent and nature of the offences brought before the court that no simple conclusions can be drawn (Cunneen 1994: 153).

According to Cunneen (1994), it is difficult to identify precursors to criminality without also assessing the ways in which recorded levels of offending reflect the criminal justice response to offending by Indigenous people. The considerable extent to which this perspective has taken hold can be seen in the overwhelming focus upon law and order characterizing Australian literature on Indigenous young people, and the substantial body of research demonstrating that Indigenous young people are over-represented at every stage of the juvenile justice system (Beresford and Omaji 1996, Cunneen 1997). Despite this attention, there is much that remains unknown about Indigenous young people's patterns of offending and how these patterns are associated with the operation of the criminal justice system. As Gale, Bailey-Harris and Wundersitz noted in 1990, 'empirical data on the nature and frequency of offending by Aboriginal youth is almost non-existent. Even less information is available on the personal characteristics of these young offenders' (1990:55). More than a decade later, the situation is largely unchanged. Moreover, we are surprisingly ill-equipped to explain why it is that adolescents from backgrounds characterized by neglect and marginalization nevertheless do not necessarily engage in criminal behaviours (Homel, Lincoln and Herd 1999), and this lack of knowledge is particularly true regarding Indigenous young people who are not officially caught up in the juvenile criminal justice system.

Importantly, there is very little research comparing young Indigenous offenders from disadvantaged backgrounds with young non-Indigenous offenders from equally disadvantaged backgrounds. Apart from the methodological difficulties involved, many researchers may be reluctant to make this comparison due to fear of being considered racist, as well as the possible political implications. If, for example, in controlling for class disadvantage, Indigenous young people are found to offend at a greater rate than their non-Indigenous counterparts, it follows that offending may be at least partially explained by culturally-specific factors (even though racism by criminal justice authorities may still be implicated). Such factors may include expressions of defiance or resistance, or, as is perhaps the concern of those who avoid confronting the issue directly, they may reflect some intrinsic aspect of Indigenous culture not well accommodated for by non-Indigenous society generally, and the criminal justice system in particular. Without making the comparison between Indigenous and non-Indigenous young people, however, we cannot begin to adequately explain reasons for offending, and we fall short of the demand that social scientists seek to provide complete descriptions of the social world.

With these issues in mind, this chapter compares self-reported offending rates of urban Indigenous young people who have not been processed by the criminal justice system, and so cannot be the subject of any over-zealous response by that system, to those reported by two other Sibling Study cohorts: the School cohort, which closely approximates a general population profile of young people, and the Vulnerable cohort, which provides a comparison group representing disadvantage, but not Aboriginality.[2] The chapter begins by examining potential differences between the three groups regarding individual, family, and social risk factors for crime, and then details the prevalence and nature of the offending of each of the three groups. In this manner, the analyses attempt to illustrate the relative contributions of cultural and non-cultural (particularly socio-economic) factors in influencing involvement in crime. That is, to the extent that the urban Indigenous cohort differs from the other two cohorts (particularly the Vulnerable cohort), it is not unreasonable to infer that there are culturally specific factors acting as 'drivers' or 'inhibitors' of offending.

The Urban Indigenous Cohort

The urban Indigenous cohort of the Sibling Study has not been discussed in detail elsewhere in this book, so we will now provide a brief description. Obtaining this group of young people required a great deal of consultation with members of the Aboriginal community. The Aboriginal Justice Advisory Committee (as it was then known) provided a community contact, a young Indigenous woman who worked in conjunction with a female Indigenous Elder. These two women obtained the sample by approaching young Indigenous people who regularly frequented a local park in a relatively disadvantaged residential area with a high density of Aboriginal households.[3] The questionnaires were interviewer-administered, and the interviewers completed the questionnaires for the young people. Respondents were advised that participation was voluntary and that they would not be identified either publicly or to the Sibling Study researchers.

It needs to be noted that the Indigenous interviewers shared some concerns with the researchers about the length and structure of the questionnaire, and, with the researchers' consent, made some modifications to the way in which the questions were asked. The changes were not dramatic, however, and a comparison of the results from the Indigenous cohort and the Indigenous respondents in the other cohorts revealed no significant differences. It should also be noted that the

---

2   The School and Vulnerable cohorts each contain a small number of Indigenous respondents (comprising just over one per cent of the School cohort and approximately 15 per cent of the Vulnerable group), who were excluded from the analyses in order to directly compare Indigenous and non-Indigenous young people. It should also be noted that the Offender cohort was not included in the analyses, as the purpose was to compare groups with social disadvantage but different ethnicity (i.e. the Vulnerable and Urban Indigenous cohorts) with those with more advantaged background characteristics (i.e. the School cohort).

3   While this chapter will refer to the urban Indigenous cohort as simply the 'Indigenous' cohort from this point forward, the group is distinctively 'urban' and any findings should not be generalized to rural or remote groups of Indigenous young people.

Indigenous cohort includes a very small number of respondents (*n*=62). Given these two limitations, the results should be taken with some caution and are best understood as exploratory.

Characteristics of the Three Cohorts

Socio-Economic Factors

While the Sibling Study cannot provide direct measures of household income, a reasonably clear picture of socio-economic status can nevertheless be obtained by examining parental unemployment, occupational status of those working, and level of parental education. Regarding parental employment, the Indigenous and Vulnerable cohorts are clearly disadvantaged, relative to the School group, albeit in different ways. As shown in Table 9.1, almost 40 per cent of the Vulnerable group are from households in which no parents are present, compared to 24 per cent of the Indigenous cohort, but only two per cent of the School cohort. Conversely, unemployment among parents is greater in the Indigenous group (42 per cent) than in either of the other two cohorts. Moreover, adding the percentage unemployed to the percentage living with no parents, we see that two-thirds (66 per cent) of the Indigenous cohort have no working parents living with them, compared to half (51 per cent) of the Vulnerable group and only 11 per cent of the School group.

Table 9.1   Cohort differences in the number of employed parents in household (column percentages)

Employed Parents in Household	Cohort		
	Indigenous	Vulnerable	School
	n=62	*n*=136	*n*=671
0	42	12	9
1	23	29	36
2	8	21	52
No Parents in Household	24	39	2

The Indigenous and Vulnerable cohorts are disadvantaged relative to the School cohort in other ways. As can be seen in Table 9.2, fathers are absent in 60 per cent of the Indigenous households and in 48 per cent of the Vulnerable households; yet this is the case in only 15 per cent of the School families. While mothers are less likely to be absent overall, they are also more likely to be absent in the Indigenous (30 per cent) and Vulnerable (43 per cent) households, compared to the School households (5 per cent). Regarding the type of parental employment reported by respondents, white-collar work is more common in the School cohort, while blue-collar work is more common among the Indigenous and Vulnerable cohorts (see Table 9.2). Moreover, paternal unemployment is more common in the Indigenous and Vulnerable groups than in the School group, although the differences are not great. Maternal unemployment is highest in the Indigenous cohort (56 per cent) and equally less likely in the School (30 per cent) and Vulnerable (26 per cent) groups. This finding may have different meanings for the three cohorts, however. In the School cohort, not working among mothers may denote traditional, stay-at-home mothers engaging in unpaid housework, while in the other two groups, it may be more indicative of involuntary unemployment.

Table 9.2   Cohort differences in parental occupation (column percentages)

			Cohort			
	Indigenous		Vulnerable		School	
Parent Occupation	Mother	Father	Mother	Father	Mother	Father
	n=62	*n*=62	*n*=136	*n*=136	*n*=671	*n*=660
Not Working	56	18	26	13	30	10
Blue-Collar	3	11	10	24	12	34
White-Collar	12	11	20	15	53	41
Not in Household	30	60	43	48	5	14

Similar patterns of relative disadvantage are demonstrated for parental levels of education. There is very little difference between the Indigenous and Vulnerable groups, with 61 and 58 per cent, respectively, in households in which one or both parents left school before completing Grade 12. In contrast, 35 per cent of parents in the School cohort left school before Grade 12.

As these findings demonstrate, the Indigenous and Vulnerable groups have lower rates of parental employment and education relative to the School cohort, and thus can be considered economically disadvantaged. Thus, if we observe differences between these two groups in attitudinal and behavioural characteristics, it may be reasonable to interpret such disparities in 'cultural', rather than 'class', terms.

Quality of Interactions With Parents

Clearly, parental levels of education and employment are only partial measures of the intra-familial factors which might serve as precursors to delinquency. For this reason, it is also useful to examine more affective characteristics of families.

It is frequently argued that Indigenous young people live in families distinguished by low levels of emotional support, where the 'breakdown in parenting' has its genesis in alcoholism, domestic violence, welfare dependence and, ultimately, state intervention (Berseford and Omaji 1996:36, see also Cunneen 1997). Again, however, there has been little research conducted with urban Indigenous young people which addresses these issues. Indeed, much qualitative evidence suggests that family bonds in Indigenous and Torres Strait Islander families are extremely strong, despite the experience of disadvantage and marginalization (Carrington 1993). It does need to be recognized, however, that strong family bonds cannot automatically be equated with effective emotional support (Tatz 2000).

The Sibling Study questionnaire included several measures of family bonding. First, respondents were asked: 'Do your parents or the adults who look after you take much interest in what you do?'. Although originally assessed according to three response choices: 'a lot of interest', 'a bit of interest' and 'very little interest', the first two categories have been collapsed into the 'moderate-high' category, as compared to 'low' interest. As can be seen in Table 9.3, the Vulnerable and Indigenous groups experience less parental interest than do those in the School-based group, with nearly one-fourth of the first two groups reporting low interest in their activities from their parents or adult carers. In contrast, 98 per cent of respondents in the School cohort report moderate-high interest from their parents.

Intra-familial affect was also measured using the Parental Bonding Instrument (Parker, Tupling and Brown 1979). Respondents were asked to report the extent to which their mothers and fathers were affectionate, understanding, and supportive, with levels dichotomized into 'moderate-high' and 'low' support.[4] As shown in Table 9.3, responses on this scale are similar to those reported for parental interest. The School cohort is least likely to report low support (4 per cent). In comparison, between 18 and 20 per cent of the Indigenous and Vulnerable cohorts report low levels of emotional support from parents.

Table 9.3   Cohort differences in parental interest and support (column percentages)

| | Cohort | | |
	Indigenous	Vulnerable	School
Parental Interest			
Low	20	23	2
Moderate-High	80	77	98
n	61	134	658
Parental Support			
Low	18	4	20
Moderate-High	82	96	80
n	39	96	564

In order to further assess the parent-child bond, participants were asked to respond

---

4   This measure comprises 16 items aimed at ascertaining the nature and extent of the parent-child bond, with participants responding to eight statements each, regarding their bond to mothers and fathers, and responses coded on a four-point Likert scale (ranging from 'very often' to 'hardly ever'). Reports for mothers and fathers were summed, and responses dichotomized, with positive responses coded 2 and negative responses coded 1. Those with two or fewer positive scores were then categorized as having a 'low' level of emotional support; all others were categorized as the recipients of 'moderate-high' levels of emotional support. The eight items assessed whether parents: 'spoke to me in a warm and friendly voice', 'gave me as much help as I needed', 'seemed to understand my problems and worries', 'was affectionate to me', 'liked talking things over with me', 'understood what I needed', 'made me feel I was wanted', and 'gave me praise'.

to the general statement: 'Parents usually love their children'. Responses were originally coded on a four-point Likert scale (ranging from 'strongly agree' to 'strongly disagree'), then dichotomized to indicate agreement and disagreement. While most young people agree that parents usually love their children, the Indigenous and Vulnerable groups are less likely to agree (82 and 84 per cent, respectively), compared to the School cohort (93 per cent).

The final intra-familial affective factor relates directly to the central focus of this chapter: offending behaviour. Respondents were asked whether they felt their parents would stick by them if they were caught doing something against the law. The four response choices were dichotomized to compare those who responded 'always' with the combined other three groups (those reporting 'mostly', 'no' and 'unsure'). The pattern of responses shown in Table 9.4 is quite different than seen for previous results. The Vulnerable cohort is least certain that their parents would always stick by them (34 per cent), the School group is somewhat more certain (44 per cent), and the Indigenous group is very confident of parental support, with 73 per cent believing their parents would always stick by them if they were caught doing something against the law.

Table 9.4   Cohort differences in confidence that parents would stick by you if caught doing something against the law (column percentages)

	Cohort		
Parents Will Stick by You	Indigenous	Vulnerable	School
	n=62	*n*=134	*n*=653
Always	73	34	44
Mostly/No/Unsure	27	66	56

Our analysis so far has examined differences in social disadvantage and affective support among the three cohorts of young people. From a structural perspective, the results demonstrate that members of the School cohort are relatively advantaged in comparison to members of the other two groups. Regarding family affection/support, the situation is somewhat more complex. The School cohort is more likely than the other two to feel that their parents are interested in their lives and provide emotional support, but the Indigenous group is most likely to feel that their parents will stick by them if they were caught doing something against the law.

From the Family to the Psyche

The following section focuses upon individual attributes associated with offending. General attitudes regarding self and peers are considered first, followed by particular beliefs regarding the law and police.

Social inclusion is likely to lead to marginalization and influence one's sense of self. The argument that Indigenous young people are 'lost', seeing little prospect for their future given their immediate histories of poverty, lack of education and lack of employment, is frequently advanced to explain subsequent engagement in criminal activity (Beresford and Omaji 1996). If Indigenous young people do not feel a part of Australian society, they are unlikely to experience any particular hopes for the future and may be more likely to display resistant and/or defiant attitudes and practices.

In order to examine participants' sense of hopelessness, respondents were asked: 'How sure are you that things will work out OK in the future?' The five possible answers were then collapsed into three responses: 'very/pretty sure' (things will work out), 'not too sure/won't work out at all' and 'don't know'. The School group is most confident about the future, with 73 per cent at least pretty sure things will work out for them (see Table 9.5). In contrast, only 57 per cent of the Vulnerable group and 46 per cent of the Indigenous group felt the same.

Table 9.5   Cohort differences in the belief that things will work out OK in the future (column percentages)

Things Will Work Out OK	Cohort		
	Indigenous $n=57$	Vulnerable $n=129$	School $n=655$
Very/Pretty Sure	46	57	73
Unsure/Things Won't Work Out	44	30	19
Don't Know	11	14	8

Where access to resources is limited, crime may become an attractive and exciting option. In fact, attitudes conducive to risk-taking and impulsivity are strongly implicated in youth crime, and it is important to examine whether these attitudes are more likely to be held by marginalized (i.e. the Indigenous or Vulnerable groups) than general (i.e. the School group) populations. Attitudes regarding risk-seeking and impulsivity are measured using items from the Low Self-Control Scale (Grasmick *et al* 1993). The first measure is comprised of two questions, assessing young people's level of agreement that: 'Sometimes it's exciting to do things if they might get me into trouble,' and 'Sometimes I do things that are a bit risky'. The measure of impulsivity was derived from three questions regarding agreement that: 'I'm more interested in what's happening now than what might happen in the future', 'I often do things without stopping to think about it' and 'Sometimes I do something risky just for the fun of it'. For each of the two measures, answers were originally assessed on a four-point Likert scale, then dichotomized to differentiate between those who strongly agreed with the statement (those in the 'high' category) with all others ('moderate-low').

As can be seen in Table 9.6, the Vulnerable group scores highest in both risk-seeking and impulsivity. Twenty-eight per cent of the Vulnerable group reports high risk-seeking, while 10 per cent of the School cohort and nine per cent of the Indigenous cohort report high levels. For impulsivity, those in the Indigenous group report similarly high levels (16 per cent), compared to the Vulnerable group (19 per cent), while only seven per cent of those in the School cohort report high levels of impulsivity.

Table 9.6   **Cohort differences in levels of risk-seeking and impulsivity (column percentages)**

		Cohort	
	Indigenous	Vulnerable	School
Risk-Seeking	*n*=54	*n*=134	*n*=662
High	9	28	10
Moderate-Low	91	72	90
Impulsivity	*n*=58	*n*=135	*n*=668
High	16	19	7
Moderate-Low	85	81	93

Offending-Related Attitudes

We move now to more specific attitudes directly related to criminal behaviour and the police. The first issue concerns attitudes towards breaking the law. Respondents were asked their level of agreement regarding the statement: 'It's OK to break the law if you can get away with it'. The item was originally coded on a four-point Likert scale (from 'strongly agree' to 'strongly disagree'), then dichotomized as either agreeing (coded 'yes') or disagreeing (coded 'no'). As shown in Table 9.7, the School group is least likely to agree with this statement (11 per cent), while approximately one-third of the Vulnerable (38 per cent) and Indigenous (34 per cent) cohorts agree. Likewise, only nine per cent of the School group agree that: 'We would be better off without the police', compared to 41 per cent of the Indigenous group and 35 per cent of the Vulnerable group. Similar results are found regarding the item: 'You can respect a police officer'. As shown in Table 9.7, 87 per cent of the School group agree that they could respect the police, compared to 56 per cent of the Vulnerable group and only 35 per cent of the Indigenous group. In summary, the results demonstrate that the Vulnerable and Indigenous groups are more likely than the School group to have negative attitudes towards the law and police, and the Indigenous group is more likely than the Vulnerable cohort to have low levels of respect for the police.

Table 9.7   **Cohort differences in attitudes related to the law and police (row percentages)**

Attitudes to the Law and Police					Cohort				
	Indigenous			Vulnerable			School		
	Yes	No	*n*	Yes	No	*n*	Yes	No	*n*
OK to Break Law	34	66	53	38	62	132	11	89	660
Better w/out Police	41	59	61	35	65	133	9	91	665
Respect for Police	35	65	48	56	44	129	87	13	629

These findings are consistent with the focus upon antagonism between police and Indigenous young people within Australian criminology (and, indeed, the wider community). It has been argued that the hostility between police and Indigenous young people is caused by such factors as the role of the police in colonization, the emphasized masculinity of the two groups, and the specific practices police adopt (Beresford and Omaji 1996, Luke and Cunneen 1995, Cunneen 1997). We would also expect Indigenous respondents to report the highest levels of anti-police sentiment if they have high levels of negative contact with the law. However, it is critical to remember that such hostility may be an indicator of resistance, as described by Beresford and Omaji:

> The attitudes and practices police adopt towards Aboriginal youth contribute to their marginalisation from society… Equally disturbing is the internalisation of a feeling of hostility to the wider society that has accompanied their poor relationships with the police (1996: 73–74).

In this manner, Indigenous young people may react to marginalization and social exclusion with resistance. How likely are they to be joined in this defiance by like-minded individuals, namely, their peers?

Attitudes Towards Peers

The importance of peer relations in terms of adolescent criminality cannot be overlooked (Ogilvie and Lynch 2001), and peer relationships may be particularly important in explaining young Indigenous offending behaviours (Ogilvie and Van Zyl 2001). The Sibling Study questionnaire contains nine items relating to peer alignment and propensity to offend. Participants were asked to report the action they would take if they had a friend who started engaging in each of the following criminal activities: shoplifting, breaking into houses, stealing cars, bullying, vandalizing things, graffiti, getting drunk (a lot), using drugs and getting into fights. Respondents were provided with six possible responses, ranging from reporting their friends (scored 1) to joining in (scored 6). Scores were then summed and a dichotomous measure constructed, with the 'high' category representing the top quartile, and all lower scores collapsed into the 'moderate-low' category. The results indicate that Indigenous respondents are the most likely to report that they would join in with offending peers, with 57 per cent indicating a high level of peer alignment, compared to 44 per cent of the Vulnerable group and 19 per cent of the School group (see Table 9.8). Surprisingly, additional analyses do not indicate that the Indigenous respondents are more peer-oriented, in terms of their friends' moral influence, as shown in Table 9.8. When asked to describe whether or not they tend to think the same as their friends regarding what is right and wrong, only 43 per cent of the Indigenous group responded affirmatively, while 70 per cent of the Vulnerable cohort and 69 per cent of the School group report that they always or often think the same as their friends.

Table 9.8   Cohort differences in peer factors (column percentages)

	Indigenous	Cohort Vulnerable	School
Peer Alignment			
High	57	44	19
Moderate-Low	43	56	81
n	61	134	665
Think Same as Friends About Right and Wrong			
Always/Often	43	70	69
Sometimes/Never	57	30	31
n	47	132	636

Self-Reported Offending

The last section of this chapter compares the offending behaviours of each of the three cohorts, using the Australian Self-Report Delinquency Scale (ASRDS) (Mak 1993) described in Chapter 2. Analyses rely on the 33-item total delinquency scale and six sub-scales.

For general offending, as well as all offence types, the young people in the Indigenous and Vulnerable cohorts have higher self-reported offending rates than do members of the School group (see Table 9.9). The majority of the Indigenous and Vulnerable groups (85 and 75 per cent, respectively) report two or more general offences, compared to half (52 per cent) the School cohort, and offending rates of the former are generally twice that of the latter for each of the sub-scales. In addition, the Indigenous cohort has higher rates than the Vulnerable group for overall offending and some offence types, but the differences are not large. In fact, the two groups are nearly identical in their reports of alcohol and drug offences and illegal vehicle use. The largest differences are for theft, public disorder, and assault, but even for these crimes, the Indigenous rates are only approximately 1.4 times higher than those of the Vulnerable group. Nonetheless, the results indicate that Indigenous young people are somewhat more likely than those in the Vulnerable cohort to be involved in property crimes or crimes against the person.

The general findings are consistent with previous research examining official statistics (Gale *et al* 1990, Cunneen 1997), with Indigenous young people over-represented compared to the general population. The results may also help explain Indigenous young peoples' high profile as offenders, as the crimes for which they are most over-represented are also those most likely to garner outrage from the public and response from the police (i.e. violent crimes and offences against the person).

**Table 9.9   Cohort differences in self-reported delinquency
(per cent of cohort reporting two or more offences)**

Offence Type	Cohort		
	Indigenous *n*=47	Vulnerable *n*=118	School *n*=589
Total Delinquency	85	75	52
Public Disorder	55	41	19
Vandalism	38	31	12
Illegal Vehicle Use	26	25	10
Theft	53	37	14
Assault	38	27	11
Alcohol/Drug Use	49	50	19

Drawing the Threads Together

This chapter began by acknowledging the paucity of empirical data (particularly self-reported data) that may be drawn upon to explain factors related to Indigenous offending and the over-representation of Indigenous young people in the criminal justice system.   Moreover, we suggested that this lack of knowledge was compounded by researchers' reluctance to consider the possibility that over-representation may be related to culturally-specific factors (as well as to racism in the system), and that such failure of nerve contradicts the first task of social scientists, to provide an accurate and informative description of the nature of the social world.

The results described in this chapter cannot resolve the many issues related to an over-representation of Indigenous offenders, nor do they provide a complete description of the social factors underpinning Indigenous offending. However, this chapter demonstrates several important findings that contribute to a better understanding of the nature and reasons for offending by Indigenous young people, and hopefully, will encourage other researchers to conduct similar investigations. For example, the analyses demonstrate the benefits and appropriateness of using this type of research design. More specifically, the use of the two comparison groups allows multiple conclusions to be drawn. First, we can demonstrate that the social/environmental precursors of Indigenous offending are quite different from those of the general population of young people (i.e. the School group). More importantly, we also highlight differences between Indigenous young people and those from equally marginalized backgrounds (at least regarding the economic and social factors considered here) who are not Indigenous (i.e. the Vulnerable cohort). If we had accepted the methodological and political difficulties discouraging a comparison between the Indigenous and Vulnerable cohorts, and restricted our analysis to a comparison of the Indigenous and School cohorts, our conclusions would have been incomplete and unable to reveal the complexity in the relationship between Indigenous status, disadvantage and involvement in crime.

The analyses demonstrate that Indigenous young people are far more likely than the School cohort to report offending behaviours, and that they are economically and socially disadvantaged compared to the general youth population. These results are not surprising and have also been reported by others (Blagg 1997, Cunneen 1999, Lincoln and Wilson 2000).

By including the Vulnerable cohort in the analyses, we were able to generate a more complete (and perhaps realistic) analysis of Indigenous offending. More specifically, the data show very similar offending rates for the Indigenous and Vulnerable cohorts, dispelling the notion that Indigenous young people are simply more apt to engage in crime. Nonetheless, the analyses also demonstrate that young people in the Indigenous cohort are somewhat more likely to engage in certain types of crime than are members of the Vulnerable group, namely offences against the person and property crimes. Because these crimes are considered more serious by the public and police, Indigenous young people may be more likely to come into contact with the criminal justice system and so be labelled as offenders by the criminal justice system and wider society. Thus, there is some support for the notion that the heightened representation of Indigenous young people as offenders is at least partially explained by the level of attention paid to the crimes they typically commit, and a more certain response by the criminal justice system to the individuals committing those offences.

The comparison of Indigenous and Vulnerable young people has other implications. For example, while the Indigenous and Vulnerable cohorts tend to experience similar levels of economic disadvantage compared to the School group, they display somewhat different attitudes towards the law and police. Specifically, the Indigenous respondents are less likely to believe in the need for police, or to respect police officers, and they are more certain that their families will support them if they break the law. These findings suggest that offending by Indigenous young people may indeed be explained (at least in part) as resistance to the law brought about by cultural oppression. It is also possible that respondents in the Vulnerable group have slightly lower rates of offending because they suffer from economic disadvantage, but not necessarily institutional or personal discrimination, and so do not feel the same need to oppose systems of oppression.

Clearly, the results in this chapter are preliminary and must be taken with some caution, particularly due to the very small sample size of the Indigenous cohort and the reliance on bivariate analyses. Nonetheless, they represent an attempt to reveal some of the little recognized underlying dynamics of an extraordinarily complex social phenomenon. Moreover, the findings are in accord with previous research that argues for the recognition of structural factors of disadvantage, together with cultural factors of marginalization, and the complex manner in which these two interact (Broadhurst 1997, Blagg 1997, Cunneen 1999, Lincoln and Wilson 2000). Further research is clearly needed to examine these issues, particularly more precise identification of the cultural factors that may propel or protect Indigenous young people from becoming involved in offending.

At the risk of 'pushing' the data, the findings suggest other, unknown positive influences operating within the Indigenous community. As stated, general offending amongst Indigenous young people is not much different from the offending of other equally disadvantaged young people (i.e. the Vulnerable group).

When we take into account the data suggesting that the offending of Indigenous young people is further propelled by defiance/resistance, it is perhaps surprising that Indigenous offending is not much higher, and this contradiction provides a tantalizing suggestion that there are culturally specific protective factors at work of which we are only dimly aware.

Chapter 10

Adolescent Victimization and Involvement in Crime

Abigail A. Fagan, Ross Homel, Ian O'Connor and Rosie Teague

Introduction

The victimization of young people is increasingly being recognized as a major social problem, with adolescents more likely than adults to be victims of crime, particularly violent assault (Australian Bureau of Statistics 1998, Finkelhor 1997, Queensland Police Service 2000, Snyder and Sickmund 1999, Stewart and Homel 1994). Moreover, young people are at-risk of victimization within their homes, as well as in their schools, neighbourhoods, and peer groups. The consequences of such experiences can be devastating and long-lasting, resulting not only in immediate physical harm or loss of property, but also in a variety of short- and long-term medical, psychological, social and behavioural problems, including involvement in crime.

This chapter utilizes data from the Sibling Study to investigate the victimization of young people in more detail. We focus on respondents' perceptions of victimization, and how such experiences may increase their likelihood of offending. The current study expands upon prior research to explore the impact of a diverse set of victimization experiences—including property crime, assault by non-family members, child abuse, and other traumatic family experiences—on varying levels of criminal involvement. Moreover, the study recognizes that not all victims become offenders and that risk and protective factors influence some children to break the law, while increasing others' resilience to crime.

The Prevalence of Victimization

It is very difficult to obtain accurate prevalence rates of the major forms of child maltreatment (i.e. physical, sexual, and emotional abuse, as well as neglect), likely due to vast disparity in the ways in which maltreatment is defined and measured (particularly when comparing self-report and official statistics); the fact that abuse is generally under-reported; and the difficulty in substantiating claims of abuse and neglect (Australian Institute of Health and Welfare 2001, Falshaw, Browne and

Hollin 1996, Howing, Wodarski, Kurtz, Gaudin and Herbst 1990, Kotch, Muller and Blakely 1999, Widom 1989a). Despite these problems, child maltreatment is widespread. According to 1995–96 statistics from the Australian Institute of Health and Welfare (Broadbent and Bentley 1997), nearly 30,000 children (5.8 victims per 1,000 children) in Australia were substantiated as victims of child maltreatment. Self-report surveys generally result in higher prevalence rates of abuse. For example, the 1985 National Family Violence Survey (NFVS) (Straus and Gelles 1990), conducted with a representative sample of households in the United States, estimated that 110 per 1,000 children were victims of severe physical abuse. In addition, Finkelhor (1994) estimates that 20 per cent of women and five to 10 per cent of men have experienced child sexual abuse.

Although maltreatment affects children of all backgrounds, certain children appear to be particularly at-risk. Girls are overwhelmingly more likely than boys to be victims of sexual abuse (Australian Institute of Health and Welfare 2001, Finkelhor and Baron 1986, Kotch *et al* 1999, Trickett and Putnam 1998), though the prevalence of child homicide, neglect, physical abuse, and emotional abuse does not appear to vary by sex (Australian Institute of Health and Welfare 2001, U.S. Department of Health and Human Services 2001b). Indigenous young people in Australia, as well as African American and Native American youth in the United States, are more likely to be victims according to official statistics (Australian Institute of Health and Welfare 2001, U.S. Department of Health and Human Services 2001b), as are those from lower-class families (Kotch *et al* 1999, Panel on Research on Child Abuse and Neglect 1993). Finally, research demonstrates that younger children are more at-risk of maltreatment than are teenagers (Australian Institute of Health and Welfare 2001, Council on Scientific Affairs 1993, Kotch *et al* 1999). It is important to note, however, that adolescents may face significant amounts of victimization, including abuse that was initiated in childhood and continues into adolescence (Brezina 1998, Lourie 1977).

While official reports of child maltreatment generally focus on four major types of victimization—physical, sexual, or emotional abuse, or neglect—young people may experience other types of victimization and/or traumatic events. For example, a substantial number of children are at-risk by witnessing parental violence (Edelson 1999, MacEwen 1994, Smith 1998), though the prevalence and consequences of this type of victimization are largely unknown, given that partner abuse itself is highly under-reported. Young people are also at high risk of victimization by non-family members. Data from the 1996 American National Crime Victimization Survey (NCVS) demonstrate that adolescents are most often victimized by strangers (responsible in 36 per cent of all cases), followed by friends (34 per cent), acquaintances (18 per cent) , and family members (11 per cent) (Snyder and Sickmund 1999). Thus, young people may be targets of assault, larceny, vandalism, bullying, and other crimes, and these acts are likely to occur outside the home, in schools, neighbourhoods, and other public places (Burrows, Homel and Gallois forthcoming, Fagan 2001a).

The demographic characteristics of adolescent victims of non-family violence are similar to those who experience maltreatment at home. Regarding gender differences, males are more likely than females to be victims of larceny, physical assault, and robbery, with differences greater for more serious types of victimization (Australia Bureau of Statistics 1998, Finkelhor and Ormrod 2000, Queensland Police Service 2000, Snyder and Sickmund 1999, Stewart and Homel 1994). However, girls comprise the majority of all officially reported cases of sexual assault (Finkelhor and Ormrod 2000, Queensland Police Service 2000). In the United States, minority groups are more likely to be victimized than whites, particularly for violent crimes (Baker, Mednick and Carothers 1989, Finkelhor and Ormrod 2000, Hashima and Finkelhor 1999, Snyder and Sickmund 1999). Finally, teenagers are more likely than younger children to be victims of most forms of crime (Finkelhor and Ormrod 2000, Queensland Police Service 2000).

Consequences of Victimization

Just as adolescent victimization can take many forms, so, too, can the consequences of such traumatic events. While this chapter focuses on criminal outcomes of victimization, it is important to realize that victimization may result in a plethora of other negative consequences, which may be severe, long lasting, and overlapping.

Child Maltreatment and Criminal Offending

There has been much research examining the relationship between childhood maltreatment and criminal offending.[1] In general, retrospective research has produced a very strong correlation between victimization and crime, with in-depth interviews of incarcerated offenders revealing that as many as 75 per cent report histories of childhood abuse and neglect (Chesney-Lind and Rodriguez 1983, Romano and De Luca 1997), and interviews of non-incarcerated young people demonstrate rates of up to 80 per cent (O'Connor 1989, Russell 1998, Welsh, Archambault, Janus and Brown 1995). Other retrospective studies, particularly those incorporating large, diverse samples of offenders, report lower rates, estimating that 5 to 35 per cent of convicted criminals report histories of childhood physical or sexual abuse (Benoit and Kennedy 1992, Dembo *et al* 1991, Dutton and Hart 1994, Harlow 1999, Lake 1995, McClellan, Farabee and Crouch 1997, Weeks and Widom 1998).

Prospective investigations, which follow maltreated children over time, have also found that victims are more likely than non-victims to become offenders (Kakar 1996, Maxfield and Widom 1996, Smith and Thornberry 1995, Widom 1989b, Zingraff, Leiter, Myers and Johnsen 1993). In addition, some studies demonstrate that victims are more likely to be arrested for violent crimes (Smith

---

1   A complete review of the literature is beyond the scope of this chapter. However, see particularly Fagan (2001b), Smith and O'Connor (1997) and Widom (1989a) for more detail regarding the relationship between childhood maltreatment and involvement in crime.

and Thornberry 1995, Widom 1989b); arrested more frequently (Smith and Thornberry 1995, Widom 1989b); and arrested at earlier ages (Widom 1989b), compared to non-victims. Neglect has also been identified as an important risk factor for later offending, and the combination of neglect and physical abuse also increases the likelihood of criminal involvement (Maxfield and Widom 1996, Smith and Thornberry 1995, Widom 1989b, Zingraff *et al* 1993). Despite this evidence, prospective studies also demonstrate that not all victims become involved in crime. For example, several investigations find that victims of sexual abuse are no more likely than non-victims to be arrested, particularly for violent crimes (Widom and Ames 1994, Zingraff *et al* 1993).

Other Forms of Victimization and Offending

While there is much research investigating the relationship between childhood maltreatment and criminal offending, there is less evidence exploring the impact of other types of victimization on crime. However, some retrospective studies report that offenders have significant histories of victimization experienced outside the home, including robbery, assault, and sexual assault (Gilfus 1992, Lake 1995, McCllelan *et al* 1997). Moreover, Fagan's (2001a) prospective study, using data from the National Youth Survey, demonstrates that adolescent victimization perpetrated by non-family members is significantly related to adult involvement in a variety of crimes, including general and index offending, as well as assault and theft. Similarly, both retrospective and prospective investigations of the effects of witnessing parental violence indicate that victims are likely to engage in child or spouse abuse (Doumas, Margolin and John 1994, Edleson 1999, Hotaling, Straus, and Lincoln 1990, Mihalic and Elliott 1997, Swinford, DeMaris, Cernkovich and Giordano 2000), violence against parents or siblings (Hotaling *et al* 1990, Langhinrichsen-Rohling and Neidig 1995, Straus 1990), violence against others (Hotaling *et al* 1990, Lake 1989), and externalizing or internalizing behaviours (O'Keefe 1994, Smith 1998).

Effects of Offending on Victimization

While there is much research indicating that victimization may lead to offending, it is also evident that offending may increase the risk of victimization. Routine activities theory posits that one's risk of victimization depends on one's lifestyle and daily activities (Cohen and Felson 1979, Jensen and Brownfield 1986). Thus, offenders may be at particular risk of victimization, due to the amount of time they spend in risky environments (including delinquent gangs or peer groups, 'hot spots' where crime is likely to occur, and so on), or engaging in dangerous and/or illegal activities (Sampson and Lauritsen 1993). Evidence supports this theory, with several longitudinal investigations demonstrating that offenders have higher rates of victimization than non-offenders (Esbensen and Huizinga 1991, Lauritsen *et al* 1991). In addition, interviews with homeless/runaway young people and prostitutes reveal high rates of victimization among these populations, suggesting, again, that those who spend time in risky environments face an increased likelihood of becoming victims of crime.

In summary, the disparity in findings between retrospective and prospective studies, as well as the fact that many victims do not become offenders, indicate the need for further exploration of the link between maltreatment and offending. Particularly needed are investigations that take into account the risk and protective factors that influence some victims to become offenders, while strengthening other victims' resiliency to crime. In addition, further research is needed not only to investigate the ways in which victimization outside the home may lead to offending, but also to compare the effects of various types of victimization on a wide variety of criminal outcomes.

Research Method

This chapter uses data from the School, Vulnerable, and Offender cohorts of the Sibling Study to explore these issues.

The prevalence of lifetime victimization was assessed based on responses to two questions. First, respondents were asked: 'Have you ever been a victim of crime?'. Because not all young people may identify certain types of experiences as 'crimes' (particularly family-perpetrated violence and/or sexual assaults), respondents were also asked: 'Sometimes bad things happen to people which affect them for a long time afterwards. Has anything like that ever happened to you?' Responses to these two questions were then combined, to obtain a total score of lifetime victimization.[2]

Bivariate Results

The Prevalence of Victimization

As shown in Table 10.1, 17 per cent of the sample (n=181) reported at least one lifetime victimization event. Detailed responses to the two victimization questions indicated that the young people suffered a wide variety of victimization experiences, with many reporting very severe episodes of violence, perpetrated by family members, friends, and strangers. For example, adolescents reported: 'I was raped by a next door neighbour four or five years ago and also (by) a family friend'; 'I was abducted. The guy who took me was going to shoot me'; and 'My father molested me. I was very hurt and still am after seven years'. Not all victimization experiences involved violent assaults, however. In fact, a significant

---

2   The limitations of this measure will be discussed in more detail later in the chapter. However, it is important to note that the two victimization questions asked in the Sibling Study did not elicit specific details regarding the nature of the traumatic experience, such as the victim/perpetrator relationship, the precise setting of the victimization experience, and so on. Thus, the results described must be taken with some caution.

number of young people reported being 'rolled' by others or having property stolen from them. Still others recounted other types of traumatic events experienced during their lives, such as: 'My stepfather was killed in a tractor accident and I witnessed it', and 'My mum left when I was three and I still haven't forgotten that night'.

Chi-square analysis was performed to identify whether or not victims differed from non-victims according to the cohort from which they were drawn and by demographic characteristics. As shown in Table 10.1, victims were significantly more likely to belong to the Vulnerable and Offender cohorts (comprising 33 and 37 per cent of these groups, respectively), than the School cohort (seven per cent). Victims were also more likely to be members of non-traditional families (i.e. those living with step-parents, single parents or no parents), compared to those from two-parent families. Although not shown in Table 10.1, older respondents, particularly those aged 16 and older, were more likely than younger children to report victimization, which is not surprising given that the survey assessed lifetime victimization, and older respondents would have had more time to be victimized. Finally, victims were somewhat more likely to be Indigenous (25 per cent) than non-Indigenous (17 per cent); and male (18 per cent) rather than female (15 per cent).

Table 10.1   Total victimization, by demographic characteristics

	% Victim	(*n*)
Total Victimization	17	(181)
*Cohort***		
School	7	(46)
Vulnerable	33	(51)
Offender	37	(82)
*Sex**		
Female	15	(75)
Male	18	(104)
*Race/Ethnicity**		
Non-Indigenous	17	(165)
Indigenous	25	(16)
*Family Structure***		
Two Parent	10	(64)
Single Parent	22	(19)
Step Parent	25	(44)
Other Family Type	35	(38)

*p < 0.10; **p <0 .05; ***p <0 .01

Because the types of victimization reported by young people varied extensively, a content analysis of responses to the two victim questions was performed, and a typography of victimization constructed. This procedure yielded four major types of victimization/trauma: 'theft', 'other violence', 'family violence' and 'other trauma'. Theft includes theft of personal property (e.g. bike, body board, clothing, etc.), breaking and entering, and motor vehicle theft. Other violence includes serious violent crimes perpetrated by non-family members, such as robbery; police harassment or assault; attempted or completed physical or sexual assault; attempted murder or abduction; stalking; and sexual harassment. Victims of family violence reported physical, sexual, or emotional abuse perpetrated by family members and witnessing violence between family members. The 'other trauma' category represents family/relationship problems and other negative events experienced within and outside the family, such as the death of a loved one; parental divorce, separation, or remarriage; problems with friends or significant others; poor relationships with parents; arrest of a family member; and so on.

Table 10.2 details the percentage of respondents reporting each type of victimization. Respondents were most likely to report having experienced theft (six per cent of the total sample) and other violence (six per cent). Other trauma was somewhat less likely to be reported (five per cent), and only 23 respondents (two per cent) reported family violence. Though these results are consistent with research demonstrating that adolescent victimization is more likely to occur outside the family than within the home (Burrows *et al* forthcoming, Fagan 2001a, Snyder and Sickmund 1999), given the general under-reporting of family violence, it is likely that family victimization is under-represented in the Sibling Study.

Chi-square analysis was conducted to discover whether or not victims of each of the four types of victimization differed from non-victims. As shown in Table 10.2, young people from all four victim categories were more likely than non-victims to be members of the Vulnerable and Offender cohorts. In addition, those experiencing other violence, family violence, and other trauma were less likely than non-victims to live in two-parent families. Finally, females were more likely than males to experience family violence, while males were more likely to report theft victimization, and Indigenous victims were more likely than non-Indigenous victims to report other trauma. Although these results parallel many of the findings demonstrated for total victimization, they should be taken with caution, as many of the categories involve very small numbers of victims.

The data also reveal that many young people suffered multiple experiences of victimization, with 181 respondents reporting a total of 206 victimization experiences.[3] In addition, bivariate analyses demonstrated a significant correlation between other trauma and other violence ($r=0.09$, $p<0.01$), as well as between other trauma and theft ($r=0.10$, $p <0.01$), suggesting that young people who reported crises in their relationships with friends and family members (i.e. other trauma) were particularly likely to experience additional forms of victimization.

---

3   Although the number of young people reporting repeat victimization is not detailed in any of the tables, adding the prevalence rates of the four types of victimization outlined in Table 10.2 results in a total of 206 victimization experiences, and Table 10.1 indicates that 181 adolescents reported one or more types of victimization.

Table 10.2   Sub-types of victimization, by demographic characteristics (per cent victimized [n])

	Theft	Other Violence	Family Violence	Other Trauma
Total Victimization (*n*)	6 (68)	6 (63)	2 (23)	5 (52)
Cohort	***	***	**[1]	***
School	2 (16)	2 (11)	1 (9)	2 (12)
Vulnerable	15 (23)	12 (18)	4 (6)	8 (12)
Offender	13 (29)	15 (33)	4 (8)	12 (27)
Sex	***			***
Female	3 (16)	5 (25)	4 (18)	4 (21)
Male	9 (52)[1]	7 (37)[1]	1 (5)[1]	5 (30)***[1]
Race/Ethnicity				
Non-Indigenous	6 (61)	6 (57)	2 (22)	5 (45)
Indigenous	11 (7)[1]	9 (6)***[1]	2 (1)**[1]	11 (7)***
Family Structure				
Two Parent	5 (32)	3 (16)	1 (7)	2 (14)
Single Parent	7 (14)	9 (17)	3 (6)	8 (15)
Step Parent	4 (3)	8 (6)	5 (4)	13 (10)
Other Type	9 (10)	15 (16)	5 (5)	10 (11)

*p < 0.10; **p <0.05; ***p <0.01.

[1] Statistic must be taken with caution, as the variable has an expected cell count less than five.

The Relationship between Victimization and Involvement in Crime

As discussed previously, research indicates both that victimization is likely to lead to involvement in crime, and that criminal involvement increases the likelihood of victimization. Bivariate and multivariate analyses were performed in order to examine these relationships in the Sibling Study. It should be noted, however, that results are based on cross-sectional data and cannot fully assess the temporal ordering of these variables.

Criminal involvement was measured using the Australian Self-Report Delinquency Scale (ASRDS) (Mak 1993), as described in Chapter 2, as well as Homel's 'crime status' variable, which was designed to capture a range of adolescent offences and involvement with formal agencies. The crime status variable was based upon young people's reports of the specific offences they committed; self-reports of whether or not they had been cautioned by police, appeared in court, or sentenced to a watch house or detention centre; and the cohort from which they were drawn. Those who reported no contact with the criminal justice system and who were not members of the Offender or Vulnerable cohorts were classified according to their level of self-reported offending. These adolescents were then classified as having reported no offences, minor offences (including shoplifting, graffiti, vandalism, and use of minor drugs or alcohol, and so on), or serious offences (including crimes such as use of 'hard' drugs, physical and sexual assault, stealing, robbery, and auto theft). Young people from the Offender cohort, as well as those reporting contact with formal agencies, were classified as belonging to one of the three groups: minor contacts (cautioned), firmer contacts (court appearance or supervision), and detention (past or current detention). A six-category scale, ranging from 'no offences' to 'detention' was then created, with higher scores indicating more serious offending and/or contact with the criminal justice system.

Using the crime status variable, the data demonstrate a strong bivariate association between victimization and offending, with those who report more serious offences and higher levels of involvement with the criminal justice system more likely to be victims. The results are strongest for total victimization. As shown in Table 10.3, six per cent of those with no offences reported one or more episodes of victimization during their lifetime, compared to 10 per cent of minor offenders, 11 per cent of serious offenders, 15 per cent of those with minor contact with the criminal justice system, 41 per cent of those with firmer contact, and 33 per cent of those in detention. Thus, those in detention were five times more likely to have a lifetime history of victimization compared to non-offenders. Similar results were found for the relationship between the four types of victimization and crime status. As shown in Table 10.3, the relationships were significant for each type of victimization, and were strongest for victims of theft, other violence and other trauma. For example, four per cent of non-offenders were victims of theft, compared to 15 per cent of those with firmer contacts and 13 per cent of those in detention. Likewise, none of the non-offenders reported being victims of other violence, compared to 19 per cent of those with firmer contacts with the criminal justice system, and 13 per cent of those in detention.

A somewhat different picture emerged for family violence, in that young people with lower levels of criminal involvement were more likely to report victimization than those with higher levels (see Table 10.3). None of the young people in the non-offending group reported a history of family violence, and there were also very small numbers of victims among the detention (one per cent) and firmer contacts (three per cent) groups. In contrast, 10 per cent of those with minor contacts with the criminal justice system reported family victimization. While these results are somewhat difficult to interpret, it is important to remember that 18 of the 23 victims of family violence were young women, and it may be that females are more likely than males to respond to family violence, particularly sexual abuse, with internalizing behaviours or less serious types of offending, such as running away or drug/alcohol use (Chesney-Lind 1997, Finkelhor 1995, Gutierres and Reich 1981, Hawke, Jainhill and De Leon 2000, Romano and De Luca 2001, Widom, Ireland and Glynn 1995).

Table 10.3 Crime status and history of victimization
(per cent of offenders reporting victimization; row percentages)

Crime Status	Victimization Type					
	Total Victim	Theft	Other Violence	Family Violence	Other Trauma	n
No Offence	6	4	0	0	2	194
Minor Offence	10	2	2	3	4	255
Serious Offence	11	5	4	2	2	249
Minor Contact	15	4	2	7	1	94
Firmer Contact	41	15	19	3	12	156
Detention	33	13	13	1	12	114
Gamma	0.48***	0.41***	0.62***	0.21*	0.44***	

*p < .10; **p < .05; ***p < .01.

A strong association between offending and victimization was also found using the ASRDS measure. The results shown in Table 10.4 are displayed in a somewhat different format than those in Table 10.3. While the latter presented row percentages, indicating the percentages of offenders reporting victimization, Table 10.4 presents column percentages, or the percentages of victims and non-victims also reporting offending behaviour. According to the information in Table 10.4, those experiencing all types of victimization are significantly more likely than non-victims to report offending behaviours. The only exception is for family violence, in that victims were no more likely than non-victims to report general offending, vandalism, illegal vehicle use, theft, and assault.

While the bivariate analyses reveal a strong correlation between victimization and criminal involvement, they cannot assess the ways in which other risk and protective factors may influence the relationship between victimization and crime. The next section describes the results of multivariate analyses that further explore these issues.

Multivariate Analysis

Two sets of multivariate analyses were performed. First, offending was utilized as a predictor of victimization (including total victimization and each type of victimization). Secondly, the impact of each form of victimization on criminal involvement was analyzed. These analyses control for a variety of risk and protective factors thought to influence these relationships.[4]

---

4   See Appendix A for a list of the risk and protective factors included in analyses.

Table 10.4   Victimization and self-reported offending (per cent of non-victims and victims reporting one or more offences; column percentages)[1]

					Victimization Type					
Offence Type	Total		Theft		Other Violence		Family Violence		Other Trauma	
	No	Yes	No	Yes	No	Yes	No	Yes	No	Yes
General	75	91	77	88	77	97	78	95	77	92
Vandalism	34	59	38	52	37	67	39	40	38	57
Disorder	51	76	54	77	53	84	55	80	54	73
Vehicle	30	57	34	57	33	65	35	50	34	61
Theft	40	64	43	59	42	74	44	35	43	69
Assault	38	61	40	65	40	68	42	40	41	57
Drugs/ Alcohol	42	76	46	74	46	83	47	85	47	73
n	761	168	864	65	872	57	909	20	878	51

[1] All relationships are significant (p <0.05), except that between family violence and general delinquency, vandalism, illegal vehicle use, theft, and assault.

The Relationship Between Offending and Victimization

The impact of offending on victimization was first assessed using logistic regression analysis, with the Homel crime status variable as the independent variable. As shown in Table 10.5, crime status was significantly related to the overall measure of victimization, as well as theft, other violence and other trauma, even when numerous risk and protective factors were included in the analyses. Thus, young people with higher levels of criminal involvement had an increased likelihood of victimization. The one exception is that crime status did not directly influence the likelihood of family violence, although this may be due to the very small number of young people (*n*=23) who reported this type of experience.

Individual, family, peer, and neighbourhood characteristics also increased the likelihood of lifetime victimization, with significant variables including previous sexual experience, parental education, parental supervision, neighbourhood wealth, and so on. For the victimization sub-types, different circumstances influenced the likelihood of different types of trauma. Theft victimization was largely predicted by family factors, family violence was generally influenced by the respondents' individual characteristics, and other trauma was largely predicted by neighbourhood factors. Finally, victims of other violence were characterized by a variety of family, peer, and neighbourhood characteristics (see Table 10.5).

In order to examine these relationships from a slightly different perspective, logistic regression analyses were performed using the ASRDS measure as the independent variable (results not shown). The results demonstrated little relationship between self-reported offending and victimization. Offending was significantly related to victimization in only nine of the 35 analyses (the seven types of offending by the five types of victimization). The relationship was strongest when predicting total victimization, and vandalism, public disorder, illegal vehicle use, theft and assault (but not general offending or drug and alcohol use) each increased the likelihood of lifetime victimization. In addition, illegal vehicle use and theft predicted other trauma, drug and alcohol use predicted family violence, and assault predicted theft victimization. Surprisingly, total offending did not increase the likelihood of total victimization or any of the victimization sub-types, even though significant relationships were found when using the Homel crime status variable. This disparity may be due to the fact that the crime status variable controls for cohort type, while the ASRDS does not.

Table 10.5   Crime status as a predictor of victimization (logistic regression, n=929)[1]

Significant Predictors	Victimization Type				
	Total Victim	Theft	Other Violence	Family Violence	Other Trauma
Crime Status	Yes	Yes	Yes	NS	Yes
Individual	Non-virgin Confused Jobless	NS	NS	Female Non-virgin Confused Makes plans	NS
Family/ Parents	Rules Lives w/ relatives Education	Friends Rules	Education	NS	Isolation
Peer	NS	NS	Friends don't care Cares for friends	NS	NS
Neighbourhood	Wealth	NS	English-speaking residents	NS	Single-parents Teens

[1] All indicated predictors are significant at p <0.05.

The Relationship Between Victimization and Offending

The impact of victimization on criminal involvement was also assessed. First, ordinary least squares (OLS) regression analysis was conducted, using the Homel crime status variable as the dependent variable. The standardized and unstandardized regression coefficients are shown in Table 10.6, and the results provide mixed evidence that victimization leads to offending. Total victimization was significantly related to the crime status variable, with victims having increased criminal involvement. This relationship remained significant even controlling for other individual, family, social and neighbourhood circumstances.[5] Experiencing theft and other trauma also increased criminal offending, but other violence and family violence did not. Although the analyses cannot identify why it is that some types of victimization, but not others, increase offending, the mixed findings underscore the importance of examining the impact of different forms of victimization on crime, as well as including other predictors of crime in multivariate analyses.

Table 10.6   Victimization as a predictor of crime status (OLS regression, *n*=935)

Victimization Type	Crime Status	
	B	Beta
Total Victimization	.310***	.074
Theft	.295**	.045
Other Violence	.084	.012
Family Violence	-.046	-.004
Other Trauma	.620***	.090

**p <0.05   ***p <0.01.

Logistic regression analysis was next performed using the ASRDS total scale and sub-scales as dependent variables. As shown in Table 10.7, very few relationships were significant. While a variety of risk and protective factors were related to the offending outcomes (not shown), the victimization variables emerged significant in only seven of the 35 models. Total victimization increased the odds of engaging in vandalism, public disorder, and illegal vehicle use, and other trauma increased the likelihood of general offending, illegal vehicle use, and theft. While it was perhaps expected that total victimization would increase offending, it is somewhat surprising that, of the four types of victimization, other trauma was most likely to lead to offending. As the types of experiences captured in this category are rarely

---

5   The significant risk and protective factors are not listed in Table 10.6, as numerous predictors were found. In fact, the variance explained in each model was very high (approximately 57 per cent in each case), demonstrating that the comprehensive models were very successful in predicting respondents' crime status.

considered by criminologists, the results emphasize the importance of examining the effects of a wide variety of victimization experiences on a wide variety of criminal outcomes, in order to reveal the complexity of the relationship between victimization and offending.

Table 10.7   Victimization as a predictor of self-reported offending[1] (logistic regression, n=834)

Victimization Type	Offence Type						
	General	Vandalism	Public Disorder	Illegal Vehicle	Theft	Assault	Drugs/ Alcohol
Total	NS	0.54	0.54	0.49	NS	NS	NS
Theft	NS	NS	NS	NS	NS	0.70	NS
Other Violence	NS	NS	NS	NS	NS	NS	NS
Family Violence	NS	NS	NS	NS	NS	NS	NS
Other Trauma	1.42	NS	NS	0.85	0.89	NS	NS

[1] Unstandardized coefficients; listed coefficients are significant at $p < 0.05$.

Conclusion

This chapter has explored the nature and prevalence of victimization among the young people in the Sibling Study, as well as the relationship between victimization and involvement in crime. Although the findings are somewhat preliminary, they have implications for the field and highlight many areas needing further investigation.

Perhaps most importantly, the data demonstrate that teenagers are subject to many different kinds of victimization, within their families as well as outside their homes. Although it is generally acknowledged that adolescents are the age group most at-risk for experiencing victimization, there is relatively little research (particularly using self-reported data) identifying the prevalence and nature of such experiences. Likewise, much more attention has been aimed at examining the consequences of victimization perpetrated by family members, particularly during childhood, and much less research has recognized the extent and consequences of non-family violence, or other types of family problems, that may occur during adolescence. Additionally, the findings indicate that different types of victimization may have differential effects on criminal involvement, and it is important that future studies assess a wider variety of victimization experiences and their consequences.

The results also indicate the importance of including other risk and protective factors for crime when investigating the relationship between victimization and offending. Bivariate analyses demonstrated a significant relationship between each form of victimization and involvement in crime (with some exceptions for family violence), but multivariate analyses indicated only mixed support for these relationships. Controlling for other factors, total victimization, theft, and other trauma increased the likelihood of involvement in crime using the Homel crime status variable, while total victimization and other trauma were likely to lead to offending using the ASRDS measure.[6] These findings indicate that victimization may influence involvement in crime indirectly. For example, it may be that family violence and other violence negatively influence other important life events, which, in turn, may increase the likelihood of offending. It is also possible that victims of other violence or family violence may experience other types of negative consequences, such as interpersonal problems, mental health deficits, increased drug or alcohol use, and so on, that were not considered in this chapter. Together, these findings emphasize the need for future research to acknowledge the complexity in the relationship between victimization and offending, and more comprehensive analyses, particularly those relying on longitudinal data, are needed.

Relatedly, the results indicate some support for the reciprocity between victimization and offending. More specifically, multivariate analyses demonstrated that those engaging in more criminal activities (as measured by the crime status variable) reported a greater number of victimization experiences (with the exception of family violence), and that some types of offending (as measured by the ASRDS) were associated with an increased likelihood of total victimization. However, these findings are based on cross-sectional data and require further exploration.

While raising important issues needing further research, the current findings must be taken with some caution, given several limitations in the data. The questions used to determine the nature and prevalence of victimization in this sample are somewhat limited and may not capture the full range of victimization experiences. This shortcoming is particularly true regarding sexual assault and family violence, which are typically under-reported and may require more sensitive and detailed definitions and measures than those utilized here (Eigenberg 1990, Finkelhor 1994, Panel 1993). In addition, this chapter is based on cross-sectional data and analyses cannot adequately examine causality between victimization and offending, or whether other risk and protective factors may intervene to influence this relationship.

---

6   Again, it is important to remember that the two dependent variables measure offending in somewhat different ways. Most importantly, the crime status variable takes cohort membership into account, while the ASRDS does not.

Appendix A: Risk and protective factors included in the analyses

Individual Characteristics
Age
Sex
Unemployed and receives a benefit
Feels it is important that people care about them
Feels life is confusing
Ability to plan for the future
Would like to change their life
Prefers physical activity

Family Characteristics
Parent white-collar job
Parental employment
Parental university education
Parental love and support
Parental supervision/rules
Parental authority
Family moved often
Lives with other relatives
Family isolation (does not often see relatives)
Number of family friends
Number of older siblings

School Characteristics
Number of schools attended
Left school for a negative reason

Neighbourhood Characteristics
High percentage of teenaged (10 to 16 year old) residents
High percentage of non-English-speaking residents
Household wealth
Concentration of single mothers

Personal Characteristics
Risk-taker
Impulsive
Egocentric
Delinquent disposition
Bad temper
Ever dieted
Currently dieting
Non-virgin

Peer Characteristics
Number of friends
Cares about friends
Wants to copy friends
Friends don't care
Deviant peers
Now in pro-social group
Was in deviant peer group
Now in deviant peer group

Chapter 11

Criminality and Conformity: Implications for the Future

Mark Lynch, Emma Ogilvie and John S. Western

The traditional criminal career which involves crimes against persons and crimes against property is relatively short. Farrington (2002), reporting on data from the Cambridge Study in Delinquent Development, suggests that the average career lasts between seven and eight years. Those who begin at an early age, between 10 and 13 years, are the most persistent offenders with a career lasting a little more than 11 years while those who begin at an older age, around 17 years, persist on average for no more than around three years. Farrington's sample was not large and the absolute figures should be treated with some caution. Nevertheless there is sufficient supporting evidence to suggest that, in relative terms, criminal careers are of short duration and the majority come to an end at around the age of 30 (Blumstein and Cohen 1987, Farrington 1992, Farrington and West 1990, Farrington 2002).

Those involved in criminal careers represent a tiny proportion of the population, for although the probability of an American male being arrested sometime in his life for a non-traffic offence is between 50 and 60 per cent, and in Great Britain the lifetime conviction probability for males is estimated to be in the same range, at around 45 per cent, those finding their way repeatedly into jail, at least in Australia, is markedly less than 0.1 per cent of the population (Yearbook Australia 1997). Perhaps there is an expanding crime problem but it hardly seems to be characterized by large numbers of people engaging in a life of crime. Nevertheless, significant government moneys are spent on matters relating to justice in the form of police services, court administration and corrective services. In the Australian context, in 1999–2000, around 6.4 billion dollars was spent on the justice system in total. Of this total recurrent expenditure, the majority, around four billion dollars, was spent on police services, followed by expenditure on corrective services of over one billion dollars. Expenditure had grown by eight per cent since 1998–99, with the greatest level of growth found in corrective services (Yearbook Australia 2002). From a slightly different perspective, Walker (1992) suggests that crime may cost Australians at least 27 billion dollars each year, which is about 7.2 per cent of the Gross Domestic Product.

So crime is a growing industry and youth crime is an important component of that industry. As we have seen in our discussion to date, criminality is matched by conformity and the two in a sense go hand in hand. Our book began with a discussion of the way in which criminality and conformity are somewhat 'slippery' concepts that sometimes fail to capture the complex realities of the lives of both offending and non-offending young people who evidence both criminality and conformity at different times and differently combined. Each of the chapters have drawn attention to aspects of trajectories through adolescence and the ways in which these trajectories are sometimes consistent with, and at other times inconsistent with, the received wisdoms of criminology.

Regarding the relationship between age and offending, we saw that the impact of some factors on offending increased with age, while the impact of others decreased. More interestingly, we also observed that some factors appeared to be particularly important at certain stages of adolescence. It was something of a surprise to observe that emotional support from parents was most important for our middle age group of 14 and 15 year olds: support enhanced conformity and reduced criminality.

In the two chapters that focused upon gender, we found that our measures of opportunity and motivation for delinquent behaviours were not good predictors of gender differences with respect to levels of offending. In addition, traditional understandings of sex roles were good predictors of conformity, but did not make the conditions for offending any more transparent. We were led to conclude that satisfactorily explaining female adolescent offending would require revisiting gender specific theories of adolescent criminality.

When we turned to analyses focusing upon the influence of social class, we were somewhat serendipitously drawn to conclude that self-esteem rather than class position was the more significant factor implicated in the offending of young people, and those lacking it were the more likely to offend. Self-esteem of course derives in part from family influences, and when we focused specifically upon this issue, the importance of growing up in a relatively stable environment became clear. Just how important a stable family environment may be was highlighted in the chapter focusing more directly upon family influences. High levels of maternal and paternal care, albeit differentially applied, tipped the balance in favor of conformity over criminality. Sibling influences were also found. In contrast to research findings reported elsewhere, our data suggest that being a sibling of a young person who has broken the law (i.e. those in the Offender cohort) makes conformity more likely. Brothers and sisters did not seem to follow each other down the offender trail. However, to complicate matters, among non-offending young people with siblings (i.e. those in the School cohort, and to a lesser extent, those in the Vulnerable cohort), levels of self-reported crime were highly correlated. Thus if one member of a sibling pair reported little deviation from the straight and narrow, the other member also conformed. But if one sibling reported substantial illegality, the other was not far behind. Conformity begets conformity and criminality begets criminality, but only for non-offenders.

Victimization, including victimization by family members, was also found to be strongly associated with offending. However, this relationship may be indirect and mediated by a wide variety of other factors. Finally, our study of urban Indigenous young people alerted us to a series of culturally specific values present amongst this group, which may act as protective factors to inhibit offending.

What are we to make of these findings? Is there some central message that they collectively convey? The obvious answer to this rhetorical question is that if there is some central message it eludes easy discernment. This is not, however, as unsatisfying a conclusion as it might appear at first sight. The findings demonstrate the point made in Chapter 1 that real people behave in ways that conform to the dominant theoretical paradigms only with great difficulty and significant over-simplification. In reality, what we see are young people behaving in ways that are sometimes consistent with the propositions of strain theory, while at other times better understood by drawing on control theory. At yet other times differential association theory could be used as an interpretive framework, as could feminist theories, theories of alienation, class-based analyses and so on and so on. Despite our best efforts, the behaviours of young people appear to be remarkably resistant to pigeon-holing. No single theoretical orientation encompasses the complexities of their behaviour.

This resistance to containment brings to the foreground the theme running throughout this book, that both offending and non-offending can derive from highly individual relationships between individuals and their material and social environment. This is not to say of course that criminality and conformity are totally idiosyncratic phenomena. The behaviours and the conditions giving rise to them are socially patterned, but the slavish adherence to a privileged theoretical position is not likely to appreciably advance either our understanding of the phenomena or the likely success of intervention programs aimed to reduce adolescent criminality.

It is to the question of intervention that we wish to turn in the final few pages of this book. Proponents of 'real-world' responses to adolescent criminality typically start from one of two approaches. There are those who argue from a favoured perspective, and while acknowledging that such a perspective only partially encapsulates the real world, assert that such an approach provides firmer ground for interventions than does the more relativistic perspective that many orientations may each have something of value to reveal—the second approach.

At first sight the first approach appears attractive, as it seems to lend itself to a reasonably straightforward shift from theory to practice in the form of particular intervention programs, and it readily accommodates evaluation exercises that provide measures of the success or failure of the interventions. The attractiveness of this stance is, however, misguided in that it assumes that the shift towards practice (by interventions) must be based on adherence to a particular theoretical orientation. This is simply not so. For example, intensive supervision orders which provide a behavioural framework with which criminal young people must comply and which are central to an intervention program, may simultaneously address issues at the heart of a diverse set of theories of adolescent behaviour, and the potency of the various elements of the intervention may vary substantially from person to person.

Every empirical demonstration of support for a particular theory of adolescent behaviour does not mean support for some other theory of adolescent behaviour is reduced by a corresponding amount. It is not a zero sum game. Different theoretical approaches are differently significant in accounting for the behaviour of different people at different points in the movement through adolescence. Recognizing this fact certainly complicates attempts at developing responses or interventions aimed at discouraging adolescent criminality, but also paradoxically places our responses on firmer, albeit vastly more heterogeneous, ground. Instead of trying to 'squint in' exactly the right way for behaviours to fit the model, the challenge becomes to develop responses that accommodate the myriad of causal relationships that underpin the behaviours of most people most of the time. Such an endeavor may be challenging, but it is far from impossible. After all, the number of causal relationships is finite, and this recognition arguably makes developing effective responses easier in as much as we avoid 'placing all our eggs in the one basket'.

In understanding why such an endeavour is not impossible we need to think about what we actually mean when we talk about responses or interventions aimed at reducing adolescent offending. For the most part, we are talking about initiatives that are planned, funded, implemented and very occasionally evaluated by the state. In using the term 'the state', we are actually referring to the activities of a wide range of government departments at different levels—national, state and local in the Australian context—providing advice to, and acting at the behest of, central government. If the type of data outlined in this book are to have a positive impact in terms of the activities of the state, the next step is for criminologists to demonstrate how such data can be taken into account by the 'machinery of government' in order that interventions that make sense criminologically are administratively feasible and capable of yielding the sorts of results elected governments responsible to their constituents demand.

There are thus two threads we need to draw together here. On the one hand we are saying we need interventions that recognize the diversity of the bases of adolescent offending, and on the other hand we need interventions that take account of the political context within which interventions are developed and implemented or alternatively stymied and discounted. The reconciliation of these two threads is a much greater challenge than is reconciling control with strain theory or differential association with class theory.

If more criminologists had greater experience with the policy-making processes of government it is likely that 'turf wars' over theoretical perspectives would be much less pronounced than has been the case to date. And equally, if more government policy-makers were familiar with criminology as a discipline, the success rates of our interventions might be much greater than is currently the case.

The following example provides a disturbing indication of just how far we have to go in improving our responses to problematic adolescent behaviour. In so doing it points to just how important it is that we seek to understand this behaviour by drawing upon findings such as those reported in the preceding chapters. The data presented below in Figure 11.1 comprise the administrative histories of all young people in Queensland who were on supervised orders at the time the Sibling Study interviews were undertaken. They draw together histories of supervised orders, police criminal histories and correctional data from 1994-95 through to 2001. What the data reveal is that having come to the attention of government in early adolescence for either offending or living at risk is a powerful predictor of subsequently becoming part of the adult correctional system. In particular we see that 84 per cent of Indigenous males who were serving a juvenile supervised order in 1994–95 subsequently entered the adult correctional system. At the other end of the spectrum, that is non-Indigenous females, we find that fully 56 per cent of those on supervised orders in 1994–95 also entered the adult correctional system. It is important to recognize here that even though these figures are disturbing, they under-estimate the seriousness of the issue because as time passes these percentages will increase.

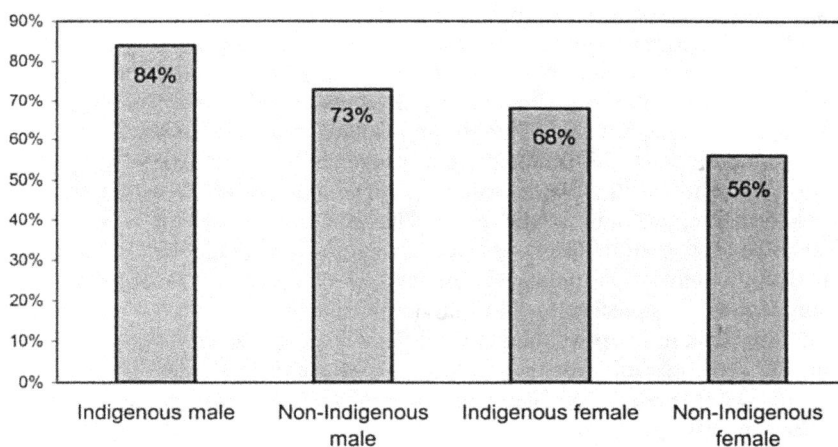

Source: Unpublished data, Crime and Misconduct Commission, 2003.

Figure 11.1   Proportion of people who served juvenile supervised orders in 1994-95 who subsequently entered the adult corrections system

It is difficult to imagine data that more obviously point to the importance of seriously grappling with the messages contained in the preceding chapters. Importantly, however, these data cannot be read as an obvious indictment of government policies concerned with crime prevention. It is too easy to judge government agencies concerned with complex social issues by the difficulty they have in changing problematic behaviours. In addition, it is easy to overlook the fact that many of the central precursors of these behaviours have been set in place long before the individuals have come to the attention of the state agencies concerned.   These data draw attention to the importance of improving communication between researchers on the one hand and government policy-makers on the other. The inability of policy to produce planned outcomes is due as much to the failure of researchers to provide the necessary evidence, as it is to the failure of policy-makers to develop evidence sensitive policy alternatives. If the evidence is not forthcoming, evidence-based policy is difficult to achieve.

It is obviously beyond the scope of this chapter to outline all the different ways in which more criminologically-informed thinking might feed into the policy process that is at the core of most government activity. Instead, the aim of this final chapter has been to bring to the foreground two key points. First, that the preceding chapters have each, selectively, demonstrated that adolescent behaviour cannot sensibly be described on the basis of adherence to any one particular theoretical orientation; secondly, that the complex bases of both criminality and conformity we have observed unambiguously point to the necessity for a better reconciliation of criminological insights and the policy practices of government.

What is being suggested is arguably little more than pointing out the need to respond to the behaviour of young people who have been caught up in the juvenile justice system in a more sociologically informed manner than is currently the case. The education system provides a model which might be followed. It recognizes that individuals participating in the system possess a wide range of both competencies and deficits. For individuals who are challenged in some way, there are special education facilities of one sort or another. For example, for individuals with exceptional competencies, there are accelerated learning opportunities. For individuals who are marginalized, assisted programs are available, and so on. Significantly, the education system recognizes and accepts that although its overarching service responsibility is to provide a uniformly acceptable quality of education, its 'clients' are characterized by diverse needs, deficits, and competencies. And accordingly, the education system (as a service provider) cannot avoid taking these differences into account when determining how best to progress its core business.

Policy-makers need to adopt a similar strategy in terms of the mechanisms employed in dealing with offending adolescents. In short, they need to seriously address some very basic questions. In the Australian context, these issues relate to how and why pre-sentence reports that are developed prior to the sentencing of young offenders are used; whether protection orders issued with respect to designated offenders increase rather than decrease the likelihood of an adverse outcome from the courts; under what circumstances police should caution rather than charge young people; for which young people are community corrections orders the most effective sanction in the long term; in what circumstance is an intensive supervision order a more beneficial response than detention (and vice versa); and so on.

These are issues of both immediate practical importance and longer-term criminological interest. There is a tendency among the research community, however, to overlook these issues. Such concerns are seen as lacking the grand theoretical compass of the great thoughts of the day. What is needed is a greater rapprochement between those who have to immediately confront the world's problems, or at least those aspects of them concerned with the offending of young people, and those who have the luxury of a little more time in which to choose a course of action and who are not immediately confronted by the consequences of that choice.

What is being suggested is that both policy-makers and researchers need to become more sophisticated in the ways in which they both recognize and respond to the diversity of factors underpinning adolescent criminality and conformity. While evidence-based policy may not necessarily be the panacea, not everything will unfold as anticipated, because inevitably, 'if we do what we've always done, we'll get what we've always had', and we ought to be able to do better than that.

Bibliography

Ageton, S. (1983), 'The Dynamics of Female Delinquency, 1976–1980', *Criminology*, vol. 21, pp. 555–84.

Agnew, R. (1985), 'Social Control Theory and Delinquency: A Longitudinal Test', *Criminology*, vol. 23, pp. 47–61.

Agnew, R. (1991a), 'A Longitudinal Test of Social Control Theory and Delinquency', *Journal of Research in Crime and Delinquency*, vol. 28, pp. 126–56.

Agnew, R. (1991b), 'The Interactive Effects of Peer Variables on Delinquency', *Criminology*, vol. 29, pp. 47–72.

Agnew, R. and Broidy, L. (1993), *Neighborhoods and Crime*, Lexington, New York.

Agnew, R and Raskin White, H. (1992), 'An Empirical Test of General Strain Theory', *Criminology*, vol. 30, pp. 475–99.

Alder, C. (1997), 'Theories of Female Delinquency', in A. Borowski and I. O'Connor (eds), *Juvenile Crime, Justice and Corrections*, Addison Wesley Longman, South Melbourne, pp. 43-59.

Alder, C. and Hunter, N. (1999), *Young Women in the Juvenile Justice System: Report of Findings 1, Young Women's Offending*, Criminology Research Council, Canberra.

Amato, P.R. and Keith, B. (1991), 'Parental Divorce and the Well-Being of Children', *Psychological Bulletin*, vol. 110, pp. 26–46.

Australian Bureau of Statistics (1998), *Crime and Safety, Australia*, Australian Bureau of Statistics, Canberra.

Australian Institute of Health and Welfare (2001), *Child Protection: Australia, 1999-2000*, Child Welfare Series No. 27, Australian Institute of Health and Welfare, Canberra.

Baker, R.L., Mednick, B.R. and Carothers, L. (1989), 'Association of Age, Gender, and Ethnicity with Juvenile Victimization in and Out of School', *Youth and Society*, vol. 20, pp. 320–41.

Bank, L., Patterson, G.R. and Reid, J.B. (1996), 'Negative Sibling Interaction Patterns as Predictors of Later Adjustment Problems in Adolescent and Young Adult Males', in G.H. Brody (ed), *Sibling Relationships: Their Causes and Consequences*, Ablex Publishing, Norwood, NJ, pp. 197–230.

Barnes, G.M. and Farrell, M.P. (1992), 'Parental Support and Control as Predictors of Adolescent Drinking, Delinquency, and Related Problem Behaviors', *Journal of Marriage and the Family*, vol. 54, pp. 763–76.

Baxter, J., Emmison, M., Western, J. and Western, M. (1991), *Class Analysis and Contemporary Australia*, Macmillan, Melbourne.

Benoit, J.L. and Kennedy, W.A. (1992), 'The Abuse History of Male Sex Offenders', *Journal of Interpersonal Violence*, vol. 7, pp. 543–48.

Beresford, Q. and Omaji, P. (1996), *Rites of Passage: Aboriginal Youth, Crime and Justice*, Fremantle Arts Centre Press, Western Australia.

Bernard, T. (1987), 'Testing Structural Strain Theories', *Journal of Research in Crime and Delinquency*, vol. 24, pp. 262–80.

Bessant, J. (2001), 'From Sociology of Deviance to Sociology of Risk: Youth Homelessness and the Problem of Empiricism', *Journal of Criminal Justice*, vol. 29, pp. 31–43.

Bessant, J., Sercombe, H. and Watts, R. (1998), *Youth Studies: An Australian Perspective*, Addison Wesley Longman, South Melbourne.

Blagg, H. (1997), 'A Just Measure of Shame? Aboriginal Youth and Conferencing in

Australia', *British Journal of Criminology*, vol. 37, pp. 481–501.

Blumstein, A. and Cohen, J. (1987), 'Characterizing Criminal Careers', *Science*, vol. 237, pp. 985–91.

Blumstein, A., Cohen, J., Roth, J. and Visher, C. (1986), *Criminal Careers and 'Career Criminals'*, National Academy Press, Washington, D.C.

Bor, W., Najman, J.M., O'Callaghan, M., Williams, G.M. and Anstey, K. (2001), 'Aggression and the Development of Delinquent Behavior in Children', *Trends and Issues in Crime and Criminal Justice*, No. 207, Australian Institute of Criminology, Canberra.

Bottcher, J. (1995), 'Gender as Social Control', *Justice Quarterly*, vol. 12, pp. 33–37.

Box, S. (1983), *Power, Crime and Mystification*, Tavistock Publications, New York.

Box, S. (1971), *Deviance, Reality and Society*, Holt, Rinehart and Winston Ltd, London.

Braithwaite, J. (1979), *Inequality, Crime and Public Policy*, Routledge and K. Paul, London.

Braithwaite, J. (1989), *Crime, Shame and Re-integration*, Cambridge University Press, Cambridge.

Braithwaite, J. and Daly, K. (1994), 'Masculinities, Violence and Communitarian Control', in T. Newburn and E.A. Stanko (eds), *Just Boys Doing Business*, Routledge, London, pp. 189–213.

Brantingham, P. and Brantingham, P. (1995), 'Criminality of Place: Crime Generators and Crime Attractors', *European Journal on Criminal Policy and Research*, vol. 3, pp. 1–26.

Brezina, T. (1998), 'Adolescent Maltreatment and Delinquency: The Question of Intervening Processes', *Journal of Research in Crime and Delinquency*, vol. 35, pp. 71–99.

Broadbent, A. and Bentley, R. (1997), *Child Abuse and Neglect, Australia 1995–96*, Australian Institute of Health and Welfare, Canberra.

Broadhurst, R. (1997), 'Aborigines and Crime in Australia,' in M. Tonry (ed), *Ethnicity, Crime, and Immigration: Comparative and Cross-national Perspectives*, University of Chicago Press, Chicago.

Broidy, L. and Agnew, R. (1997), 'Gender and Crime: A General Strain Theory Perspective', *Journal of Research in Crime and Delinquency*, vol. 34, pp. 275–306.

Brook, J.S., Whiteman, M., Gordon, A.S. and Brook, D.W. (1988), 'The Role of Older Brothers in Younger Brothers' Drug Use Viewed in the Context of Parent and Peer Influences', *The Journal of Genetic Psychology*, vol. 151, pp. 59-75.

Brown, S. (1998), *Understanding Youth and Crime: Listening to Youth?*, Open University Press, Buckingham, UK.

Brownfield, D. and Sorenson, A.M. (1994), 'Sibship Size and Sibling Delinquency', *Deviant Behavior: An Interdisciplinary Journal*, vol. 15, pp. 45-61.

Burrows, T., Homel, R. and Gallois, C. (forthcoming), 'Women Victims of Assault: Age Differences in Victim-Aggressor Relationship and Location', *Australian and New Zealand Journal of Criminology*.

Burton, V.S. and Cullen, F.T. (1992), 'Empirical Status of Strain Theory', *Journal of Crime and Justice*, vol. 15, pp. 1-30.

Cairns, R.B. and Cairns, B.D. (1994), *Lifelines and Risks: Pathways of Youth in Our Time*, Cambridge University Press, Cambridge.

Campbell, A. (1993), *Men, Women and Aggression*, Basic Books, New York.

Carey, G. (1992), 'Twin Imitation for Antisocial Behavior: Implications for Genetic and Family Research', *Journal of Abnormal Psychology*, vol. 101, pp. 18–25.

Carrington, K. (1993), *Offending Girls: Sex, Youth and Justice*, Allen and Unwin, St. Leonards, NSW.

Catalano, R.F. and Hawkins, J.D. (1996), 'The Social Development Model: A Theory of

Antisocial Behavior', in J.D. Hawkins (ed), *Delinquency and Crime: Current Theories*, Cambridge University Press, Cambridge.

Cernkonovich, S.A. and Giordano, P. (1979), 'A Comparative Analysis of Male and Female Delinquency', *Sociological Quarterly*, vol. 20, pp. 131–45.

Cernkonovich, S.A. and Giordano, P. (1992), 'School Bonding, Race, and Delinquency', *Criminology*, vol. 30, pp. 261-91.

Chesney-Lind, M. (1997), *The Female Offender: Girls, Women and Crime*, Sage Publications, Thousand Oaks, CA.

Chesney-Lind, M. and Rodriguez, N. (1983), 'Women Under Lock and Key', *The Prison Journal*, vol. 63, pp. 47–65.

Clarke, R. (1995), 'Situational Crime Prevention: Everybody's Business', Proceedings of a Conference: *Crime Prevention: Everybody's Business*, Crime Prevention Council of Australia, Western Australia Branch, Western Australia, pp. 5-21.

Clarke, R. and Cornish, D. (1985), 'Modeling Offenders' Decisions: A Framework for Research and Policy', in M. Tonry and N. Morris (eds), *Crime and Justice: An Annual Review of Research*, Vol. 6, University of Chicago of Press, Chicago.

Clarke, R. and Felson, M. (1993), *Routine Activity and Rational Choice*, Transaction Publishers, New Brunswick, NJ.

Clarke, R and Felson, M. (1998*), Opportunity Makes the Thief: Practical Theory for Crime Prevention,* Home Office, Policing and Reducing Crime Unit, Research, Development and Statistics Directorate, London.

Cloward, R. and Ohlin, L. (1960), *Delinquency and Opportunity*, Free Press, Glencoe, IL.

Cohen, A. (1955), *Delinquent Boys*, Free Press, Glencoe, IL.

Cohen, L.E. and Felson, M. (1979), 'Social Change and Crime Rate Trends: A Routine Activities Approach', *American Sociological Review*, vol. 46, pp. 505–24.

Coleman, J.C. and Hendry, L.B. (1999), *Nature of Adolescence* (3rd ed.), Routledge, London.

Conger, R.D. and Rueter, M.A. (1996), 'Siblings, Parents, and Peers: A Longitudinal Study of Social Influences in Adolescent Risk for Alcohol Use and Abuse', in G.H. Brody (ed), *Sibling Relationships: Their Causes and Consequences*, Ablex Publishing, Norwood, NJ.

Council on Scientific Affairs, American Medical Association (1993), 'Adolescents as Victims of Family Violence', *Journal of the American Medical Association*, vol. 270, pp. 1850–56.

Crenshaw, K. (1991), 'Mapping the Margins: Intersectionality, Identity Politics and Violence Against Women of Color', *Stanford Law Review*, vol. 43, pp. 1241–99.

Crew, B. (1991), 'Sex Differences in Criminal Sentencing: Chivalry or Patriarchy?', *Justice Quarterly*, vol. 8, pp. 59–83.

Criminal Justice Commission (1995), 'Children, Crime and Justice in Queensland', *Research Paper Series*, vol. 2, pp. 1–19.

Cullen, F.T. (1984), *Rethinking Crime and Deviance Theory – The Emergence of a Structuring Tradition*, Rowman and Allanheld, Totowa, NJ.

Cunneen, C. (1994), 'Enforcing Genocide?', in R. White and C. Alder (eds), *The Police and Young People in Australia*, Cambridge University Press, Cambridge.

Cunneen, C. (1997), 'Indigenous Young People and Juvenile Crime', in A. Borowski and I. O'Connor (eds), *Juvenile Crime, Justice and Corrections*, Addison Wesley Longman, South Melbourne.

Cunneen, C. (1999), 'Criminology, Genocide and the Forced Removal of Indigenous Children from their Families', *Australian and New Zealand Journal of Criminology*, vol. 32, pp. 124–38.

Cunneen, C. and White, R. (1995), *Juvenile Justice: An Australian Perspective*, Oxford

University Press, Melbourne.

Daly, K. (1994), *Gender, Crime and Punishment*, Yale University Press, New Haven, CT.

Daly, K. (1998), 'Gender, Crime and Criminology', in M. Tonry (ed), *The Handbook of Crime and Punishment*, Oxford University Press, New York.

Daly, K. and Chesney-Lind, M. (1988), 'Feminism and Criminology', *Justice Quarterly*, vol. 5, pp. 497–538.

Daly, K. and Maher, L. (1998), 'Crossroads and Intersections: Building From Feminist Critique', in K. Daly and L. Maher (eds), *Criminology At the Crossroads: Feminist Readings in Crime and Justice*, Oxford University Press, New York.

Dembo, R., Grandon, G., LaVoie, L., Schmeidler, J. and Burgos, W. (1986), 'Parents and Drugs Revisited: Some Further Evidence in Support of Social Learning Theory', *Criminology*, vol. 24, pp. 85–101.

Dembo, R., Schmeidler, J., Williams, L., Berry, E., Getreu, K., Wish, E.D., Genung, L. and La Voie, L. (1991), 'Recidivism Among High-risk Youths: Study of a Cohort of Juvenile Detainees', *The International Journal of the Addictions*, vol. 26, pp. 121–77.

Denno, D.W. (1994), 'Gender, Crime and Criminal Law Defenses', *Journal of Criminal Law and Criminology*, vol. 85, pp. 80–180.

Doumas, D., Margolin, G. and John, R.S. (1994), 'The Intergenerational Transmission of Aggression Across Three Generations', *Journal of Family Violence*, vol. 9, pp. 157–74.

D'Souza, N. (1990), 'Aboriginal Children and the Juvenile Justice System', *Aboriginal Law Bulletin*, vol. 44, p. 2.

Dutton, D.G. and Hart, S.H. (1994), 'Evidence for Long-Term, Specific Effects of Childhood Abuse and Neglect on Criminal Behavior in Men', *International Journal of Offender Therapy and Comparative Criminology*, vol. 36, pp. 129–37.

Dwan, K. and Western, J. (2003), 'Patterns of Social Inequality in Australia', in I. McAllister, S. Dowrick and R. Hassan (eds), *The Cambridge Handbook of Social Sciences in Australia*, Cambridge University Press, Cambridge.

Edelbrock, C., Rende, R. and Plomin, R. (1995), 'Twin Study of Competence and Problem Behavior in Childhood and Early Adolescence', *Journal of Child Psychology and Psychiatry*, vol. 36, pp. 775–85.

Edleson, J.L. (1999), 'Children's Witnessing of Adult Domestic Violence', *Journal of Interpersonal Violence*, vol. 14, pp. 839–70.

Eigenberg, H.M. (1990), 'The National Crime Survey and Rape: The Case of the Missing Question', *Justice Quarterly*, vol. 7, pp. 655–72.

Elliott, D. and Ageton, S. (1980), 'Reconciling Race and Class Differences in Self Reported and Official Estimates of Delinquency', *American Sociological Review*, vol. 45, pp. 95–110.

Emler, N. and Reicher, S. (1995), *Adolescence and Delinquency: The Collective Management of Reputation*, Blackwell, Oxford.

Empey, L. and Lubeck, S. (1971), *Explaining Delinquency*, DC Heath, Lexington, MA.

Empey, L. and Stafford, M. (1991), *American Delinquency* (3rd ed.), Wadsworth, Belmont, CA.

Esbensen, F.A. and Huizinga, D. (1991), 'Juvenile Victimization and Delinquency', *Youth and Society*, vol. 23, pp. 202–28.

Fagan, A.A. (2001a), *The Cycle of Violence Expanded: Assessing the Impact of Gender and Type of Perpetrator on the Relationship Between Adolescent Violent Victimization and Adult Offending and Drug Use*, Unpublished PhD Dissertation, University of Colorado, Boulder, CO.

Fagan, A.A. (2001b), 'The Gendered Cycle of Violence: Comparing the Effects of Child

Abuse and Neglect on Criminal Offending for Males and Females,' *Violence and Victims*, vol. 16, pp. 457-74.

Fainstein, S., Gordon, I. and Harloe, I. (1992), *Divided Cities*, Blackwell, Oxford.

Falshaw, L. and Browne, K. (1997), 'Adverse Childhood Experiences and Violent Acts of Young People in Secure Accommodation', *Journal of Mental Health*, vol. 6, pp. 443–55.

Falshaw, L., Browne, K.D. and Hollin, C.R. (1996), 'Victim to Offender: A Review', *Aggression and Violent Behavior*, vol. 1, pp. 389–404.

Farrington, D.P. (1986), 'Age and Crime', in M. Tonry and N. Morris (eds), *Crime and Justice: An Annual Review of Research*, University of Chicago Press, Chicago.

Farrington, D.P. (1992), 'Criminal Career Research in the United Kingdom', *British Journal of Criminology*, vol. 32, pp. 521–36.

Farrington, D.P. (1994), 'Early Developmental Prevention of Juvenile Delinquency', *Criminal Behavior and Mental Health*, vol. 4, pp. 209–27.

Farrington, D.P. (1995), 'The Development of Offending and Anti-Social Behavior from Childhood: Key Findings from the Cambridge Study', *Journal of Child Psychology and Psychiatry*, vol. 36, pp. 929–64.

Farrington, D.P. (1997), 'Human Development and Criminal Careers', in M. Maguire, R. Morgan and R. Reiner (eds), *The Oxford Handbook of Criminology* (2nd ed.), Clarendon Press, Oxford.

Farrington, D.P. (2002), 'Key Results from the First Forty Years of the Cambridge Study in Delinquent Development', in T.P. Thornberry and M.D. Krohn (eds), *Taking Stock of Delinquency: An Overview of Findings from Contemporary Longitudinal Studies*, Kluwer/Plenum Press, New York.

Farrington, D.P., Barnes, G.C. and Lambert, S. (1996), 'The Concentration of Offending in Families', *Legal and Criminological Psychology*, vol. 1, pp. 47-63.

Farrington, D.P., Jolliffe, D., Loeber, R., Stouthamer-Loeber, M. and Kalb, L.M. (2001), 'The Concentration of Offenders in Families, and Family Criminality in the Prediction of Boys' Delinquency', *Journal of Adolescence*, vol. 24, pp. 579-96.

Farrington, D.P. and West, D.J. (1990), 'The Cambridge Study in Delinquent Development: A Long-Term Follow-Up of 411 London Males', in H.J. Kerner and G. Kaiser (eds), *Criminality: Personality, Behavior and Life History*, Springer Verlag, Berlin.

Feeney, J.A. and Noller, P. (1996), *Adult Attachment*, Sage Publications, London.

Feeney, J.A., Noller, P. and Hanrahan, M. (1994), 'Assessing Adult Attachment', in M. Sperling and W. Berman (eds), *Clinical and Developmental Perspectives*, Free Press, New York.

Felson, M. (1995), 'Those Who Discourage Crime', in J.E. Eck and D. Weisburd (eds), *Crime and Place*, Vol. 4, Criminal Justice Press, Washington, D.C.

Felson, M. (1998), *Crime and Everyday Life* (2nd ed.), Sage Publications, Thousand Oaks, CA.

Felson, M. and Clarke, R.V. (1998), *Opportunity Makes the Thief*, Police Research Series No. 98, Home Office Policing and Reducing Crime Unit, London.

Finkelhor, D. (1994), 'Current Information on the Scope and Nature of Child Sexual Abuse', *Sexual Abuse of Children*, vol. 4, pp. 31–62.

Finkelhor, D. (1997), 'The Victimization of Children and Youth: Developmental Victimology', in R.C. Davis, A.J. Lurigio and W.G. Skogan (eds), *Victims of Crime* (2nd ed.), Sage Publications, Thousand Oaks, CA, pp. 86–107.

Finkelhor, D. and Asdigian, N.L. (1996), 'Risk Factors for Youth Victimization: Beyond a Lifestyles/Routine Activities Theory Approach', *Violence and Victims*, vol. 11, pp. 3–19.

Finkelhor, D. and Baron, L. (1986), 'High-Risk Children', in D. Finkelhor (ed), *A*

Sourcebook on Child Sexual Abuse, Sage Publications, Beverly Hills, CA., pp. 60–88.

Finkelhor, D. and Ormond, R. (2000), *Characteristics of Crimes Against Juveniles*, Office of Juvenile Justice and Delinquency Prevention, Washington, D.C.

Finnane, M. (1994), 'Larrikins, Delinquents and Cops: Police and Young People in Australian History', in R. White and C. Alder (eds), *The Police and Young People in Australia*, Cambridge University Press, Cambridge.

Flood-Page, C., Campbell, S., Harrington, V. and Miller, J. (2000), *Youth Crime: Findings from the 1998/99 Youth Lifestyles Survey*, Home Office Research Study No. 209, Home Office, London.

Gale, F., Bailey-Harris, R. and Wundersitz, J. (1990), *Aboriginal Youth and the Criminal Justice System: The Injustice of Justice?*, Cambridge University Press, Cambridge.

Gans, H. (1993), 'From 'Underclass' to 'Undercaste': Some Observations About the Future of the Post-Industrial Economy and its Major Victims', *International Journal of Urban and Regional Research*, vol. 17, pp. 322–35.

Gibbs, J.J., Giever, D. and Martin, J.S. (1998), 'Parental Management and Self-Control: An Empirical Test of Gottfredson and Hirschi's General Theory', *Journal of Research in Crime and Delinquency*, vol. 35, pp. 40-70.

Gilfus, M.E. (1992), 'From Victims to Survivors to Offenders: Women's Routes of Entry and Immersion into Street Crime', *Women and Criminal Justice*, vol. 4, pp. 63–90.

Gottfredson, M. and Hirschi, T. (1990), *A General Theory of Crime*, Stanford University Press, Stanford, CA.

Graham, J. and Bowling, B. (1995), *Young People and Crime*, Home Office Research Study No. 145, Home Office, London.

Grasmick, H.G., Tittle, C.R., Bursik, R.J. and Arneklev, B.J. (1993), 'Testing the Core Empirical Implications of Gottfredson and Hirschi's General Theory of Crime', *Journal of Research in Crime and Delinquency*, vol. 30, pp. 5–29.

Greenburg, D. (1999), 'The Weak Strength of Social Control Theory', *Crime and Delinquency*, vol. 45, pp. 66–81.

Greenwood, P., Model, K., Rydell, C. and Chiesa, J. (1996), *Delivering Children From a Life of Crime: Measuring Costs and Benefits*, Report prepared for the University of California at Berkley and the James Irvine Foundation, The Rand Corporation, Santa Monica, CA.

Greenwood, P., Petersilia, J. and Zimring, F.E. (1980), *Age, Crime and Sanctions: The Transition from Juvenile to Adult Court*, The Rand Corporation, Santa Monica, CA.

Grossman, F.K., Beinashowitz, K., Sakurai, M., Finnin, L. and Flaherty, M. (1992), 'Risk and Resilience in Young Adolescents', *Journal of Youth and Adolescence*, vol. 21, pp. 529–50.

Gutierres, S.E. and Reich, J.W. (1981), 'A Developmental Perspective on Runaway Behavior: Its Relationship to Child Abuse', *Child Welfare*, vol. LX, pp. 89–94.

Hagan, J. (1992), 'The Poverty of a Classless Criminology: The American Society of Criminology 1991 Presidential Address', *Criminology*, vol. 30, pp. 1–19.

Hagan, J., Gillis, A. and Simpson, J. (1985), 'The Class Structure of Gender and Delinquency', *American Journal of Sociology*, vol. 90, pp. 1151–78.

Hagan, J., Simpson, J.H. and Gillis, A.R. (1979), 'The Sexual Stratification of Social Control: a Gender Based Perspective on Crime and Delinquency', *British Journal Of Sociology*, vol. 30, pp. 25–41.

Hahn Rafter, N. and Heidensohn, F. (eds) (1995), *International Feminist Perspectives in Criminology: Engendering a Discipline*, Open University Press, Buckingham, UK.

Hamnet, C. (1994), 'Social Polarisation in Global Cities: Theory and Evidence', *Urban Studies*, vol. 31, pp. 401–24.

Harlow, C.W. (1999), 'Prior Abuse Reported by Inmates and Probationers', U.S. Department of Justice, Washington, D.C.

Hashima, P.Y. and Finkelhor, D. (1999), 'Violent Victimization of Youth Versus Adults in National Crime Victimization Survey', *Journal of Interpersonal Violence*, vol. 14, pp. 799–820.

Haskell, M.R. and Yablonsky, L. (1982), *Juvenile Delinquency*, Houghton Mifflin Co., Boston.

Hawdon, J. (1996), 'Deviant Lifestyles: The Social Control of Daily Routines', *Youth and Society*, vol. 28, pp. 162–88.

Hawke, J.M., Jainchill, N. and De Leon, G. (2000), 'The Prevalence of Sexual Abuse and Its Impact on the Onset of Drug Use Among Adolescents in Therapeutic Community Drug Treatment,' *Journal of Child and Adolescent Substance Abuse*, vol. 9, pp. 35–49.

Heidensohn, F. (1985), *Women and Crime*, Macmillan, London.

Heidensohn, F. (1996), *Women and Crime* (2nd ed.), MacMillan, London.

Heimer, K. and DeCoster, S. (1999), 'The Gendering of Violent Delinquency', *Criminology* vol. 37, pp. 277–312.

Herrenkohl, T. I., Maguin, E., Hill, K.G., Hawkins, J.D., Abbott, R.D. and Catalano, R.F. (2000), 'Developmental Risk Factors for Youth Violence', *Journal of Adolescent Health*, vol. 26, pp. 176–86.

Hil, R. (2000), 'A Gloomy Vista? 'Globalisation', Juvenile Crime and Social Order: An Australian Perspective', *Crime, Law and Social Change: An International Journal*, vol. 33, pp. 369–84.

Hill, G.D. and Atkinson, M.P. (1988), 'Gender, Familial Control, and Delinquency', *Criminology*, vol. 26, pp. 127–47

Hindelang, M.J. (1973), 'Causes of Delinquency: A Partial Replication and Extension', *Social Problems*, vol. 20, pp. 471–87.

Hirschi, T. (1969), *Causes of Delinquency*, University of California Press, Berkeley, CA.

Hoffman, J. and Su, S. (1997), 'The Conditional Effects of Stress on Delinquency and Drug Use: A Strain Theory Assessment of Sex Differences', *Journal of Research in Crime and Delinquency*, vol. 34, pp. 46–78.

Homel, R., Lincoln, R. and Herd, B. (1999), 'Risk and Resilience: Crime and Violence Prevention in Aboriginal Communities', *Australian and New Zealand Journal of Criminology*, vol. 32, pp. 182–96.

Hotaling, G.T., Straus, M.A. and Lincoln, A.J. (1990), 'Intra-family Violence and Crime and Violence Outside the Family', in M.A. Straus and R.J. Gelles (eds), *Physical Violence in American Families*, Transaction Publishers, New Brunswick, NJ, pp. 431–72.

Howing, P.T., Wodarski, J.S., Kurtz, P.D., Gaudin, J.M. Jr. and Herbst, E.N. (1990), 'Child Abuse and Delinquency: The Empirical and Theoretical Links', *Social Work*, vol. 35, pp. 244–49.

Hudson, A. (1990), 'Elusive Subjects': Researching Young Women in Trouble', in L. Gelsthorpe and A. Morris (eds), *Feminist Perspectives in Criminology*, Open University Press, Philadelphia, PA.

Jensen, G.F. and Brownfield, D. (1986), 'Gender, Lifestyle, and Victimization: Beyond Routine Activities Theory', *Violence and Victims*, vol. 2, pp. 85–99.

Jenson, J.M., Potter, C.C. and Howard, M.O. (2001), 'American Juvenile Justice: Recent Trends and Issues in Youth Offending', *Social Policy and Administration*, vol. 35, pp. 48–68.

Johnson, R., Marcos, A. and Bahr, S. (1987), 'The Role of Peers in the Complex Etiology of Adolescent Drug Use', *Criminology*, vol. 25, pp. 323–57.

Jones, M.B., Offord, D.R. and Abrams, N. (1980), 'Brothers, Sisters, and Antisocial Behaviour', *British Journal of Psychiatry*, vol. 136, pp. 139–45.

Juby, H. and Farrington, D.P. (2001), 'Disentangling the Link Between Disrupted Families and Delinquency', *British Journal of Criminology*, vol. 41, pp. 22–40.

Junger–Tas, J., Terlouw, G. and Klein, M. (1994), *Delinquent Behavior Among Young People in the Western World, First Results of the International Self-report Delinquency Study*, Ministry of Justice, Amsterdam.

Kakar, S. (1996), *Child Abuse and Delinquency*, University Press of America, Lanham, MD.

Karniol, R., Gabay, R., Ochion, Y. and Harari, Y. (1998), 'Is Gender or Gender-Role Orientation a Better Predictor of Empathy in Adolescence?', *Sex Roles*, vol. 39, pp. 45–59.

Katz, J. (1988), *The Seductions of Crime: Moral and Sensual Attractions of Doing Evil*, Basic Books, New York.

Keating, D.P. and Hertzman, C. (1999), *Developmental Health and the Wealth of Nations*, Guilford Press, New York.

Kempf, K. (1993), 'The Empirical Status of Hirschi's Control Theory', in F. Adler and W.S. Laufer (eds), *New Directions in Criminological Theory: Advances in Criminological Theory*, Transaction Books, New Brunswick, NJ.

Kennedy, L. and Forde, D. (1995), *Self–Control, Risky Lifestyles, Routine Conflict and Crime, A Re-Specification of the General Theory of Crime*, University of Alberta, Edmonton.

Kornhauser, R. (1978), *Social Sources of Delinquency*, University of Chicago Press, Chicago.

Kotch, J.B., Muller, G.O. and Blakely, C.H. (1999), 'Understanding the Origins and Incidence of Child Maltreatment', in T.P. Gullotta and S.J. McElhaney (eds), *Violence in Homes and Communities: Prevention, Intervention, and Treatment*, Vol. 11, Sage Publications, Thousand Oaks, CA, pp. 1–38.

Kratoscki, P.C. and Kratoscki, J.E. (1975), 'Changing Patterns in the Delinquent Activities of Boys and Girls: A Self Reported Delinquency Analysis', *Adolescence*, vol. 10, pp. 83–91.

Kruttschnitt, C., Heath, L. and Ward, D. (1986), 'Family Violence, Television Viewing Habits, and Other Adolescent Experiences Related to Violent Criminal Behavior', *Criminology*, vol. 24, pp. 235–67.

LaGrange, T. and Silverman, R. (1999), 'Low Self–Control and Opportunity: Testing the General Theory of Crime as an Explanation for Gender Differences in Delinquency', *Criminology*, vol. 37, pp. 41–71.

Lake, E.S. (1989), *Cognitive Factors and Social Controls Influencing the Intergenerational Transmission of Violent Behavior*, UMI Dissertation Services, Ann Arbor, MI.

Lake, E.S. (1995), 'Offenders' Experiences of Violence: A Comparison of Male and Female Inmates as Victims', *Deviant Behavior*, vol. 16, pp. 269–90.

Langhinrichsen-Rohling, J. and Neidig, P. (1995), 'Violent Backgrounds of Economically Disadvantaged Youth: Risk Factors for Perpetrating Violence?', *Journal of Family Violence*, vol. 10, pp. 379–97.

Laub, J.H. and Lauritsen, J.L. (1993), 'Violent Criminal Behaviour Over the Life Course: A Review of the Longitudinal and Comparative Research', *Violence and Victims*, vol. 8, pp. 235–52.

Lauritsen, J.L. (1993), 'Sibling Resemblance in Juvenile Delinquency: Findings from the National Youth Survey', *Criminology*, vol. 31, pp. 387–409.

LeBlanc, M. and Loeber, R. (1998), 'Developmental Criminology Updated' in M. Tonry (ed), *Crime and Justice: An Annual Review of Research*, Vol. 23, University of Chicago Press, Chicago, pp. 115–98.

Lincoln, R., Lynch, M. and Ogilvie, E. (1998), *Peer Networks and Other Influences on Aboriginal Offending*, Criminology Research Council, Canberra.

Lincoln, R. and Wilson, P. (2000), 'Aboriginal Criminal Justice: Background and Foreground' in D. Chappell and P. Wilson (eds), *Crime and the Criminal Justice System in Australia: 2000 and Beyond*, Butterworths, Sydney.

Loeber, R. and Farrington D.P. (1994), 'Problems and Solutions in Longitudinal and Experimental Treatment Studies of Child Psychopathology and Delinquency', *Journal of Consulting Clinical Psychology*, vol. 62, pp. 887–900.

Loeber, R. and Stouthamer-Loeber, M. (1986), 'Family Predictors as Correlates and Predictors of Juvenile Conduct Problems and Delinquency', in M. Tonry and N. Morris (eds), *Crime and Justice: An Annual Review of Research*, University of Chicago Press, Chicago.

Lourie, I.S. (1977), 'The Phenomenon of the Abused Adolescent: A Clinical Study', *Victimology: An International Journal*, vol. 2, pp. 268–76.

Lubeck, S. and Garrett, P. (1990), 'The Social Construction of the 'At-Risk' Child', *British Journal of Sociology of Education*, vol. 11, pp. 327-40.

Lucashenko, M. (1997), 'Violence Against Indigenous Women: Public and Private Dimensions', in S. Cook and J. Bessant (eds), *Women's Encounters with Violence, Australian Experiences*, Sage Publications, Thousand Oaks, CA.

Luke, G. and Cunneen, C. (1995), *Aboriginal Over-Representation and Discretionary Decisions in the New South Wales Juvenile Justice System*, Juvenile Justice Advisory Council of New South Wales, Sydney.

Lynch, M. and Ogilvie, E. (1999), 'Access to Amenities: The Issue of Ownership', *Youth Studies Australia*, vol. 18, pp. 17–22.

Maher, L. (1997), *Sexed Work, Gender, Race and Resistance in a Brooklyn Drug Market*, Clarendon Press, Oxford.

Maher, L. (2000), 'Gangs: Cabra Girls (Australia)', in N. Hahn Rafter (ed), *Encyclopedia of Women and Crime*, Onyx Press, Phoenix, AZ.

Mak, A.S. (1990), 'Testing a Psychosocial Control Theory of Delinquency', *Criminal Justice and Behavior*, vol. 17, pp. 215–30.

Mak, A.S. (1991), 'Psychosocial Control Characteristics of Delinquents and Nondelinquents', *Criminal Justice and Behavior*, vol. 18, pp. 287–03.

Mak, A.S. (1993), 'A Self-Report Delinquency Scale for Australian Adolescents', *Australian Journal of Psychology*, vol. 45, pp. 75–79.

Matsueda, R. (1988), 'The Current State of Differential Association Theory', *Crime and Delinquency*, vol. 34, pp. 277–306.

Maxfield, M.G. and Widom, C.S. (1996), 'The Cycle of Violence: Revisited Six Years Later', *Archives of Pediatrics and Adolescent Medicine*, vol. 150, pp. 390–95.

Mazerolle, P., Brame, R., Paternoster, R., Piquero, A. and Dean, C. (2000), 'Onset Age, Persistence, and Offending Versatility: Comparisons Across Gender', *Criminology*, vol. 38, pp. 1143–72.

McCarthy, B., Hagan, J. and Woodward, T. (1999), 'In the Company of Women: Structure and Agency in a Revised Power Control Theory of Gender and Delinquency', *Criminology*, vol. 37, pp. 761–88.

McClellan, D.S., Farabee, D. and Crouch, B.E. (1997), 'Early Victimization, Drug Use, and Criminality: A Comparison of Male and Female Prisoners', *Criminal Justice and Behavior*, vol. 24, pp. 455–76.

McCord, J. (1979), 'Some Child-Rearing Antecedents of Criminal Behavior In Adult Men', *Journal of Personality and Social Psychology*, vol. 37, pp. 1477–86.

McCord, J. (1990), 'Long-Term Perspectives On Parental Absence', in L. Robins and M. Rutter (eds), *Straight And Devious Pathways From Childhood to Adulthood*,

Cambridge University Press, New York.

McGue, M., Sharma, A. and Benson, P. (1996), 'Parent and Sibling Influences on Alcohol Use and Misuse: Evidence from a U.S. Adoption Cohort', *Journal of Studies on Alcohol*, vol. 57, pp. 8–18.

Mears, D., Ploeger, M. and Warr, M. (1998), 'Explaining the Gender Gap in Delinquency: Peer Influence and Moral Evaluations of Behavior', *Journal of Research in Crime and Delinquency*, vol. 35, pp. 251–66.

Merton, R. (1938), 'Social Structure and Anomie', *American Sociological Review*, vol. 3, pp. 672–82.

Messerschmidt, J. (1994), 'Schooling, Masculinities and Youth Crime', in T. Newburn and E.A. Stanko (eds), *Just Boys Doing Business*, Routledge, London.

Messerschmidt, J. (1995), 'From Patriarchy to Gender: Feminist Theory, Criminology and the Challenge of Diversity', in N. Hahn Rafter and F. Heidensohn (eds), *International Feminist Perspectives in Criminology: Engendering a Discipline*, Open University Press, Buckingham, UK.

Mihalic, S.W. and Elliott, D. (1997), 'A Social Learning Theory Model of Marital Violence', *Journal of Family Violence*, vol. 12, pp. 21–47.

Miller, J. (1998), 'Up it Up: Gender and the Accomplishment of Street Robbery', *Criminology*, vol. 36, pp. 37–67.

Mingione, E. (1993), 'The New Urban Poverty and the Underclass', *International Journal of Urban and Regional Research*, vol. 17, pp. 324–26.

Moffitt, T.E. (1993), 'Adolescence-Limited and Life-Course Persistent Antisocial Behavior: A Developmental Taxonomy,' *Psychological Review*, vol. 100, pp. 674–701.

Mollenkopf, J. and Castells, M. (1991), *Dual City*, Russell Sage Foundation, New York.

Mukherjee, S. (1983), *Youth Crime Project: Age and Crime*, Australian Institute of Criminology, Canberra.

Mukherjee, S. (1997), 'The Dimensions of Juvenile Crime', in A. Borowski and I. O'Connor (eds), *Juvenile Crime, Justice and Corrections*, Addison Wesley Longman, South Melbourne.

Muncie, J. (1999), *Youth and Crime: A Critical Introduction*, Sage Publications, London.

Mustaine, E. and Tewksbury, R. (1997), 'Obstacles in the Assessment of Routine Activity Theory', *Social Pathology*, vol. 3, pp. 177–94.

Mustaine, E. and Tewksbury, R. (1998), 'Predicting Risks of Larceny Theft Victimization: A Routine Activity Analysis Using Refined Lifestyle Measures', *Criminology*, vol. 36, pp. 829–57.

Mustaine, E. and Tewksbury, R. (2000), 'Comparing the Lifestyles of Victims, Offenders, and Victim-Offenders: A Routine Activity Theory Assessment of Similarities and Differences for Criminal Incident Participants', *Sociological Focus*, vol. 33, pp. 339–62.

Naffine, N. (1996), *Feminism and Criminology*, Temple University Press, Philadelphia.

National Crime Prevention (1999), *Pathways to Prevention: Developmental and Early Intervention Approaches to Crime in Australia*, National Crime Prevention, Attorney-General's Department, Canberra.

O'Connor, I. (1989), *Our Homeless Children: Their Experiences*, Human Rights and Equal Opportunity Commission, Sydney.

Offer, D. and Offer, J. (1972), 'Development Psychology of Youth', in S. Shamsie (ed), *Youth: Problems and Approaches*, Lea and Febiger, Philadelphia.

Ogilvie, E. (1996), 'Masculine Obsessions: An Examination of Criminology, Criminality and Gender', *Australian New Zealand Journal of Criminology*, vol. 29, pp. 205–26.

Ogilvie, E. (1999), *Offensive Girls: An Investigation of Gender and Adolescent Criminality*, Unpublished PhD Thesis, The University of Queensland, St. Lucia, QLD.

Ogilvie, E. and Lynch, M. (2001), 'Responses to Incarceration: A Qualitative Analysis of Adolescents in Juvenile Detention Centres', *Current Issues in Criminal Justice*, vol. 12, pp. 330–46.

Ogilvie, E. and Lynch, M. (2002), 'Gender, Race, Class and Crime in Australia' in P. Grabosky and A. Graycar (eds), *Handbook of Australian Criminology*, Cambridge University Press, Cambridge, pp. 196-210

Ogilvie, E., Lynch, M. and Bell, S. (2000), 'Gender and Official Statistics: The Juvenile Justice System in Queensland', *Trends and Issues in Crime and Criminal Justice*, No. 162, Australian Institute of Criminology, Canberra.

Ogilvie, E. and Van Zyl, A. (2001), 'Indigenous Youth, Custody and the Rites of Passage', *Trends and Issues in Crime and Criminal Justice*, No. 204, Australian Institute of Criminology, Canberra.

O'Keefe, M. (1994), 'Linking Marital Violence, Mother-Child/Father-Child Aggression and Child Behavior Problems', *Journal of Family Violence*, vol. 9, pp. 63–78.

Osgood, D., Wilson, J., O'Malley, P., Bachman, J. and Johnston, L. (1996), 'Routine Activities and Individual Deviant Behavior', *American Sociological Review*, vol. 61, pp. 635–55.

Panel on Research on Child Abuse and Neglect, Commission on Behavioral and Social Sciences and Education, National Research Council (1993), *Understanding Child Abuse and Neglect*, National Academy Press, Washington, D.C.

Parker, G., Tupling, H. and Brown, L. (1979), 'A Parental Bonding Instrument', *British Journal of Medical Psychology*, vol. 52, pp. 1–10.

Passas N. and Agnew, R. (eds) (1997), *The Future of Anomie Theory*, Northeastern University Press, Boston.

Paternoster, R. and Mazerolle, P. (1994), 'General Strain Theory and Delinquency: A Replication and Extension', *Journal of Research in Crime and Delinquency*, vol. 31, pp. 235–63.

Perrone, S. and White, R. (2000), 'Young People and Gangs', *Trends and Issues in Criminal Justice*, No. 167, Australian Institute of Criminology, Canberra.

Piquero, A.R. and Chung, H.L. (2001), 'On the Relationship Between Gender, Early Onset, and the Seriousness of Offending', *Journal of Criminal Justice*, vol. 29, pp. 189–206.

Queensland Police Service (2000), *1999–2000 Statistical Review*, Statistical Services, Information Management Division, Queensland.

Raskill, P. and Urquhart, R. (1995), *Who Gets What Where: An Exploratory Analysis of Differences in the Distribution of Income and Wealth Between Australian Cities*, Paper presented to the 1995 National Social Policy Conference, University of New South Wales, Sydney.

Reinarman, C. and Fagan, J. (1987), 'Social Organization and Differential Association: A Research Note from a Longitudinal Study of Violent Juvenile Offenders', *Crime and Delinquency*, vol. 34, pp. 307-27.

Reiss, A.J. and Farrington, D.F. (1991), 'Advancing Knowledge About Co-Offending: Results from a Prospective Longitudinal Survey of London Males', *Journal of Criminal Law and Criminology*, vol. 82, pp. 360–95.

Rigby, K. and Schofield, P. (1985), *A Children's Attitude to Authority Scale*, School of Social Studies, South Australia Institute of Technology, Adelaide.

Robins, L.N. (1966), *Deviant Children Grown Up*, The Williams and Wilkins Company, Baltimore, MD.

Robins, L.N. and Rutter, M. (1990), *Straight and Devious Pathways from Childhood to Adulthood*, Cambridge University Press, Cambridge.

Rojek, D.G. and Erickson, M.L. (1982), 'Delinquent Careers: A Test of the Career

Escalation Model', *Criminology*, vol. 20, pp. 5–28.

Romano, E. and De Luca, R. (1997), 'Explaining the Relationship Between Child Sexual Abuse and Adult Sexual Perpetration', *Journal of Family Violence*, vol. 12, pp. 85–98.

Romano, E. and De Luca, R. (2001), 'Male Sexual Abuse: A Review of Effects, Abuse Characteristics, and Links with Later Psychological Functioning', *Aggression and Violent Behavior*, vol. 6, pp. 55–78.

Rosen, L. and Neilson, K. (1978), 'Broken Homes and Delinquency', in L.D. Savitz and N. Johnston (eds), *Crime in Society*, John Wiley and Sons, New York.

Rowe, D.C. (1985), 'Sibling Interaction and Self-Reported Delinquent Behavior: A Study of 265 Twin Pairs', *Criminology*, vol. 23, pp. 223–39.

Rowe, D.C. (1986), 'Genetic and Environmental Components of Antisocial Behavior: A Study of 265 Twin Pairs', *Criminology*, vol. 24, pp. 513–34.

Rowe, D.C. and Britt, C.L. (1991), 'Developmental Explanations of Delinquent Behavior Among Siblings: Common Factor vs Transmission Effects', *Journal of Quantitative Criminology*, vol. 7, pp. 315–32.

Rowe, D.C. and Gulley, B.L. (1992), 'Sibling Effects on Substance Use and Delinquency', *Criminology*, vol. 30, pp. 217-33.

Rowe, D.C. and Farrington, D.P. (1997), 'The Familial Transmission of Criminal Convictions', *Criminology*, vol. 35, pp. 177–201.

Rowe, D.C., Linver, M.R. and Rodgers, J.L. (1996), 'Delinquency and IQ: Using Siblings to Find Sources of Variation', in G.H. Brody (ed), *Sibling Relationships: Their Causes and Consequences*, Ablex Publishing, Norwood, NJ, pp. 147–72.

Rowe, D.C. and Osgood, D.W. (1984), 'Heredity and Sociological Theories of Delinquency: A Reconsideration', *American Sociological Review*, vol. 49, pp. 526–40.

Rowe, D.C. and Plomin, R. (1981), 'The Importance of Nonshared Environmental Influences in Behavioral Development', *Developmental Psychology*, vol. 17, pp. 517–31.

Rowe, D.C., Rodgers, J.L. and Meseck-Bushey, S. (1992), 'Sibling Delinquency and the Family Environment: Shared and Unshared Influences', *Child Development*, vol. 63, pp. 59–67.

Rowe, D.C., Vazsonyi, A. and Flannery, D. (1995), 'Sex-Differences in Crime: Do Means and Within-Sex Variation Have Similar Causes?', *Journal of Research in Crime and Delinquency*, vol. 31, pp. 84–100.

Russell, L.A. (1998), *Child Maltreatment and Psychological Distress Among Urban Homeless Youth*, Garland Publishing, Inc., New York.

Rutter, M., Giller, H. and Hagell, A. (1998), *Antisocial Behavior by Young People*, Cambridge University Press, Cambridge.

Sampson, R.J. and Laub, J.H. (1993), *Crime in the Making: Pathways and Turning Points Through Life*, Harvard University Press, Cambridge, MA.

Sampson, R.J. and Lauritsen, J.L. (1993), 'Violent Victimization and Offending: Individual-, Situational-, and Community-Level Risk Factors', in A.J. Reiss and J.A. Roth (eds), *Understanding and Preventing Violence*, Vol. 3, National Academy Press, Washington, D.C., pp. 1–114.

Sassen, S. (1989), *The Global City*, Princeton University Press, Princeton, NJ.

Schalling, D., Edman G. and Asberg, M. (1983), 'Impulsive Cognitive Style and Inability to Tolerate Boredom: Psychobiological Studies of Temperamental Vulnerability', in M. Zuckerman (ed), *Biological Bases of Sensation Seeking, Impulsivity and Anxiety*, Lawrence Erlbaum Associates, Hillsdale, NJ.

Schwartz, M. and Milovanovic, D. (eds) (1996), *Race, Gender, and Class in Criminology: The Intersection*, Garland, New York.

Seydlitz, R. (1990), 'The Effects of Gender, Age, and Parental Attachment On Delinquency: A Test For Interactions', *Sociological Spectrum*, vol. 10, pp. 209–25.

Sherman, L. (1995), 'Hot Spots of Crime and Criminal Careers of Places', in J. Eck and D. Weisburd (eds), *Crime and Place*, Willow Tree Press, Washington, D.C.

Shoemaker, D.J. (1990), *Theories of Delinquency: An Examination Of The Explanations of Delinquent Behavior* (2nd ed.), Oxford University Press, New York.

Shoemaker, D.J. (1996), *Theories of Delinquency: An Examination of Explanations of Delinquent Behavior* (3rd ed.), Oxford University Press, New York.

Short, J. and Nye, I. (1958), 'Extent of Unrecorded Juvenile Delinquency', *Journal of Criminal Law, Criminology and Police Science*, vol. 49, pp. 296–302.

Silva, P. and Stanton, W. (eds) (1997), *From Child to Adult: The Dunedin Multidisciplinary Health and Development Study*, Oxford University Press, Auckland.

Simpson, S.S. (1991), 'Caste, Class and Violent Crime: Explaining Difference in Female Offending', *Criminology*, vol. 29, pp. 115–35.

Simpson, S.S. and Ells, L. (1994), 'Is Gender Subordinate to Class? An Empirical Assessment of Calvin and Puley's Structural Marxist Theory of Delinquency', *Journal of Criminal Law and Criminology*, vol. 85, pp. 453–80.

Slomkowski, C., Rende, R., Conger, K.J., Simons, R.L. and Conger, R. (2001), 'Sisters, Brothers, and Delinquency: Evaluating Social Influence during Early and Middle Adolescence', *Child Development*, vol. 72, pp. 271–83.

Smith, C. and Thornberry, T.P. (1995), 'The Relationship Between Childhood Maltreatment and Adolescent Involvement in Delinquency', *Criminology*, vol. 33, pp. 451–77.

Smith, J.L. (1998), *The Effects of Domestic Violence on Children: Children's, Mother's, and Teacher's Reports*, Unpublished PhD Thesis, The University of Queensland, St. Lucia, QLD.

Smith, J.L. and O'Connor, I. (1997), 'Child Abuse, Youth Homelessness, and Juvenile Crime', in A. Borowski and I. O'Connor (eds), *Juvenile Crime, Justice and Corrections*, Addison Wesley Longman, South Melbourne, pp. 121–51.

Snyder, H.N. and Sickmund, M. (1999), *Juvenile Offenders and Victims: 1999 National Report*, Office of Juvenile Justice and Delinquency Prevention, Washington, D.C.

Sochting, I., Skoe, E.E. and Marcia, J.E. (1994), 'Care-Oriented Moral Reasoning and Prosocial Behavior: A Question of Gender or Sex Role Orientation', *Sex Roles*, vol. 31, pp. 131–47.

Sokol-Katz, J., Dunham. R. and Zimmerman, R. (1997), 'Family Structure Versus Parental Attachment in Controlling Adolescent Deviant Behavior: A Social Control Model', *Adolescence*, vol. 32, pp. 199–215.

Sommers, I. and Baskin, D. (1993), 'The Situational Context of Violent Female Offending', *Journal of Research in Crime and Delinquency*, vol. 30, pp. 136–62.

Steffensmeier, D. (1991), 'National Trends in Female Arrests, 1960–1990: Assessment and Recommendations for Research', *Journal of Quantitative Criminology*, vol. 9, pp. 411–41.

Steffensmeier, D. and Steffensmeier, R. (1980), 'Trends in Female Delinquency: An Examination of Arrest, Juvenile Court, Self-Report, and Field Data', in J.F. Sheley (ed), *Criminology: A Contemporary Handbook*, Wadsworth, Belmont, CA.

Stewart, A. and Homel, R. (1994), *Correlates of Victimization for Crimes Against the Person: An Analysis of the 1991 Queensland Crime Victim Survey*, Paper presented at the Crime Victims Surveys in Australia Conference, Griffith University, Brisbane, QLD.

Stormshak, E.A., Bellanti, C.J. and Bierman, K.L. (1996), 'The Quality of Sibling Relationships and the Development of Social Competence and Behavioral Control in Aggressive Children', *Developmental Psychology*, vol. 32, pp. 79–89.

Strang, H. and Braithwaite, J. (eds) (2001), *Restorative Justice and Civil Society*, Cambridge University Press, Cambridge.

Straus, M.A. (1990), 'Ordinary Violence, Child Abuse, and Wife Beating: What Do They Have in Common?', in M.A. Straus and R.J. Gelles (eds), *Physical Violence In American Families*, Transaction Publishers, New Brunswick, NJ, pp. 402-30.

Straus, M.A. and Gelles, R.J. (1990), 'How Violent Are American Families?', in M.A. Straus and R.J. Gelles (eds), *Physical Violence In American Families*, Transaction Publishers, New Brunswick, NJ, pp. 95–112.

Sutherland, E.H. (1947), *Principles of Criminology* (4th ed.), J.B. Lippincott, Philadelphia, PA.

Sutherland, E.H. and Cressey, D.R. (1979), *Criminology*, J.B. Lippincott, Philadelphia, PA.

Swinford, S.P., DeMaris, A., Cernkovich, S.A. and Giordano, P.C. (2000), 'Harsh Physical Discipline in Childhood and Violence in Later Romantic Involvements: The Mediating Role of Problem Behaviors', *Journal of Marriage and the Family*, vol. 62, pp. 508–19.

Tatz, C. (2000), *Aboriginal Youth Suicide in New South Wales, The Australian Capital Territory and New Zealand: Towards a Model of Explanation and Alleviation*, Criminology Research Council, Canberra.

Thompson, W.E., Mitchell, J. and Dodder, R.A. (1984), 'An Empirical Test of Hirschi's Control Theory of Delinquency', *Deviant Behavior*, vol. 5, pp. 11-22.

Thornberry, T. (1987), 'Toward an Interactional Theory of Delinquency', *Criminology*, vol. 25, pp. 863–91.

Tittle, C. and Meier, R. (1990), 'Specifying the SES/Delinquency Relationship', *Criminology*, vol. 28, pp. 271–99.

Tremblay, M. and Tremblay, P. (1998), 'Social Structure, Interaction Opportunities, and the Direction of Violent Offenses', *Journal of Research in Crime and Delinquency*, vol. 35, pp. 295–315.

Trickett, P.K. and Putnam, F.W. (1998), 'Developmental Consequences of Child Sexual Abuse', in P.K. Trickett and C.J. Schellenbach (eds), *Violence Against Children in the Family and the Community*, American Psychological Association, Washington, D.C., pp. 39–56.

Triplett, R. and Myers, L. (1995), 'Evaluating Contextual Patterns of Delinquency: Gender-Based Differences', *Justice Quarterly*, vol. 12, pp. 59–81.

U.S. Department of Health and Human Services (2001a), *Youth Violence: A Report of the Surgeon General*, U.S. Department of Health and Human Services, Centers for Disease Control and Prevention, National Center for Injury Prevention and Control; Substance Abuse and Mental Health Services Administration, Center for Mental Health Services; and National Institutes of Health, National Institute of Mental Health, Rockville, MD.

U.S. Department of Health and Human Services (2001b), *Child Maltreatment 1999*, U.S. Government Printing Office, Washington, D.C.

Wadsworth, M. (1979), 'The Broken Family and Juvenile Delinquency: Scientific Explanation or Ideology', *Social Problems*, vol. 21, pp. 726–29.

Walker, J. (1992), 'Estimates of the Costs of Crime in Australia', *Trends and Issues in Crime and Justice*, No. 39, Australian Institute of Criminology, Canberra.

Warr, M. (1993), 'Age, Peers, and Delinquency', *Criminology*, vol. 31, pp. 17–40.

Weeks, R. and Widom, C.S. (1998), 'Self-Reports of Early Childhood Victimization Among Incarcerated Adult Male Felons', *Journal of Interpersonal Violence*, vol. 13, pp. 345–61.

Welsh, L.A., Archambault, F.X., Janus, M.D. and Brown, S.W. (1995), *Running for Their Lives: Physical and Sexual Abuse of Runaway Adolescents*, Garland Publishing, Inc.,

New York.
West, D.J. and Farrington, D.P. (1977), *The Delinquent Way of Life: Third Report of the Cambridge Study in Delinquent Development*, Heinemann, London.
Western, J.S. (1983), *Social Inequality in Australian Society*, Macmillan, Melbourne.
Western, J.S. and Lanyon, A. (1999), 'Anomie in the Asia Pacific Region: The Australian Study', in P. Atteslander, B. Gransow and J. Western (eds), *Comparative Anomie Research*, Ashgate Publishing, Ltd., Aldershot, Hampshire.
White, R. (1990), *No Space of Their Own: Young People and Social Control in Australia*, Cambridge University Press, Cambridge.
White, R. (1994), 'Street Life: Police Practices and Youth Behavior', in R. White and C. Alder (eds), *The Police and Young People in Australia*, Cambridge University Press, Cambridge.
White, R. and Alder, C. (eds) (1994), *The Police and Young People in Australia*, Cambridge University Press, Cambridge.
Widom, C.S. (1989a), 'Does Violence Beget Violence: A Critical Examination of the Literature', *Psychological Bulletin*, vol. 106, pp. 3–28.
Widom, C.S. (1989b), 'The Cycle of Violence', *Science*, vol. 244, pp. 160–66.
Widom, C.S. and Ames, M.A. (1994), 'Criminal Consequences of Childhood Sexual Victimization', *Child Abuse and Neglect*, vol. 18, pp. 303–18.
Widom, C.S., Ireland, T. and Glynn, P.J. (1995), 'Alcohol Abuse in Abused and Neglected Children Followed-Up: Are They at Increased Risk?', *Journal of Studies on Alcohol*, vol. 56, pp. 207–17.
Wilcox-Rountree, P. and Warner, B. (1999), 'Social Ties and Crime: Is the Relationship Gendered?', *Criminology*, vol. 37, pp. 789–813.
Wilkinson, K., Stitt, B.G. and Erickson, M.L. (1982), 'Siblings and Delinquent Behavior: An Exploratory Study of a Neglected Family Variable', *Criminology*, vol. 20, pp. 223–39.
Williams, J. and Gold, M. (1972), 'From Delinquent Behavior to Official Delinquency', *Social Problems*, vol. 20, pp. 209–29.
Wilson, J.Q. and Herrnstein, R. (1985), *Crime and Human Nature*, Simon Schuster, New York.
Wilson, M. and Daly, M. (1998), 'Sexual Rivalry and Sexual Conflict: Recurring Themes in Fatal Conflicts', *Theoretical Criminology*, vol. 2, pp. 291–310.
Wilson, W.J. (1987), *The Truly Disadvantaged*, University of Chicago Press, Chicago.
Wolfgang, M.E., Figlio, R.M. and Sellin, T. (1972), *Delinquency in a Birth Cohort*, University of Chicago Press, Chicago.
Worrall, A. (1990), *Offending Women, Female Lawbreakers and the Criminal Justice System*, Routledge, London.
Wright, E.O. (1985), *Classes*, New Left Books, London.
Wright, R. and Bennett, T. (1990), 'Exploring the Offenders' Perspective: Observing and Interviewing Criminals', in R. Wright and T. Bennett (eds), *Measurement Issues in Criminology*, Springer Verlag, New York.
Wundersitz, J. (1996), 'Juvenile Justice', in K.M. Hazlehurst (ed), *Crime and Justice: An Australian Textbook in Criminology*, LBC Information Services, North Ryde, NSW.
Wyn, J. and White, R. (1997), *Rethinking Youth*, Allen and Unwin, St. Leonards, NSW.
Yearbook Australia 1997, No. 79, Australian Bureau of Statistics, Canberra.
Yearbook Australia 2002, No. 84, Australian Bureau of Statistics, Canberra.
Zager, M.A. (1994), 'Gender and Crime', in T. Hirschi and M.R. Gottfredson (eds), *The Generality of Deviance*, Transaction Publishers, New Brunswick, NJ.
Zingraff, M.T., Leiter, J., Myers, K.A. and Johnsen, M.C. (1993), 'Child Maltreatment and Youthful Problem Behavior', *Criminology*, vol. 31, pp. 173–202.

Subject Index

empathy 94-6

family disruption/family breakdown 117, 124, 140, 146-7
family stability 111-5
female 6, 12, 14-5, 39, 65, 76, 79, 80, 82, 85, 97, 125, 143, 145, 159, 176, 188, 191
feminist 24, 65-6, 84, 97, 189

gender differences in 7, 19, 24-6, 32, 39, 41, 65, 66-8, 71, 73-4, 80, 82, 94-5, 130-1, 136
   class 100
   delinquency, opportunities for 67
   orientation to others 88
   parental supervision 123
   victimization 18, 20
gender identity 82
general strain theory 5

Homel crime status variable 181, 183
household possessions 106

identity; see also gender identity 49, 78, 82-3
impulsivity, see self-control 164-5
Index of Relative Disadvantage 11-2, 16-7, 54, 59, 101
Indigenous 10-11, 15, 20, 76, 77, 97, 99, 157-70, 172, 176-7, 188, 191
Instrumentality 94-6
intervention(s) 20, 63, 161, 189-90

juvenile justice 18, 75, 136, 157-8, 192

law, the 41, 66, 70, 79, 88, 92, 121, 154-5, 163, 165, 169, 199
   attitudes towards; see also Attitude to Authority Scale 165, 169
Low Self-Control Scale 9, 164

masculinity 10, 19, 78, 85-6, 95, 166

neglect, see child maltreatment; victimization 1, 158, 171-4
neighbourhood 5, 9, 20, 54-5, 58-62, 70, 83, 106, 109, 181, 183, 186

offences, types of, see delinquency, types of 14, 23, 25, 32, 35-42, 45 46-7,

49, 50-3, 57, 65, 108, 109
offending, see delinquency 1, 3, 9-10, 13-5, 18-21, 23, 25, 27-30, 32, 33-40, 42-53, 56-63, 65-8, 70-1, 73, 76, 78, 80-1, 85, 87, 94-7, 99, 117, 141-3, 148, 150, 155, 157-9, 163, 166-70, 174, 179-85, 188-92
orientation to others 85-8, 93-6

Parental Bonding Instrument 9, 56, 126, 162
parental care 123-5, 130, 133, 139
parental supervision 20, 123, 127-8, 130, 132-3, 135, 137-9, 181, 186
parenting practices and 19, 121, 125
parents 3, 7, 17-8, 24, 29, 40, 42, 55-7, 62, 92, 101, 103-4, 106, 110-13, 117, 119, 121-5, 127, 130-1, 133-4, 137, 139-41, 146, 160-3, 174, 176, 182, 188
   employment status of 60, 102, 107-9, 114-6
   quality of interactions with 161
peer alignment 85, 89-90, 93-6, 166
peers, delinquent 7, 89, 95-6, 142
   attitudes to
police services 187
power control theory 65
propensity to reject norms 94-6
protective factors 14, 20, 141, 170-1, 175, 180-1, 183, 185-6, 189

rational choice theory 36, 38, 41-2
research design 2, 9-0, 21, 141
risk-seeking, see self-control 85, 94-7, 164-5
risk factors 159
risk taking; see also Low Self-Control Scale 84, 94

self-control; see also Low Self-Control Scale 3, 63, 65, 91, 122
self-esteem 19, 83, 85, 93-4, 104-6, 109, 111-5, 117, 119, 188
   and delinquency 107, 109, 111-2, 115
   and socio-economic status 113-4
self-interest 85, 91-6
self-obsession 85-8, 92-6
sex roles 188
sibling effect(s) 10, 143, 148, 150, 154

Author Index

For Product Safety Concerns and Information please contact our EU
representative GPSR@taylorandfrancis.com
Taylor & Francis Verlag GmbH, Kaufingerstraße 24, 80331 München, Germany